The Seven Hunters: Comparative calm on lighthouse relief day at the east landing on Eilean Mòr

THE FARTHEST HEBRIDES

Alasdair Alpin MacGregor

With forty-three Illustrations,
twenty-six of which are reproduced from
Photographs by the Author

Breaking the silence of the seas
Among the farthest Hebrides.

WILLIAM WORDSWORTH

London
MICHAEL JOSEPH

First published in Great Britain by
MICHAEL JOSEPH LTD
26 Bloomsbury Street
London, W.C.1
1969

7181 0691 1

Set and printed in Great Britain by
Tonbridge Printers Ltd, Peach Hall Works, Tonbridge, Kent
in Plantin ten on twelve point, and bound by
James Burn at Esher, Surrey

FRANCES BENNETT,
without whose meticulous help
the manuscript of this volume
might never have reached
the Printer

Preface

ON NO small and impoverished islands has so much been written as on the Hebrides—impoverished largely on account of their physical ancientness and an obstinacy and intractability arising therefrom. Notwithstanding, their literature, both as regards quantity and quality, is quite astonishing. Much of this has resulted from the serious scientific interest they have evoked in so many diverse fields during the last few decades.

This is true not only of the more accessible, but also of the farthest and remotest, some of them inhabited until comparatively recent times.

This volume is, perhaps, exceptional in that it embraces for the first time all those Hebridean outliers to which so much and such varied attention is now being given—archaeological, historical, geographical, geological, biological, ornithological, oceanographical, physiographical, meteorological, and sociological. Never before have the Farthest Hebrides been submitted to so wide a range of dedicated scientific investigation.

Largely in deference to my own Hebridean lineage, as also to the fact that I already had written a few books on the Hebrides, a singular privilege was bestowed upon me when, at the invitation of *The Times*, I travelled to St. Kilda in August, 1930, as its Special Correspondent, lived there for some time with the remnant of its steadily diminishing population just prior to its being evacuated at the end of that month, and actually participated in the toils this entailed.

With the abandonment of St. Kilda in 1930, Britain, demographically, contracted forty miles. With the more recent desertion of the Monach Isles, it contracted another four.

It is certainly paradoxical that, in an age when man has virtually eliminated distance and the major difficulties and dangers it once entailed, so many of our lesser British Isles should now be regarded as no longer habitable except by seals and seabirds, and the ghosts of the departed.

For my having devoted to St. Kilda nearly a third of my text, I make no apology. Although now without a native population for

7

nearly forty years, it is today what it has always been, namely, one of the most fascinating groups of oceanic isles in the world. No isles so small, anywhere, have inspired a literature as vast, varied, and dramatic. St. Kilda's arduous occupation throughout the centuries is something quite unique. Its cliffs are stupendous; its bird-life prodigious; its geology enthralling; its abiding loneliness overwhelming.

During a blitz on London, much of my early photographic material was destroyed, more by the gushing hoses of over-exuberant firemen than actually by fire. To Mary Studdy and to Tom Weir I am immensely grateful for their having come so generously to my aid with photographs filling at least some of the gaps thus created in my own collection. The former has helped me splendidly with Sùla Sgeir: the latter no less commendably with the Shiants. For my Soay sheep illustration, I thank Dr. Peter Jewell of the Department of Zoology at University College, London. For two appropriate St. Kilda illustrations, I am grateful to the Marconi Company. For those of Rockall, I am beholden to the Air Ministry.

Alasdair Alpin MacGregor.

The King's Barn,
Odiham,
Hampshire.
June, 1969.

Contents

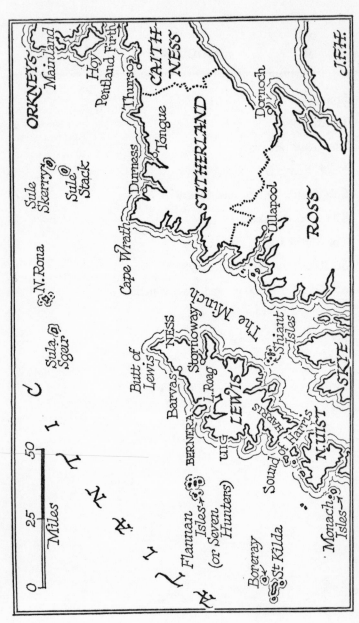

Map showing the Farthest Hebrides (Rockall excepted), drawn for the Author by the late Frank Horrabin

Illustrations

11

13

PHOTOGRAPHIC ACKNOWLEDGMENTS

Mary Studdy for numbers 10, 11, 12, 13, 14 &
15. Tom Steel for numbers 23, 24, 25, 26, 27
& 28. Peter Jewell for number 29. The Marconi
Company for numbers 40 & 41. The Air
Ministry for numbers 42 & 43.

CHAPTER ONE

The Seven Hunters

Three men alive on Flannan Isle,
Who thought of three men dead.

STUDENTS OF the present century's English verse will recognise these lines. With them, Wilfred Wilson Gibson concludes *Flannan Isle,* those truly imaginative verses afforded the notice they merited through their inclusion in that splendid anthology of modern verse chosen by Sir Algernon Methuen, and first published by his firm in 1921, a few years before his death. Ever since childhood days in the Scottish Highlands, I have known of the tragedy and of the mystery these verses commemorate.

Lying out in the North Atlantic, some twenty miles off Gallan Head, in the Outer Hebrides, and beset by a number of smaller islets and skerries, is a group of seven uninhabited islands known as the Flannan Isles, or the Seven Hunters. It was in the year, 1900, just a twelvemonth after the lighthouse had been completed on Eilean Mor, largest of them, that there occurred a mysterious incident which, to this day, remains one of the many insoluble problems of the seas. Passing vessels failed to pick up the light where it was expected, and in consequence were confused as to their exact whereabouts. The light, it was thought, had burned itself out for some strange reason. For several days a tempest had been raging. When eventually it subsided sufficiently to enable the lighthouse relief vessel to reach the scene, not a trace of humanity could be found anywhere, either dead or alive. The three lightkeepers had vanished!

In order to be able to appreciate the dramatic setting of this tragedy and mystery, some descriptive details of the Seven Hunters may not be inappropriate at this juncture. To be precise, they lie in latitude 58° 17′ north, and longitude 7° 35′ west. That is to say, some twenty miles west of Lewis, in the Outer Hebrides. Though there are seven main islands, they are so small and compact that

at times, when at sea, it is no easy matter to differentiate among
them.

The Seven Hunters fall naturally into three groups. Eilean Mor
and Eilean Tighe form the northern. Soray, Sgeir Toman, and
Sgeir Righinn constitute the southern. Eilean a' Ghobha and Roareim
form the western group. On the whole, these seven islands vary
little in appearance. All attain a remarkable altitude, having regard
to their limited area. Their cliffs of weather-beaten gneiss tower
above the Atlantic rollers at altitudes varying from 150 feet, as
in the case of Roareim, to more than 260 feet in the case of Eilean
Mor. Some conception of the remarkable height attained by these
cliffs in proportion to the area of the respective islands may be had
when it is remembered that Eilean Mor, largest of the Seven Hunters,
has an area of just under thirty-nine acres, that Eilean Tighe, the
second island in point of size, is only eighteen acres in extent, that
Eilean a' Ghobha, the second in point of height, with cliffs rising
165 feet, is twelve acres, that Roareim's area is roughly seven acres,
and that Sgeir Righinn, smallest of the group, occupies no more than
three acres.

When viewed from the sea and at some little distance, the Seven
Hunters appear for all the world like a set of gigantic cliffs, each
surmounted by a flat plateau. All share the distinction of proffering
no point at which a landing may be effected without difficulty, and
danger, because of the restless winds and tides, and of the vagaries
of the North Atlantic swell. Only during the summer or early autumn,
and under the most felicitous conditions, is it possible to land with
a modicum of safety.

The history of these ancient fragments of the earth goes back a
long way. Ecclesiological remains on Eilean Mor have been assigned
to a date that would suggest the occupation of the group in early
Christian times, probably by hermit monks of the Old Celtic Church.
But George Buchanan, the celebrated Latinist and historian of
sixteenth-century Scotland, ascribes the Seven Hunters' earliest
remains to the Druids. He refers to the group as the *Insulae Sacrae,*
since at that period, and indeed for some centuries previously, they
bore a reputation for sanctity. Situated close to the lighthouse is
the ancient drystone structure known as *Teampull Beannachadh,*
Temple of Blessing, which has been likened in appearance to a large
dog-kennel.[1] Its external length and breadth are twelve feet and

[1] See *Ronay,* by Malcolm Stewart (Oxford University Press, 1933).

nine to ten feet, respectively. It attains an internal height of about
six feet to the apex of the sloping roof, which is still almost complete.
At the west end there enters a small, low doorway. Authorities are
uncertain as to whom this building belonged. "Two saints seem to
contest for the honour of giving their name to the Flannan Isles,"
wrote Dr. John MacCulloch, the geologist, who visited these islands
during his geological researches in the Outer Hebrides. "St. Flannan
was Bishop of Killaloe in 639," continues the 'Stone Doctor'; "and
he is canonised in the Irish Calendar, but St. Flann was the son of
Maol-duine, Abbot of Iona, who died in 890, and who is to decide?"

An authority of a date more recent disposes of the difficulty,
however, by ascribing this and other structures on the Flannans to
the men who used to voyage annually from the Lewis to these remote
outposts for the purposes of collecting sea-birds and their eggs and
feathers, and of capturing what they could of the wild sheep browsing
on the grassy plateau of each of the larger of them. It is not the
least unlikely that these hardy seamen from Lewis constructed on
the Flannans one or more buildings for their own accommodation
during the expedition.

The Flannans, it should be mentioned, form part of Uig, westernmost parish of the Island of Lewis; and to this day the only regular
communication between them and the rest of the world (apart from
the Northern Lighthouse Board's vessels effecting reliefs or landing
stores) is maintained by the people of the Island of Bernera, in Uig,
whence sheep-owners and shepherds sail out to them twice annually,
within the same week if possible, to attend to and exchange some
fifty-five sheep. In fact, for many generations now, the grazing rights
of the Seven Hunters have belonged to the natives of the Great
Bernera—that rocky and extensive island situated in wild Loch Roag.
During the summer months, however, they are visited spasmodically
by lobster-fishermen, and also by trawlermen, who are often accused,
and not unjustifiably, of having added an odd Flannan sheep to their
larder!

Toward the west of Eilean Mor there is another ruin, the condition
of which renders it impossible today to postulate either its original
shape, or the purpose to which it was put. It is known traditionally
in Lewis by a Gaelic name denoting the Bothies of MacPhail's Sons;
but who MacPhail was, or what he and his sons were doing on the
Seven Hunters, no one can tell.

Two ruined structures are to be seen on Eilean Tighe, Island of the House, as might be expected from the name. The walls of one of these are about three feet in height, and three in thickness. On the east side may be traced the remains of a doorway.

*   *   *

That from early times the Seven Hunters have been noted for the excellence of their pasturage, supporting a large number of sheep, is shown by the quaint account of them given by Donald Monro, High Dean of the Isles. Toward the middle of the sixteenth century the venerable Dean wrote of these "Sevin Haley Iles" as follows: –

"First, furth 50 myle in the Occident seas from the coste of the parochin Vye in Lewis, towarts the west northwest lyes the seven iles of Flanayn, claid with girth, and Haley iles, verey natural gressing within thir saids iles; infinit wyld scheipe therein, quhilk na man knawes to quhom the said sheipe apperteines within them that lives this day of the countrymen; bot M'Cloyd of the Lewis, att certaine tymes in the zeir, sendis men in, and huntis and slayis maney of thir sheipe. The flesche of thir sheipe cannot be eaten be honest men for fatnesse, for ther is na flesche on them, bot all quhyte lyke talloune, and it is verey wyld gusted lykways. The saids iles are nouder manurit nor inhabit, bot full of grein high hills, full of wyld sheipe in the sevin iles forsaid, quhilk may not be outrune. They perteine to M'Cloyd of the Lewis."

The Seven Hunters are of further interest in that some very queer customs were observed there by those who yearly visited them on fowling or sealing expeditions, and to collect in addition feathers, down, quills, and possibly seabirds' eggs. Martin Martin,[1] from whom we learn most of what we know of the Hebrides during the seventeenth century, informs us that, if the seamen from Lewis happened to be sailing in the direction of the Seven Hunters before an east wind, and the wind suddenly went round to the west, they would

[1] About 1695 M. Martin, Gent. (d. 1719) made the itinerary which found expression in *A Description of the Western Isles of Scotland*, printed in London in 1703 for Andrew Bell, at the Cross-Keys & Bible, in Cornhill, near Stocks-Market. Martin had written it at the request of Sir Robert Sibbald (1641–1722), President of the Edinburgh Royal College of Physicians, and in his day a noted antiquarian.

Dr. Johnson had seen in his father's bookshop in Lichfield a copy of Martin's unique publication. The copy preserved in the National Library of Scotland bears in Boswell's hand an inscription showing it to have been that which he and Johnson took with them on their famous tour to the Hebrides in 1773.

abandon every intention of landing, and immediately sail back to Lewis again, even though they might have been within a stone's-throw of the usual place of disembarkation. Again, if the crew should include in its number any apprentice untutored in the recognised punctilios of fowling, it was incumbent that he should be placed under the direction of a member of the fowling party who would instruct him as to how he ought to conduct himself when afoot on the hallowed soil of these Isles. Once the boat had been lashed to the rocks, the crew scaled the cliff from the wonted landing-place by means of a wooden ladder held in position by a huge stone in order to prevent its slipping back into the sea. The ledge of rock on which it was customary to land was held in great veneration, since the crew regarded it as the spot at which it had pleased God to deliver them from the perils of the ocean. When all the fowlers were ashore, they bared their heads, and made the wonted sun-wise turn known as *deasil*. While so doing, they thanked God for their safe deliverance. They then removed their upper garments, and placed them on a stone reserved for them. Thereafter they approached the Chapel, wherein they engaged in prolonged prayer and meditation.

For a member of the party to kill a fowl before everyone had ascended the ladder, or after vespers, was deemed an unpardonable crime, whereas the killing of a fowl with a stone was looked upon at all times as "a great barbarity, and directly contrary to antient custom." No one was permitted to take away with him from the Flannans any sheep-suet. Neither was he allowed to appropriate or eat anything on these islands unbeknown to the other members of the expedition. Furthermore, the use of certain words was strictly taboo among the seamen whilst they were ashore. Consequently, they referred to water as *burn*, and not as *uisge*. A rock was spoken of as *cruey* (from the Gaelic, *cruaidh*, meaning hard); while *vah* (*uamh*, a cave) signified the sea-shore. Likewise, it was unlawful to allude to St. Kilda as Hirta, the ancient Gaelic name by which it is still known throughout the Highlands and Islands of Scotland. St. Kilda had to be referred to as "the High Country". Even the name, Flannan, had to be eschewed during these visits. When it was found necessary to mention any of these islands, they were obliged to do so by calling it "the Country".

Apart from the abundance and variety of seabird-life, there is little else of interest about the Seven Hunters except the lighthouse mystery, to which we shall turn in a moment. The chief mammals of importance are the sheep that, as in the case of North Rona (now likewise unpeopled), are landed there from Lewis for grazing. But much more numerous than the sheep are the grey seals haunting the waters around these precipitous isles. It is exceedingly doubtful, however, whether the seal ever breeds on the Seven Hunters, for even so agile a creature must find it very difficult to land on these steep, rock-bound outposts. Neither rats nor mice are to be found; but rabbits have now overrun Eilean Mor, and have destroyed much of its rich pasturage. The rabbits were introduced many years ago by some short-sighted lightkeepers.

The list of birds, resident and migratory, compiled by Eagle Clarke, who spent a couple of weeks on Eilean Mor in 1904, reaches a total of 112 species. Clarke also collected 11 species of Coleoptera, and 35 species of Diptera.

The most important of the Seven Hunters' birds is Leach's fork-tailed petrel. The puffin is very common, nesting largely in the innumerable rabbit burrows. The eggs of the fork-tailed petrel are rare; and collectors usually offer good prices for them—although the wife of a lightkeeper told me at the shore-station of Breascleit some years ago that a taxidermist in Oban was offering her husband tuppence per egg. "My husband wouldn't *blow* a petrel's egg for tuppence!" she remarked with a suggestion in her voice of grievance mixed with a certain amount of pride and Scots independence.

Great risk is often entailed in procuring seabirds' eggs on the Flannan Isles. The method of getting them off inaccessible ledges from above, equipped with bamboo-rod, to the end of which is attached a piece of looped wire and a hanging net-bag, is still employed by the lightkeepers, just as it was by the natives of St. Kilda up to the time of the evacuation of their fastness in the autumn of 1930. This method requires both skill and patience. Flannan light-keepers have told me that sometimes they 'play' an egg for twenty minutes or half an hour before they are successful in scooping it into the net-bag. Their wives at the shore-station use these eggs extensively in cooking and baking. In order to ensure that they are as fresh as possible, the keepers resort regularly to the same nests.

The guillemots and razor-bills lay their eggs on the very edge of the ledges. The result is that, if the hen bird be startled when on her nest, she frequently precipitates her eggs into the sea, or gets them smashed on the rocks below. The kittiwake, on the other hand, builds on the ledge a nest of grass and clay or mud. Her eggs, therefore, are less liable to fall out when she moves or is disturbed. The mud for her nest-building she carries in beakfuls from the freshwater mud-holes as may be found on such islands.

Having regard to what befell the first Flannan lightkeepers, the following, taken down from a framed copy still hanging in the lighthouse tower, is not without interest:

The Commissioners of Northern Lighthouses hereby give Notice, that on the night of Thursday the 7th of December next, and every evening thereafter from the going away of daylight in the evening till the return of daylight in the morning, a Light will be exhibited from a Lighthouse which has been erected on Eilean Mor, one of the Flannan Islands. The Light will be a Group Flashing White Light showing 2 flashes in quick succession every half minute. The power of the Light will be equal to about 140,000 standard candles. The Light will be visible all round and will be elevated 330 feet above high water spring tides, and allowing fifteen feet for the height of the eye will be seen at about 24 nautical miles in clear weather, and at lesser distances according to the state of the atmosphere. When close to, the stacks lying to the westward of Eilean Mor will obscure the Light over two small angles. The top of the Lantern is about 75 feet above the island.

By order of the Board.

Edinburgh, 30th, Oct., 1899. *James Murdoch, Secretary.*

With the rapid development of shipping during the nineteenth century, the Seven Hunters constituted a serious menace, particularly in the night-time and in time of fog. Situated close to the course usually adopted by vessels bound by way of the Butt of Lewis and the Pentland Firth for ports on the east coast of Scotland and England, or for Scandinavian and Baltic ports, these unlit, inhospitable outposts claimed many a victim. A crew, whose ship crashed on the Flannans, stood little chance of being rescued. Even if survivors succeeded in obtaining a footing on one of these islands, they ultimately succumbed to starvation and exposure. Disaster followed upon disaster, until at length representation was made that led to the decision to construct a lighthouse on Eilean Mor. In 1895 this arduous and perilous responsibility was undertaken by the Northern Lighthouse Board. As it was necessary first of all to blast two landing-places and two zigzag staircases out of solid gneiss (one of each on the west side of the island, and one of each on the east), to erect cranes and derricks at both landing-places, and to carry all the requisite material two hundred feet up the face of the cliffs by means of wire pulleys—all of which had to be accomplished in the midst of raging seas—it was not until December, four years later, that the lighthouse itself was ready for service. The lantern-tower, some seventy-five feet in height, was installed with a light of 140,000 candle-power visible, under normal conditions, over a range of forty miles. The Flannan Isles light-station had been operating just a year when there occurred the tragedy, the precise nature of which still remains unknown, and is likely to remain so forever. Then, as now, the station was manned by three lightkeepers, each of whom served two months at it, and was relieved in rotation by the fourth, who resided in the shore-station at Breascleit, on Loch Roag. Weather permitting, the relief in those days was carried out regularly by the *Hesperus*, one of the splendid little ships in the service of the Northern Lighthouse Board. When the *Hesperus* arrived off Eilean Mor on December, 26th, 1900, the relief, owing to inclement seas, already was some days overdue. In the meantime a passing vessel, the *Archer*, had reported by morse to the shore-station that, when passing the Flannans in the darkness, she had failed to pick up their light. The three men believed to have been on duty at the time were James Ducat, Thomas Marshall, and Donald MacArthur. The fourth lightkeeper, Joseph Moore, was now returning from the shore-station to relieve one of the three. As the *Hesperus* hove-to off the east landing-stage, which was the more suitable on this occasion because of the direction of the wind, skipper and crew were surprised that the lightkeepers did not answer to the customary signals, for the relief-steamer as a rule was observed when she was still a goodly distance from the islands. Surprise turned to dismay when, on closer examination, the east landing-place showed none of the usual indications that the *Hesperus* was expected. The idea that, perhaps, preparations to receive the relief had been made at the *west* landing was not entertained for a moment. Three skilled lightkeepers, all by this time inured to the conditions of storm and prolonged isolation associated with the Seven Hunters, were not likely to expect the arrival of the *Hesperus* at the *west* landing-place when the skipper found the *east* the more practicable!

With some difficulty Joseph Moore was put ashore on Eilean Mor, together with the usual mails and provisions. In the ordinary way, the lightkeeper, whose turn it was to be relieved, would have been waiting at the landing-place, ready to be transferred aboard; and the *Hesperus* would have returned with him that afternoon to the shore-station at Breascleit. True it was that a day or two earlier a passing vessel had reported the extinction of the Flannan Light, and that the natives dwelling among the remote sea-creeks of western Lewis had failed to observe the beam on particular nights. However, this caused no alarm at the time, as the neighbourhood for some weeks had been wrapped in sea-fog of varying density. But no light shone when the fog had cleared away! It now was certain that something of a serious nature had happened.

While the relief-steamer lay off the landing-place at a distance sufficient to prevent her being brought into sudden contact with the cliffs with a change of wind, Moore hurried up the long, zigzag staircase to the lighthouse. The gate admitting one to the enclosure, in which lay the lighthouse, the keepers' dwelling-house, and the more adjacent out-buildings, was closed. So, too, were all outer doors. Moore immediately flung them open, and made his way to the living-room. He found it empty. The clock on the mantelshelf had ticked itself to a standstill. In the fireplace lay the cold, dead cinders of the last warmth enjoyed by the missing lightkeepers. Chill welcome, indeed, on a mid-winter's day in the North Atlantic! Imagining for a moment that, maybe, they had overslept, Moore then dashed into the bedroom. He found it lifeless. In bewilderment, he hastened back to the landing-place to seek help. On learning his story, two more men were got ashore with some difficulty. The three of them now proceeded to make the fullest investigation. They ransacked the lighthouse-tower and adjoining buildings. No trace could they find of the lightkeepers. Then they scoured the surface, cliffs, and caverns of Eilean Mor, but with equally little result. Again examining the landing-place at which they had just disembarked, they found it precisely in the order in which it had been left when the previous relief had been carried out on December, 6th, just twenty days earlier. They then clambered down to the west landing-place. Though there was evidence at this point of recent storms, the crane, fixed as it still is in a concrete base some eighty feet above the sea, appeared to have escaped damage. Its jib was lowered and fastened to the rock in the usual fashion; and the tarpaulin remained tightly wrapped round the barrel of the crane, protecting the hawser from sea-spray and the corroding influences of other epigene agents. Yet, on closer inspection it was discovered that a box kept in a hollow in the rocks, some forty feet above the level of the crane platform, had been dislodged—that is to say, at a height approximately 120 feet above the sea. This box contained a number of spare ropes and crane-handles. Several of the latter were found scattered upon the face of the cliffs some little distance below this point. It looked very much as though a tremendous wave had come tearing up from the west, had carried away the box, had broken it open, and had scattered its contents about the cliffs, or swept them into the sea. One or two of the ropes, I believe, actually were found entwined round the crane. Further evidence that this side of Eilean Mor had been subjected to a storm of the most violent character lay in the facts that a great stone exceeding a ton in weight had been moved a considerable distance, having regard to its massiveness, and that much of the iron railings fringing the lower part of the stone staircase had been dis-located and twisted.

However, the evidence at the west landing-place gave no definite clue as to what had occurred, though its storm-shattered appearance, when considered in conjunction with some of the evidence obtained in the habitable part of the lighthouse premises, seemed to suggest at least one plausible explanation. It was discovered that the oil-skins and sea-boots of Ducat and Marshall were missing. Joseph Moore, who knew well the ways of his fellow-lightkeepers, was able to con-firm that, only when they were obliged to inspect the landing-stages in time of storm, did they wear this equipment. The third man apparently had gone out as though in a hurry, leaving both his oil-skin and sea-boots behind him. These were found in their proper place in the lighthouse premises. This gave weight to the theory that, during one of the many storms engulfing the Seven Hunters that wild December, the lightkeepers, anxious lest everything had not been made doubly fast at the west landing-place, ventured to reach the scene, and were either carried off by a terrific gale, or swept away by a stupendous wave that had left the trail of havoc already described. One such wave, as we know, had made its fury felt on objects more than a hundred feet above the ocean's level.

Although this theory gained considerable currency and acceptance, the lighthouse world had difficulty in accepting it. To men in the service of the Northern Lighthouse Board, it seemed unreasonable —nay, untenable—that, when a storm of such violence was raging, three tried and experienced keepers would all have ventured forth to a spot as perilous as can be the west landing-place on Eilean Mor under such circumstances.

Certain bare facts we do possess. The record of happenings on the Seven Hunters had been kept punctiliously by Ducat, the principal keeper. From the log found by those who made the search, it was evident that on December, 12th and 13th, a furious gale had been blowing from a westerly direction, and that this gale had subsided considerably by the 14th. The last entry made on the slate by Ducat was timed 9 a.m., and dated Saturday, December, 15th. Therefore, whenever the tragedy occurred, it obviously was *after* that! Possibly later in the morning of the same day, or perhaps in the afternoon. Though other meteorological sources indicated that by the 15th the gale had fallen almost to a fresh breeze, the seas around the Seven Hunters, in all probability, were still running high with freakish swells that at unexpected moments crashed upon their cliffs.

The condition in which the lighthouse and its habitable premises were found helped the investigators to fix the time of the fatality more precisely. The final entry on the slate, as we have seen, was 9 a.m. But it was observed that the morning's routine duties had been performed subsequent to that hour. The big lamps in the lantern-tower had been trimmed in readiness for another night's vigil: the canteens and oil fountains were primed: the lens and mechanism had been cleaned and polished in the usual way after a night's revolving. All this took time. Furthermore, everything in the kitchen was in order. Utensils used in the preparation and consumption of that morning's breakfast were all clean and in their place. This seems to add to the conviction that doom befell the keepers in the late forenoon, before lunch-time. Finally, Captain Holman of the S.S. *Archer* reported that, at midnight on the 15/16th December, he had passed the Seven Hunters on a course on which, even having regard to weather conditions, he was bound to have picked up the Flannan Light, had it been showing. That midnight he saw no light! So, while we are able to fix with a degree of certainty the day of this haunting tragedy, and even the hour of day within reasonable limits, the cause and nature of it still remains a mystery.

Nearly seventy years have come and gone since that wild December. No one is any nearer a solution. The sea, unlike humans, has a terrifying way of keeping its secrets.

When staying with my kinsfolk in Lewis a few years ago, I happened one evening to visit the keepers at the lighthouse perched above the wild, northern tides at the Butt of Lewis. They chanced at the time to be speaking by wireless to their comrades on the Flannans, as they do at least twice at stated periods every day, transmitting news to them, receiving news from them, and also discussing matters of a domestic nature. Soon the Flannan Light was streaking the tides of the North Atlantic with unerring precision, and with an effulgence which convinced me that the man devoid of a sense of reverence were better dead! By this time a gale of considerable velocity had reached its maximum. It was then that I had that terrifying and awe-inspiring experience known only to those intimately acquainted with the sea and the art of pharology—the experience of being high up in a lighthouse-tower when it is rocking visibly around and beneath one, and the foam and spindrift of turbulent seas are blinding the lantern with dark, foreboding shadows. As I left the keepers in their grim setting to find my way home across the vast Lewisian moors, now overcast by an angry night, my mind was turned to;

Three men alive on Flannan Isle,
Who thought of three men dead!

In December, 1938, when our Hebrides were swept by gales and dashed by mounting seas, making it impossible to effect the normal reliefs at several lighthouses, another three men alive on Flannan Isle were among those in distress. When the Northern Lighthouse vessel, *Pole Star,* arrived from the shore-station at Breascleit late that month in order to carry out the routine relief, it was discovered that two of the three lightkeepers had fallen ill, and that for several days and nights Donald MacLeod, an occasional hand, had been attending to the light alone, and at the same time nursing his companions. Though he had been in regular wireless communication with the the lightkeepers at the Butt throughout his ordeal, turbulent seas and similar distress at other lighthouses in the *Pole Star's* circuit had rendered impossible an earlier relief. The strain upon MacLeod had been enormous. For all our modern appliances, tragedy might still befall at the Flannans. Only the lightkeepers' most rigid self-discipline reduces the likelihood at such perilous outposts.

Although the mystery of the Flannan lightkeepers has remained unsolved all these years, now and again an echo of it may still be heard. In 1967 a certain James Armour wrote from Wisconsin to the

Scottish Field, recalling how, in the course of conversations he had had at Oban about 1926 with a Captain Allan MacDonald, a member of the *Hesperus's* crew in 1900, MacDonald told him that, since Joseph Moore, the relief lightkeeper, could scarcely have been left alone on Eilean Mor, he volunteered to remain there with him until other arrangements could be made. For this he was afterwards presented with a gold watch inscribed to commemorate his courageous and meritorious services on that occasion.

*　　*　　*

It was not until August, 1946, that a happy concatenation of circumstances enabled me to disembark at the Flannan Isles under the most favourable conditions, both as regards the means of reaching them, and as regards weather. The Northern Lighthouse authorities in Edinburgh, with whom I have had some contact throughout most of my life, granted me a passage on the *Pole Star.* The day chosen was an admirable one for my purpose, since it was what in lighthouse parlance is termed a coal-and-water day. As the unloading of these commodities takes several hours, even when the sea around this cluster of isles is calm, I was afforded ample time ashore on Eilean Mor. Half-yearly—in April, and again in August, before the northern winter sets in—the *Pole Star* sails at that time for the Flannans from her base at Stromness, by way of Breascleit, in order to land 1,250 gallons of water and several tons of coal, the former mainly for cooking and drinking purposes, the latter for domestic use, and also for generating steam to operate the cable-haulage system whereby stores are transported between landing-stage and lighthouse. In addition to coal and water, roughly 1,200 gallons of paraffin and 150 gallons of petrol have to be landed, the paraffin for the lamps, the petrol for the charging of batteries. Water is landed in 7-gallon ankers, made of wood so as to ensure its purity. Water from metal receptacles never tastes as good. Paraffin is put ashore in steel drums, each holding 40 gallons.

In response to a telegram stating precisely when the vessel was expected to land such stores, and at the same time effect the relief then due, I flew to Stornoway's airport, and in the late evening of the same day left for Breascleit on the boat-bus, as the islanders call the last outward-bound conveyance after the arrival, at Stornoway, of the mailboat from Kyle of Lochalsh. I had but crossed the vast, moorland interior of Lewis, when I observed the Standing Stones of Callernish, silent and ominous against the gathering dark. Soon a glimpse of Loch Roag was to be had. Before reaching the pink-washed shore-station, situated a hundred yards above the road leading on to Carloway, to Bragair and Barvas, and eventually to the Butt of Lewis, the mast-tops of a vessel appeared among the hills and rocks: the *Pole Star* was already at her anchorage off Breascleit. My journey now took on the quality of adventure. I spent the night at the shore-station, where I was entertained most hospitably. Lighthouse institutions are famed for their hospitality. When on the point of turning in, I drew aside the casement, just to make sure that the ship to which I now pinned my immediate aspiration was still there. I could discern her bare masts, thrust up into the starlight. It augured well; and I retired with an easy mind.

When breakfasting about five the following morning, we tuned in to a conversation between the ship and the Flannan lightkeepers. The former endorsed that she was bringing, in addition to the relieving keeper, the usual autumn stores, plus *me*: the latter responded that they were looking forward to our arrival, and that weather conditions out there indicated a landing at the east side. An hour later I was aboard the *Pole Star* as she raised anchor and began to sail cautiously down Loch Roag toward the open Atlantic. A curious morning fog now descended in patches, suffused here and there by a crimson glow lent to it by a rising sun as yet unseen. Wisps of vapour from the still sea condensed everywhere around us. This weird setting resembled what one imagines the earth may have looked like when cooling down in the eras of primordial chaos. It was not unlike the effect one got at dawn over a ruined and smouldering city, after a night's ordeal with incendiary bombs.

Had the fog increased, we would have been delayed indefinitely, since, owing to violent magnetic disturbance off Cruitir (a rock in mid-channel at the mouth of East Loch Roag), mariners cannot sail these waters by compass, and must therefore rely, for a mile or two, on the recognised landmarks. A submarine deposit of iron ore in this locality plays tricks with the compass. Within an hour, however, we were steaming past Berisay and the Old Hill. Strong lighting by this time enabled me to locate, on the former isle, the ruins of the fortress occupied early in the seventeenth century by that redoubtable pirate, Neil MacLeod, one of the last of the MacLeods of Lewis—the very Neil who, as the Lord Advocate informed King James in 1613, "died at his executioun verey christianlie".

When the Seven Hunters appeared on the horizon ahead of us, bright sunshine and unusually good visibility prognosticated a profitable day ashore. From the camera's viewpoint, it was a day such as one gets at the Flannan Isles but once or twice in a whole year, and such as seldom falls when the *Pole Star* is due there to carry out the routine relief and to land supplies. All this inspired in me a sense of the wonderment navigators in ancient times must have felt when sailing uncharted seas in search of unknown landfalls. It may be regretted that all the world's landfalls have now been tabulated.

Scarcely had the anchor found bottom off the East Landing when the motor-launch was lowered. To and fro between vessel and island, all day long, she now began to ply. Every fifteen minutes or so, she was alongside again, unloading empties, and taking aboard as many sacks of coal or ankers of water as conditions so favourable would allow. Not even the steward's temptatious recital of the breakfast menu could restrain me from going ashore on her third trip. The sun by this time had waxed strong behind us, lighting up the eastern shores of such isles as lay before us. By this time, moreover, I had surveyed them at leisure from this anchorage, had watched and listened to groups of seabirds at their various pursuits and antics, and had taken a dozen or more photographs.

The approximate hour of arrival was already known, for, as I have mentioned, we had been in touch with the lightkeepers by wireless early that morning. Thus, the steam-engine driving the huge drum round which the cable coils and uncoils was soon working at full pressure. From the concrete platform at the East Landing to the very threshold of the lighthouse runs the steep railway, up and down which the truck now began to travel. An antiquated bit of machinery, consuming three tons of coal in performing a day's work. Yet, it is reliable, and not too inefficient. No sooner had a netful of stores been raised by derrick from the launch below, and packed into the truck, than it set off on its acclivitous journey, a speaking-tube enabling those engaged in loading it to inform the engine-man at the lighthouse immediately it was full enough to ascend again. Slowly, but so surely, it climbs. When returning, it comes tearing down the line under gravity, pulling the cable after it, and unwinding the drum. At a point some yards from its terminus at the landing-stage, the engine-man slows it down by retarding the speed of the drum. The length of cable already unwound tells him just where the truck is, in its downward rush, so that he knows exactly when to steady it up. On so remote a rock-station, doubtless, some oil-driven device would be more economical; and it is probable that by this time, but for the war, it would have been installed.

*   *   *

I was scarcely a moment ashore before realising that, in order to cover the ground swiftly, yet safely, I would have to discard my footgear, for this would reduce enormously the likelihood of my slipping on the rocks and cliffs, or on succulent vegetation, especially on such of it as sloped suddenly and precipitously seawards. The bare foot, allowing one to make primitive use of the toes, affords the surest foothold of all, as every scrambler in places rough and perilous is aware. Only when picking one's way over rocky or stony surfaces did one find movement irksome. The asperities of the gneiss, where it had weathered in planes well off the horizontal, made the going slow, and not too pleasant, particularly to one whose soles in recent years had been but little inured to rude travel. Nevertheless, without some sort of tackle, the cliffs of the Seven Hunters, though they rise to no great altitude, remain inaccessible except, perhaps, to cragsmen as surefooted and intrepid as were the St. Kildans I once knew.

Since the greater part of Eilean Mor is covered with closely knit sward (much of it consisting of sea-thrift growing, as it does on maritime rocks, in dense, cushion-like rosettes), progress on the whole could be made on ground as sure as it was agreeable. Yet, even there, one was obliged to tread with caution, especially by the edge of cliffs falling perpendicularly, since rabbits have so undermined the top-soil with burrows hidden by thrift and branching matricary that the foot often slips down into one of them, causing a stumble and a tumble. Indeed, the leg, with amazing suddenness, may disappear right up to the thigh. Were this to happen where, at best, the footing at the cliff's margin is steep and slender, it might prove fatal.

The sea-parrots, or puffins, nest in these rabbit burrows. Often, as you pass prudently across them, even as late in the year as August, you will hear, underfoot, a concealed puffin growling its resentment at your intrusion. The puffin thus disturbed emits a weird, unbird-like sound.

The lightkeepers, who are afforded unique opportunities on such rock-stations for studying bird-life, and often take advantage of them, told me that most of the seabirds had left the Flannans a month or so earlier. They usually depart about the end of June or the beginning of July, after the summer nesting. But there were still considerable numbers to be seen, this tenth day of August. Inland, one noticed a few land-birds—sparrows, finches, and the like. Solans were busy fishing close inshore, dropping plumb upon their prey, as is their mode. Gulls were sitting on old nests among cliffs and caverns, and upon the tufty slopes honeycombed with burrows, and covered so largely with matricary in flower, white or dark yellow. Puffins still occupied many of the burrows. Groups of them continued to alight everywhere around me, demonstrating their tameness and curiosity. A few shags stood like rows of dark sentinels on the ridges of neighbouring skerries; while a variety of gulls kept on coming and going throughout the entire day. As I moved about the cliffs, the seafowl seemed to be keeping an eye on me, and to be asking themselves how I dared invade their condominium in this way.

One other item of biological interest might be mentioned. On Soray (Soraidh) there existed a solitary sheep. It was the only one which the Lewis shepherds had been unable to round up when, in 1938, they paid their annual visit to the Seven Hunters to transport, to the mainland of Lewis, those wintered there. Ever since, that lone creature had lived on Soray. I was able to pick it out with the naked eye, and eventually to scrutinise it with the lighthouse telescope, just as the crew of the *Pole Star* had done with the ship's telescope on approaching the East Landing early that morning. Most of the day this sheep lay near the skyline, watching from afar our diverse activities on Eilean Mor. Despite its eight years of solitary confinement, so far as one could judge at this distance, it looked well. It certainly seemed active enough when, during our visit, it stretched its limbs and began to browse upon the considerable pasturage it had had to itself all those years.

By 6 p.m. that evening, with the sun still shining brightly and our respective tasks nearing completion, preparations were being made for our return to Breascleit. All stores had been put ashore, and consigned to their apportioned places: all empties of one kind or another were aboard. The keeper we were relieving was ready to embark with us. All day long he had worked hard with the crew and his fellow-keepers in unloading and transshipping the vast quantities of goods landed that day. Having used up my films by this time, and expended much energy in so doing, I was glad of the meal one of the lightkeepers had prepared for me in their warm, homely living-room. It included three eggs laid that very day by the few hens kept on Eilean Mor. I had now traversed every axis of that island, as it were, and had taken a couple of dozen photographs. I had crossed and re-crossed the railway several times in my bare feet, careful not to get involved with truck or cable. Once or twice, when passing by the points, I had the mischievous urge to shift them over, so that the truck, when next it descended, might have run down to the *West* Landing, instead of to the East, where its return was awaited. But I realised in time that, had I practised any such prank, this would be the last occasion on which the authorities might place at my disposal facilities I so greatly appreciated, and a ship aboard which I felt myself so favoured a passenger. All the same, the temptation to divert that truck by the simple device provided was hard to resist, since all my life I have enjoyed playing with anything in the nature of wheels and rails.

In due course we sailed away from these haunted and haunting isles. When approaching the Old Hill once more, I clambered up to the bridge to take the last exposure on the last of my films. This I had reserved for the isle next to the Old Hill—for Berisay, where Neil MacLeod and his pirate accomplices held out until that wily bird, MacKenzie of Kintail, dislodged them by cruel stratagem. In order to enable me to do this to advantage, Captain Williamson took his vessel somewhat closer than usual. Three hours' steaming from the Flannans brought us back to our anchorage off Breascleit.

Of the many marvellous days with which my life has been endowed, none has been more marvellous than this. In ruminating upon it, I find myself looking back along the *Pole Star's* wake at the Seven Hunters, back through pre-human vistas to those aeons when the first, fierce stars were dispelling primeval dark.

The lighthouse on Eilean Mor, largest of the Seven Hunters

Temple of Blessing. In the Distance *Eilean a' Ghobha* (The Smith's Isle), and two of the four rocks known as The Stacks. In the middle-distance the hutch on its narrow-gauge rail-track with sacks of coal ascending to the lighthouse on coal-and-water day

Ruins of the ancient structure on Eilean Mor known traditionally as the Bothies of MacPhail's Sons (*Page 17*)

Cliffs at the north-east end of North Rona, near the customary landing-place, seen from that barren part of the island known as Fianuis

CHAPTER TWO

North Rona:
The Seals' Isle

IN THE North Atlantic, at a distance of 44 miles north-north-east from the Butt of Lewis and a mile more from Cape Wrath in a westerly direction, lies North Rona, the isle referred to in olden times as Ronay or Roney. Its name today is almost invariably prefaced by *North* so as to distinguish this remote lump of Lewisian gneiss from *South* Rona, the isle of the Inner Hebrides situated 98 sea miles to the south of it, just off Raasay, no distance from the northern end of Skye. If we exclude Rockall, that dot of rock rising some 70 feet out of the Atlantic wastes 184 miles west of St. Kilda, described so aptly by Captain Basil Hall in 1810 as "the most isolated speck in the world," this Isle of the Seals (for such does its name denote, *ròn* being the Gaelic for a seal) may well be regarded as the loneliest of the isles of Britain once inhabited, and over an appreciable period of time.

With an area of roughly 300 acres, covered mainly with coarse grass and sedge, North Rona, now a National Nature Reserve, forms part of the Lewis parish of Barvas, as does also no less distant and inaccessible Sùla Sgeir. It is lonelier far, one would say, than St. Kilda, for, although nearly forty years have elapsed since the St. Kildans were transferred to, and settled upon, the Scottish mainland, the *Hebrides* and *Dunara Castle*, sister-ships belonging to the Glasgow shipping concern of MacCallum, Orme, and Company, did pay frequent visits throughout the summer months to Hirta, largest of the St. Kilda group of islands, and that upon which men and women and children had contrived to exist uninterruptedly for at least a thousand years.

Until fairly recently, only once a year, and then for no longer than a summer day's daylight provided conditions for landing and embarking were favourable, did Rona, authentically and officially, occupy man's vision, and feel the weight of his feet. That was when the men from Ness, that rugged and densely populated parish of Lewis terminating in its inhospitable Butt, and regarded as the most fertile in all the Outer Hebrides, sailed thither every July primarily for the purpose of attending to the 150 to 200 sheep pastured there by Alasdair MacFarquhar, a farmer residing at North Dell, but a couple of miles from the Butt, and a little less from the Port of Ness, that *geo* or harbour where they embarked, and whither they returned at dusk. *Un*officially, however, trawlermen operating in North Atlantic and Icelandic waters, especially when obliged in wild, wintry weather to seek shelter in its bay, with a larder running a bit low, did land from time to time, if only to help themselves to one or two of Alasdair's sheep.

Long regarded as one of the remotest islands of Britain, North Rona has become much better known in recent years, partly on account of its having been declared in June, 1956, along with Sùla Sgeir, a Natural Nature Reserve, and partly because of its fairly regular inclusion in those popular island cruises organised annually by the National Trust for Scotland.

Since roughly a quarter of this island's area of 300 acres is occupied by the Atlantic, or grey, seal at its breeding season, the Nature Conservancy is concerned mostly with protecting and studying this species at that time. It breeds in great numbers on the lower ledges of its rocky coast where it is not entirely shoreless, and also on the adjacent skerries. Each year, between the early days of September and the end of December, no fewer than 8,000 of these quite large creatures, varying widely in age, frequent it. In fact, North Rona's herd is the world's largest. Densely occupying Fianuis, the island's northern and comparatively low promontory, it has been estimated that some 2,500 seal pups are born there annually. To quote Dr. J. Morton Boyd, the Conservancy's regional officer for West Scotland, this island then displays in its seals what is perhaps the finest spectacle of wild life in Britain. "It is at once beauty and ugliness, tenderness and savagery, strength and weakness, calm and storm, light and darkness—all on a grand scale in the idiom of the lone isle and the wide ocean."[1] Young seals he and his companions tagged there have been found afar only a few months after their leaving it. Recoveries have been made from Caithness and Aberdeenshire, from the Orkneys and from the Shetlands, from the Faeroes and from Iceland,

[1] *Scotland's Magazine*, February, 1962.

from Norway, from Lewis, and from Donegal. His team rendered habitable Rona's old manse, stretching over its semi-underground ruin a tarpaulin supported by a ridge-pole, and made secure against the winds by guy-ropes attached to ponderous stones. Heated with bottled gas and illuminated with pressurised paraffin, this made a comfortable refuge. "The days follow one another at great pace," Boyd records. "A routine of heavy work (each young seal is a struggling hundred-weight of muscle and fat), cooking, note-making, radio-link with the Butt of Lewis, and deep sleep. The team endures the aches of muscles brought suddenly into violent use after months of compara-tive idleness; and the discomforts and filth of wild weather on the seal grounds are amply repaid by sunshine, rare spectacles, and the comradeship in the little pool of light in the benighted ocean."

Apart from sheep, Rona's most important, and certainly its largest, mammal is the seal, although one must mention that whales are often sighted at no great distance offshore. One must also mention that the island possesses neither rabbits nor reptiles; while careful observations conducted a few years ago by thoroughly competent naturalists failed to show the existence there either of rats or of mice.

My earliest desire to visit this isle began with Alick MacFarquhar's telling me, many years ago now, of an occasion when, just before dawn, he and his shepherds arrived off it to hear the seals making music around their boat "like a great, Gaelic congregation singing the metrical psalms".

The problem that used to confront Alasdair MacFarquhar in regard to sheep-stealing on North Rona today exercises to some extent the Nature Conservancy in regard to the seals. It is thought that now and again foreign fishing-vessels visit the island intent upon obtaining and marketing calf-skins and seal-meat while the seals are breeding there. The damage for which one such visit can be respon-sible is quite considerable. This identical problem faces the Con-servancy where St. Kilda's thousand or more Soay sheep are concerned.

*   *   *

North Rona's bird-life, generally speaking, is not unlike that of other remote Hebridean islands similar in structure, such as the Shiants, the Flannans or Seven Hunters, Mingulay, Berneray, and the St. Kilda group. More than fifty Rona species, resident and migratory, have been listed by the ornithologist, T. H. Harrisson. Commonest is Leach's fork-tailed petrel, that *rara avis* elsewhere. Next in numbers comes the fulmar. In Britain the former, rarest of our four nesting pelagics, breeds only on North Rona, the Flannans, and St. Kilda, burrowing out a tunnel or corridor roughly a couple of inches in diameter and often as much as three or four feet deep. At the inner extremity of this, and on the bare soil, although sometimes in a nest of grass, moss, and sheeps' wool, it lays its single, chalky-white egg. So seldom is this bird seen ashore, even during the nesting-season, that sailors (among whom it is known as Mother Cary's chick) long shared the notion that it deposited its egg in the sea, and that incubation took place under its wing.

North Rona's members of the species nest almost exclusively in the burrows they have made in the dilapidated walls of its deserted village, and in the grassy and thrift-covered banks which, in its immediate vicinity, still delineate much of the arable territory of a departed people. These birds' concentration in this comparatively small area has facilitated greatly the study of them in a peculiar way because, as is generally admitted, their species, as I already have indicated, is the most oceanic of all British breeding birds, and nests in places inaccessibly underground. Furthermore, on land it is entirely nocturnal.

There now comes to mind a relevant passage written by my friend, the late Douglas M. Reid, for many years science master at Harrow, with whom I spent several memorable days at Stoer House, in distant Sutherland, shortly before his death there in 1959, at the age of 61. On July, 31st, 1930, Douglas and Malcolm Stewart (to whom we shall be referring later) were landed on North Rona. Having rendered reasonably wind- and water-proof the old manse, they occupied it until August, 4th, when the steam-drifter, *Sophos,* retrieved them. Of the island's fork-tailed petrels Douglas wrote subsequently:

"This scourge lives in burrows in the roofs of the houses and remains quiet all day. Once you have got yourself comfortably tucked in for the night and have at last really got to sleep, these birds begin to take a hand in things. First of all they sit round in a circle and talk to each other in an extremely loud voice which sounds something like this—Puie-e-e-e brrrrrrrr—the latter part like a very bad and very prolonged gear-change. This ultimately, after a series of nightmares, wakes you up. While you are still trying to adjust your ideas to account for it all, something walks unhurriedly across your face and reaching your forehead says 'Pui-e-e brrrr—' and all your returning senses fly to pieces and you make a wild grab and catch nothing. And so the night goes on. . . ."[1]

A truly fascinating account of this petrel's aerial activity is that published by the naturalists, John A. Ainslie and Robert Atkinson, in 1937, as the result of the intensive study they had made of it on North Rona for 27 consecutive days and nights between July, 16th, and August, 12th, of the previous year. "The most remarkable feature of the habits of Leach's Petrel," they record, "is the extraordinary night flighting above the nesting colony in which the birds indulge. No birds were seen anywhere near the island during the day. Usually the first signs of life in the evening were one or two birds leaving the colony and flying out to sea, anything up to 20 minutes before any incoming birds were noted. Shortly afterwards, a single bird would be seen rapidly circling round in the half-darkness; and then others would appear, and calling would begin from 2 to 20 minutes later. Soon the air was filled with flying, calling shapes swooping among and above the dark ruins. Every bird seemed to be in a great hurry: there was a feeling of enormous energy and purpose about these dashing flights. Birds were everywhere, brushing the grass, skimming along the walls, turning aside at the last moment to avoid ourselves. Often we heard collisions. Once we saw two birds collide head-on in mid-air. Both tumbled to the ground, but fluttered away unharmed. Harrisson has seen the same. Outlandish calls came from the darkness on every side, from the air, from the hollow walls, and from underground, where they mingled with the chicks' excited peeping. Away from the sea-cliffs, Rona is far noisier by night than by day. The frantic energy of the flying birds, their extraordinary calls, the whole midnight ritual above the dim ruins on a deserted island, in an empty sea, makes a never-to-be-forgotten impression."[2]

North Rona measures approximately a mile and a half in length from north to south, and attains toward the south a maximum breadth of about a mile. It is composed of Lewisian gneiss, the oldest known rock in the world. Its total area, as we have seen, is in the neighbour-

---

[1] *Cornhill Magazine,* September, 1931.

[2] Excerpt from the description of the breeding habits of Leach's Fork-tailed Petrel by John A. Ainslie and Robert Atkinson, *British Birds* (Witherby), No. 8, Vol. XXX, January, 1937.

hood of 300 acres. "The island has the shape of a decanter with the neck toward the north," wrote Captain Burnaby, who visited it in the early spring of 1852; and his description is accepted by more recent investigators as being quite appropriate. The impression it makes upon one approaching it for the first time is at once startling and enduring; and the experience of setting foot on such territory, as the writer well knows, defeats all powers of tongue or pen, for the nature of such experience is basic, elemental, remote. The abiding solitude, disturbed only by the breaking seas, by the occasional bleat of sheep, by the haunting calls of seafowl, and often by the roar of wind among the cliffs and caverns, never fails to convey one back and back to Time primordial.

The island on the whole is flat, particularly the Fianuis part of it, which possesses a storm-beach, and is almost completely barren. Toward the south-east, however, it rises steeply in the form of a ridge to an altitude of 355 feet. It is entirely cliff-bound, and there- fore almost entirely shore-less. Only at two spots—one at the Geodha Stoth, on the east: the other at Stoc a' Phriosain, on the south—is a landing possible. Even there, the greatest difficulty and peril are frequently experienced, except in very calm weather and in the absence of a swell. Of the two, the Geodha Stoth is the more practic- able, because of the comparative low-ness of the cliffs just there. As compared with the landing-place at Stoc a' Phriosain, however, it lies some distance from the site of the ruined village of Rona. This is a great disadvantage when heavy gear and equipment and provisions of any kind have to be landed, and then carried to the base of operations usually selected by scientific or other expeditions visiting this lone outpost. Stoc a' Phriosain, on the other hand, has the advantage of being situated immediately below the island's ruined homes.

Rona's cliffs in places are of considerable height, and fall steeply to the Atlantic. They are the resort of countless seabirds. In this respect they resemble those of Sùla Sgeir, that lone and precipitous gannetry lying roughly a dozen miles to the westward. These cliffs are exposed to the unbridled fury of the Atlantean storms. Out of them the sea has scooped innumerable caves and geos. The best known of the former is the Tunnel Cave, to which the name, Sgeildige, has been given. A rounded arch, some fifty feet in height, forms its entrance. Certainly a hundred feet in length, Sgeildige is to be found on the west side of the isthmus linking Fianuis with the main part of the island. The writer of a book dealing with Rona and Sùla Sgeir, published in 1933, mentions Poll Thothatom as an excellent example of a geo.[1]

According to Sir Archibald Geikie, who landed on Rona in 1894, the sea has piled up, in the form of a huge ridge more than 70 feet in height, great quantities of blocks of rock along the north-western coast, with the result that, in time of gales and heavy swells, tons of sea water, thrown up over this ridge, have descended eastward to the sea in streams that have cut their courses down through the turf surface to the naked gneiss. As is remarked in the appropriate publication of the Scottish Mountaineering Club, little wonder the family once living on North Rona found it necessary to occupy a dwelling constructed largely underground!

Off Rona's south-west, and separated from it merely by a few yards, lie the two rocks, Har Sgeir and Loba Sgeir. At the north end is situated a third such skerry. Another, larger than any of these and known as Gealdruig Mor, lies some 600 yards to the south of the south-east end; while roughly 300 yards east of Loba Sgeir is a sunken reef. Apart from these, the waters about North Rona are deep, presenting no real hindrance to navigation.

Except at its northern and south-western extremities, Rona supports a flourishing vegetation. There is neither heather nor peat; but rough grass grows profusely, and to an unusual height in places. This grass affords rich pasturage for about two hundred sheep. In the absence of peat, the natives burned dried divots, and driftwood when procurable.

The complete absence of heather, peat, and even bracken surprises one arriving there for the first time from the Lewis mainland, which is largely one vast peat-land. North Rona, geologically, is simply the northernmost extension above water of the Outer Hebrides. Yet, the surface of sandy soil covering its gneiss to a depth of but a few inches differs in that it supports a turf matting of considerable toughness. Such as was removed for fuel throughout the centuries when the island was inhabited—removed mainly from the locality to the west of its fallen and overgrown township—has never managed to replace itself. As Fraser Darling states in his *Island Years,* such scars never heal completely in our northern lands, where, in any case, the soil is apt to be very thin and of poor quality. What amazed him during his prolonged stay on North Rona was this turf's resis-

[1] *Ronay,* by Malcolm Stewart (Oxford University Press 1933).

tance to the fury of the Atlantic gales during the winter months. "I have seen the turf torn from the rocks by the wind and rolled inland," he writes, "and even stones as big as a man's head pushed from their bed an inch or two on the turf and rolled two or three yards uphill. The wind on Rona has to be felt to be realised."

Fraser Darling's summary of the island's botany makes interesting reading. It should be noted in this connection that Robert Atkinson listed as many as forty-two plant species. Only those with a high tolerance of salt, such as sea-pink, sea-milkwort, the annual poa-grass, and chickweed, grow profusely. The others are limited by the salt-laden gales raging over the island throughout much of the year. Darling refers to the extraordinary growth of chickweed on the eastern side of Fianuis, where, to a depth of a foot, it covers an area of some twenty acres.

The island has no running water apart from those temporary streams of brine sent over by gales from the north-west, and mentioned by Geikie as having cut channels down through the turf to the gneiss. But seldom does Rona pine for moisture: rain is one of its most insistent visitors. On the lower ground, water may be found readily by digging, especially to the south of the ruined village. In olden times the island possessed several wells. Though the sites of many of these are known, only that located near Poll Heallair, in the south, is now serviceable.

*   *   *

Probably the earliest record we possess of North Rona is that contained in the celebrated *Descriptione of the Western Isles of Scotland called Hybrides,* by Donald Monro, High Dean of the Isles, who made his historic itinerary about the middle of the sixteenth century. Dean Monro mentions its having been exceptionally fertile, "and inhabit and manurit be simple people, scant of ony religione". In his day it carried both sheep and cattle, with the flesh of which the inhabitants paid to MacLeod of Lewis, their overlord, the greater part of their dues. Quantities of the meal of bere, transported from Rona to Lewis in the skins of native sheep, and also seafowl taken on the cliffs and skerries, comprised the remainder of their payment in kind. This rental was collected by MacLeod's steward on his annual visit. Monro mentions, too, that the inhabitants used to catch many whales "and uthers grate fisches". In referring

A sombre day among the half-buried ruins of North Rona's village

Every year, in July, at this precise spot among the ruins of the manse, a fulmar petrel hatches from a solitary egg a chick resembling a lady's powder-puff. (*Page 60*)

Fianuis, the northern extremity of North Rona, famed as a breeding-ground of the Atlantic grey seal. (*Page 34*)

Atlantic seal pup at three weeks of age

to St. Ronay's (Ronan's) Chapel, he tells us that within this building they used to retain a spade and a shovel, and that, whenever any member of the community died, his neighbours purported to discover on the morrow that these implements were marking the spot at which the grave was to be delved. The Dean concludes with an account of Rona's distant associate, Ione Sùla Sgeir, and of the yearly excursion to this isle made by men from Ness, in order to collect a boat-load of seabirds and their down and feathers.

The next account of North Rona and its community is that supplied to Sir Robert Sibbald more than a century later by the Lord Register, Sir George MacKenzie of Tarbat. This enables us to picture fairly clearly the conditions endured by this remote colony. According to it, Rona for many generations had been inhabited by five families. Its population seldom exceeded thirty, all living on commonwealth lines. When a family had more children than its neighbours, the additional parental burden arising therefrom was taken off its shoulders by a family numbering less. The island by this time had passed out of the possession of the luckless MacLeods of Lewis and into the possession of the MacKenzies of Seaforth. It was therefore the property of the Earl of Seaforth. When Seaforth's boat arrived annually in the summertime, it took off with it, besides the customary dues in kind, such population as there was in excess of thirty. Then, as in Dean Monro's time, the inhabitants paid yearly to their overlord a quantity of meal stitched up in sheep-skins, together with seafowls' feathers. Their sheep, according to the Lord Register, grew wool of a bluish colour.

The natives of Rona enjoyed at that time the Romish faith, the same authority informs us. One of their number, acting as chief, issued commands and instructions to the rest of the community. So content were they all with their lot that they bewailed the misfortune of those supernumeraries who, each year, were taken off to the Lewis mainland by Seaforth's boat. Whereas the island itself yielded fuel only in the form of turf, the natives believed that the seas, by God's special dispensation, would always cast upon the cliffs an abundance of timber.

That they were not as scant of religion as they were reported to have been a century earlier is also shown by Sir George MacKenzie where he alludes to the chapel situated in the midst of the isle, and to their convening at it twice or thrice daily. One of Rona's families at this period enjoyed the distinction of being hereditary custodians. When its paterfamilias stood at the altar, the inhabitants fell on their knees to join with him in prayer.

*   *   *

Unquestionably, the most illuminating of the several accounts of North Rona is Martin Martin's, which first appeared in 1703. Martin obtained his information largely from several of the natives of Lewis who had been there, but principally from the Rev. Daniel Morrison, minister of Barvas, when he returned from a visit to this remote fragment of his parish. Rona at that time formed part of the Barvas minister's glebe. When Morrison landed there, the inhabitants received him affectionately. Adopting the usual salutation, they addressed him as follows: "God save you, pilgrim! You are heartily welcome here, for we have had repeated apparitions of your person among us (after the manner of the second-sight); and we heartily congratulate your arrival in this our remote country." One of their number then proceeded to express his high esteem for the minister by walking round him sunwise, blessing him at the same time, and wishing him every happiness. Morrison strove hard to convince these parishioners of his that he already was sufficiently sensible of their kindly intention without the necessity for expressing it in so extravagant a way. But this frankness on the minister's part was received with profound misgiving. They could not understand why he should have taken exception to the performance of this ancient and innocent ceremony, assuring him that they not only regarded this homage as due to him in his especial position, but that they would continue to perform it, whether he liked it or not!

Following upon this pleasant disputation, the Rev. Daniel Morrison was conducted to the little village where all the inhabitants resided, and where he entered some three enclosures. The indwellers saluted him severally and, taking him by the hand, gave expression to the phrase (in the Gaelic, of course), "Traveller, you are welcome here!" They then escorted him to the house that had been assigned for his lodging. There he found that a seat had been provided for him in the nature of a bundle of straw set down on the floor. Some time then elapsed in general discussion. Thereafter the islanders retired to their respective dwellings. A sheep was then killed by each of the five families. The skins of these were flayed off in a manner such as rendered them easily convertible into sacks. These, filled with barley-meal, were immediately presented to the minister as a mark of their esteem. "Traveller," said their spokesman, "we are very sensible of the favour you have done us in coming so far with a design to instruct us in our way to happiness, and at the same time to venture yourself on the great ocean; pray be pleased to accept of this small present, which we humbly offer as an expression of our sincere love to you."

These skin sacks of barley-meal the minister accepted gratefully, for he was touched by the air of hospitality and of goodwill with which the islanders responded to his visit. On the minister's man they bestowed some pecks of meal, because they, in like manner, regarded him as a traveller. However, no such beneficence was showered on the boat's crew, since its members, having been at Rona on previous occasions, were not regarded as strangers. On the other hand, they willingly supplied the crew with board and lodgings during the minister's sojourn in their midst.

Martin mentions the chapel dedicated to Saint Ronan, or Saint Ronay, and encircled by a stone wall. This place of worship the inhabitants kept in a state of great perfection. Every day they swept it. On Sunday mornings they assembled there to repeat the Lord's Prayer, the Creed, and the Ten Commandments. On the altar lay a big plank, some ten feet in length. In this plank holes had been made at intervals of roughly a foot apart. In each of these was placed a stone to which the natives ascribed a different virtue. One such stone was held to possess the power of promoting speedy delivery to a woman in travail.

Saint Ronan, by the way, is mentioned by the Venerable Bede. There's a tradition in northern Lewis that he lived near Eorrapaidh (Eoropie), at Temple Rona, not far from the Butt. Disconsolate with having heard the women of Ness scolding one another in a fashion truly unchristian, tradition has it that he prayed God to bear him to some distant land where he would be beyond the reach of their voices. On the following morning he heard a voice bidding him to proceed to the shore at Ness. This he did. There he found a large whale awaiting him. On the back of this creature he was carried to Rona, where he built what, to this day, forms the eastern end of its ancient *teampull*. Saint Ronan is believed to have died on Rona early in the eighth century.

It is gratifying to find his chapel among the ancient chapels, oratories, and hermitages listed in the Ordnance Survey's *Britain in the Dark Ages*.[1]

At the time of the Rev. Daniel Morrison's visit, the natives owned both cows and sheep. They had, in addition, a supply of barley and oats. They led a harmless existence, "being perfectly ignorant of most of those vices that abound in the world". Of wealth in the form of money they knew nothing, and had no occasion for it. They neither bought nor sold. Such commodities as they needed, they obtained by barter. Though they are said to have been fastidious in their dealings with one another as regards such expressions of private property as their respective fishings, they were strict in their observance of the Tenth Commandment. Contented with their lot as regards food, shelter, and raiment, they did not covet; and, although they always maintained a hospitable attitude toward strangers, they took very little interest in the rest of mankind. Apart from the esteem and affection in which they held the parish minister and the inhabitants of northern Lewis, they were interested in nobody but in themselves.

Rona supported five families at the time of Daniel Morrison's visit. Each occupied its own dwelling-house, to which were attached a barn and a byre. The houses were built of stone. Their roofs were thatched with straw kept down by straw ropes poised with heavy stones. In order to act as a wind-break, and also to keep off rain and snow, a stone porch was erected in front of each door. In matters of clothing, the natives dressed in the same, simple way as did their Ness neighbours; and, of course, they spoke the same tongue.

When one of their number arrived on the mainland of Lewis, few things astonished him more than to discover that there were so many people in the world. One of the greatest curiosities was the sight of a horse. For countless generations Rona's soil had been furrowed with the ancient *cas-chrom* or 'bent-foot' plough. At no time do its inhabitants appear to have possessed a horse. When a Rona boy on a visit to Lewis heard a horse neigh, he enquired whether the animal was laughing at him! According to Martin, the natives were always "mightily pleased at the sight of horses," albeit this scarcely can be

---

[1] In the light of recent researches in Anglo-Saxon art and culture, the title of this publication is inexcusably misleading. Though primarily a map of Britain in the period between the end of Roman rule and the time of King Alfred (roughly 410 A.D. to 870 A.D.), it is prefaced by some splendid archaeological and historical matter.

said of the boy who, noticing a colt running toward him, instantly fled with fright, and leapt into a patch of nettles!

Parenthetically, as it were, this recalls the St. Kildan who, on his arrival in Glasgow, felt as though he had dropped out of the clouds. When he saw a pair of horses drawing a coach, which he took to be a tiny house with two men seated inside, he was of opinion that the horses actually were drawing the coach with their tails. Greatly taken with the movement of the coach's wheels, he thought that only a coachman who was mad would sit on the roof of the little house when he might have been safer and more comfortable on the back of one of the horses! Another native of Rona, afforded the opportunity of travelling as far afield as Coul, in Ross-shire, was dumfounded by everything that came his way. Few things surprised—nay, terrified—him more than the noise made by those who walked across the floor of the room above him. He verily believed that the house was toppling about his ears.

The story is recorded of a native who was desirous of taking unto himself a wife. Having been given a shilling by a seaman who at one time had landed on North Rona, he straightway handed it to the Rev. Daniel Morrison with the instruction that he should purchase therewith a wife for him in Lewis, and send her out to Rona. He had been assured by the donor of the shilling that it represented great wealth. As it so happened, his matrimonial wish was gratified the following year. In such lonely and austere surroundings, and as might have been expected, the inhabitants harboured many superstitions. They believed, for example, that, only after the death of the Earl of Seaforth or of the minister, was the cuckoo ever heard or seen on Rona.

Somewhere about 1689 a plague of rats, in some unaccountable manner, visited Rona, and devoured all the islanders' corn. Shortly afterwards seamen are said to have landed, and deprived the island of its bull. It is thought that, as the result of misfortunes such as these, together with the fact that for a whole year weather conditions had prevented the landing of supplies from Lewis, the entire population perished. The Steward of St. Kilda, as it happened, had been driven on to Rona by a storm; and there, at the side of a rock, he found a dead woman with a dead child at her breast. Some years later the minister sent forth a new colony to the island, duly provisioned. The boat sent to Rona the following year by the minister for the purpose of landing further supplies and of collecting dues was lost, with the result that at this stage there ensues a period during which nothing is known of happenings on Rona. How the new plantation fared is not told. There can be little doubt that it suffered great privation, if not extinction.

*   *   *

From the time of the Rev. Daniel Morrison's visit, which must have been prior to 1703, until about 1812, we appear to know nothing of Rona nor of Sùla Sgeir. In 1812 the former was visited occasionally by boats from the *Fortunée,* then engaged in cruising in these waters. Two years later Dr. John MacCulloch, the tiresome 'Stone Doctor', landed on Rona. From the fact that the women and children fled and hid themselves on his arrival, he deduced that visits to Rona at this time must have been few and far between.

MacCulloch failed to effect a landing on Sùla Sgeir. But he was justifiably proud of his having succeeded in setting foot on Rona. "To have visited Barra and Rona," he wrote, "gives a claim to distinction scarcely less in their estimation than to have explored the source of the Nile or the Niger." In olden times Barra or, more often, North Barra was the name given to Sùla Sgeir.

MacCulloch found on North Rona in 1814 one cottar and his family. The cottar's name was Kenneth MacCraigie. For services rendered, Kenneth received from him food for himself and his family, and two pounds paid in garments which had to clothe six persons—the total population of Rona at the time. Kenneth apparently was tied to the island for a term of eight years. In order to remove from him and his family the temptation that probably would have resulted in their drowning, he was not permitted a boat. The family possessed a cow brought from Lewis when in milk. From the milk of sheep were made cheeses, some of which MacCulloch took away with him.

Rona's soil, MacCulloch informs us, was of a good quality, producing barley, oats, and potatoes. As there existed no peat on the island, the inhabitants used turf for fuel. The oil of the cuddy supplied them with artificial light; "but with characteristic improvidence," writes MacCulloch, "there are no means of lighting the fire, should it ever be extinguished. Well may the vestals of their cottage watch the smoky embers and trim the dying lamp!"

If one thing more than another impressed MacCulloch, it was the solidarity and durability of North Rona's primitive, dry-stone houses. Today, owing to the state of collapse into which they now have fallen, it is difficult to ascertain whether originally there were four houses or five. Solid slabs of rock, probably obtained at Sceapull, in the extreme south-west of the island, many of them weighing two and three hundredweight, lie upon one another in such a way as to have resisted the elements that, long ere this, would have razed to the ground buildings constructed of lime and stone and cement. Of course, the fact that these houses were built half underground has protected them considerably from the violence of the North Atlantic gales. The houses averaged six feet in height—three feet above the level of the ground, and three feet below. So as to avoid the prevailing south-west wind, all the doors faced east. MacCulloch is sufficiently absorbing on the matter of these dwellings to justify our quoting a relevant passage:

"Such is the violence of the wind in this region that not even the solid mass of a highland house can resist it. The house is therefore excavated in the earth, the walls required for the support of the roof scarcely rising two feet above the surface. The roof itself is but little raised above the level, and is covered with a great weight of turf, above which is the thatch; the whole being surrounded with turf stacks to ward off the gales. The entrance to this subterranean retreat is through a long, dark, narrow, and tortuous passage like the gallery of a mine, commencing by an aperture not three feet high and very difficult to find. With little trouble it might be effectually concealed; nor, were the fire suppressed, could the existence of a house be suspected, the whole having the appearance of a collection of turf stacks and dunghills. Although our conference had lasted some time, none of the party discovered that it was held on the roof of the house. . . . The interior strongly resembles that of a Kamchatkan hut; receiving no other light than that from the smoke hole, being covered with ashes, festooned with strings of dried fish, filled with smoke, and having scarcely an article of furniture. Such is life on North Rona. . . ."

*   *   *

The last family to inhabit North Rona was that of a shepherd named Donald MacLeod, known among the people of Ness as King of Rona. In 1844 Donald and his dependants returned to Lewis. Except for the annual sheep-shearing excursions from Ness, and for the solitary and voluntary exile on the island of two men who perished there in 1885, and to whom we shall allude later, it has remained unpeopled ever since. Six years after this final evacuation (1850), Sir James Matheson, who in 1844 had purchased the Lewis from the trustees of the MacKenzies of Seaforth, offered this lone, Atlantic outpost as a gift to the government with the suggestion that it might be used as a penal settlement. The government wisely declined the offer.

Accounts of more recent visits to Rona are of less interest, since they are all subsequent to the evacuation. In 1857, and again in 1860, T. S. Muir went there to carry out those minute investigations of an archaeological and ecclesiological nature recorded in his extensive writings. Accurate plans and measurements of the chapel, known as Teampull Rona, were made by him. The chapel is, of course, the most interesting structure on the island. At the time of Muir's visit, it consisted for the most part of a rounded heap of stones, roofed over with turf. The cell within measured 11 feet 6 inches in length, and 7 feet 6 inches in width at the floor. Its maximum height was 9 feet 3 inches. Other details may be found in Muir's very complete description. Muir had the advantage of being able to set down the chapel's details and measurements when it was much less of a ruin than it is today. At the present time it is falling rapidly into dilapidation. As Malcolm Stewart observes in the delightful volume to which we already have alluded, "it would be absolutely unforgivable if this unique building were permitted to become a total ruin". Nowadays it is the habitat of representatives of the feathered clans. Its corners and crannies are the nesting-place of the fulmar.

After T. S. Muir's visit of 1860, North Rona would appear to have received from antiquarians little or no attention until 1958. In the summer of that year, and as part of a more comprehensive research programme, members of the Glasgow University North Rona Expedition undertook to survey and describe its ancient structures. No excavation was undertaken on this occasion. However, it soon became clear that much tumbled and buried material would have to be removed before any precise planning could be accomplished. This commendable enterprise, essentially undergraduate in character, was made possible mainly through the exemplary coöperation of Glasgow University, the Carnegie Trust for the Universities of Scotland, and the financial generosity of Mr. Charles Hepburn, a Glasgow citizen who gave considerable financial assistance. Others helped significantly. To a degree in which Glasgow has always been noted in such regard, firms and individuals bequeathed or lent equipment. In the matter of transport the expedition was fortunate when Lieutenant-Commander R. C. Dumas, of Aultbea, and the crew of M.F.V. 289 undertook to land its members on Rona, and to retrieve them in due course. Apart from my merely mentioning that the pottery recovered has been deposited in Glasgow University's celebrated Hunterian Museum, it would be foolish of me, with my somewhat superficial archaeological knowledge, to attempt a serious account of Rona's antiquities when this has been done so commendably, and as recently as June, 1962, by Helen G. Nisbet and R. A. Gailey.[1] Incidentally, on July, 10th, 1958, after an eleven-hours' sail, there arrived at Stornoway aboard the *Mary Rose o' Morar*, (skipper and owner Dr. Robert Morrison of Bridge of Weir, a member of the Royal Ocean Racing Club), the first mail to leave North Rona for over a century—probably the first ever to leave it. This consisted of postal communications from members of this Glasgow University Expedition to relatives and friends throughout Scotland. The Post-Office might well have commemorated the occasion with a special stamp of appropriate design.

During the last fifty or sixty years, both Rona and Sùla Sgeir have been visited, though not very frequently, other than by the men from Ness, who yearly sail to the former principally to attend to the sheep, and to the latter to obtain for human consumption some of its baby solan geese. The Duchess of Bedford landed on Rona in 1907, and again in 1910. In 1914, just three weeks after the outbreak of the Great War, the cruiser, *Sappho*, went there to search it in response to the rumour that the enemy was using it as an aircraft base—a purpose to which it scarcely could have lent itself at that time, as was demonstrated subsequently. In December, 1915, the Second and Fourth Battle Squadrons, accompanied by the *Iron Duke*, proceeded westward from the Orkneys to carry out target-practice at Sùla Sgeir; and in 1924 some of the Commissioners of Historic Monuments disembarked at Rona.

In the summer of 1927 the late Dr. John Wilson Dougal, of Edinburgh, sailing northward with Alick MacFarquhar from Port of Ness, spent a considerable time with his geological hammer both on Rona and on Sùla Sgeir. In the autumn of 1930, and again in

[1] *A Survey of the Antiquities of North Rona*, published separately in June, 1962 by the Royal Archaeological Institute.

1931, Malcolm Stewart, aforenamed, and another of the Brethren of the Hammer, to use the term Sir Archibald Geikie applied to his geological fraternity, landed on Rona, and in the summer of 1932 visited Sùla Sgeir.

*   *   *

Long, long ago (so the following impossible folk-tale has it!) there lived on Rona an old man and his wife, whose humble home was built in such a way as to be an infallible retreat should any strange vessel land a crew intent on plunder and kidnapping. One day the old man was alarmed at noticing an unknown vessel lying off the wonted landing-place. On his observing a small boat leave for the shore, he instantly concealed his wife. Captain and members of the crew duly landed, and searched diligently for the only cot on Rona inhabited at the time. Eventually they discovered it.

"Do you live here alone?" asked the captain of the old man.

"Yes, sir," replied the latter.

"And where's your wife?" the captain proceeded.

"She's dead, sir!"

"And what of your family?"

"They are scattered over the face of the earth," responded the old man.

"And where is Donald now?" enquired the captain, when the old man had enumerated that name among the list of his sons.

"Oh, he ran away to sea," came the rueful reply.

"And you're quite sure you have no wife?" the captain persisted.

"No, she's dead many years."

"What would you say was the most important thing you possess on this Island?" continued the captain.

"The fire, sir," answered the old man, "because, when once it goes out, there's no way of re-kindling it."

"Now, you are perfectly sure there's no woman living with you here?'

Once again the old man assured the captain of his wife's decease some years previously.

"Well, then, to whom does *this* belong?" asked the captain, meanwhile picking up a mutch he had seen lying on the settle.

This undeniable piece of evidence obliged the old man to bring forth his wife. The captain then purported to abduct her. He directed his sailormen to carry the fire out of the house, and to extinguish it, to kill the stirk grazing by the doorway, and take its carcass to the small boat, along with the old woman. They duly rowed out to the ship, leaving the old man alone on Rona, in great tribulation.

An hour or so later the small boat returned to the shore with the old woman, now clad in the most expensive finery, and accompanied by the captain, who handed her over to her husband again. From his pocket the captain produced a flint. This he handed to the old man, showing him in so doing how, from henceforth, he could create fire at will. He then asked him the value of the stirk that had been slain, and proceeded to compensate him four-fold. Thereafter he turned to the old man and said: "Father, do you not know me? *'S mise do mhac, Dhomhnuill!* I am none other than your son, Donald, who ran away to sea!"

Great was the joy then on Rona. Without much difficulty, Donald persuaded his agèd parents to quit their desolate habitation, and settle at Ness, where, I am told, their descendants still reside. This story is somewhat fantastic; but I record it just as it was related to me at a ceilidh while living early in the nineteen-twenties at what was then the remote sheep-farm of Galson, in northern Lewis.

According to one of the many folk-tales still recounted round the peatfires of Ness, the possession of Rona was long in dispute between the men of Sutherland and the Morrisons of Ness. The Sutherlanders claimed it on the pretext that it lay nearer to their shores than to the shores of Lewis. However, it was agreed eventually—so Hebridean folk-lore has it—that the contestants should race for Rona on a certain day, and that the island should belong to those who first succeeded in kindling a fire upon it. On the appointed day it seemed as though the Sutherlanders were likely to win the race, and kindle their fire. Indeed, they assuredly would have succeeded, had not one of the Morrisons sent a flaming arrow from their boat, which set fire to the parched grass. Since that day, North Rona has been regarded as the property of the people of Ness.

Captain F. W. Thomas, R.N., the distinguished folklorist, who contributed so many fascinating papers to the *Proceedings of the Society of Antiquaries of Scotland* during the latter half of the nineteenth century, reminds us that it was customary among the Northmen, when they desired to lay prescriptive claim to land, or to render it hallowed, to raise a fire upon it. Similarly, a fire kindled at the mouth of a river in ancient times was held to constitute a title to the territory through which the river flowed. The Norse settlement on Iceland is said to have commenced with the shooting of a burning arrow.

Perhaps the most ancient of the traditionary tales connected with North Rona is that which seeks to explain the extensive scratchings on the southern cliffs at a spot called *Leac na Sgròb*, meaning literally Slab of the Scratches. It is said that some time during the eighth century the saintly Ronan, unable to meditate as was his desire when associated with the old-world Temple of Eorrapaidh, near the Butt of Lewis, sought the undisturbed solitude of Rona. How he managed to find his way across the wild, intervening sea, the story does not relate; but it does relate that, on his arrival there, he did not find the repose he had anticipated, since the island was tenanted by the devil in the form of a six-legged monster with long, sharp claws. For a considerable time the feud continued between saint and devil, neither gaining the mastery of the other. At length St. Ronan succeeded in driving his evil adversary to the edge of the cliffs; and it was in the monster's last, desperate effort to prevent his being driven out into the sea that, with his long claws, he scratched the rock at the spot since known as *Leac na Sgròb*, Slab of the Scratches.

The geologist explains the "devil's scratches" in another way. He sees them simply as slickensides produced by differential land movement.

*   *   *

In the unkempt graveyard of North Rona, situated to the north of the chapel, there are several truncated crosses of plain stone. The tallest, pierced by three small, round holes in triangular position where the arms intersect, stands only 2½ feet above the ground. The most conspicuous object in this ancient place of burial, however, is a stone of comparatively modern date which Malcolm Stewart describes as "a real blot on the landscape". This stone has offended the eye of almost every visitor to Rona since its erection. The Duchess of Bedford wrote of it as follows: "The horrible modern tombstone erected to the memory of the last two inhabitants who died there in 1885, and placed in the little chapel-yard amongst the old locally carved stone crosses, had been re-whitewashed. If ever I commit sacrilege, it will be here." This stone is painted over as a matter of routine by the Ness shepherds on their annual visit. It bears the following legend:

SACRED

TO

THE MEMORY OF

MALCOLM M'C DONALD

NESS

WHO DIED AT RONA

FEB 18 1885 AGED 67

ALSO M M'C KAY

WHO DIED AT RONA SAME TIME

"Blessed are the dead

who die in the Lord."

Two Ness-men, Malcolm MacDonald and Murdoch MacKay, the former a native of Adabrock, the latter a native of Lionel, had taken exception to the autocratic conduct of the clergyman, MacBeth, who, despite his not having completed the curriculum usually required for such a position, had been appointed Free Church minister at Ness. Though a man of overpowering will, he was very popular with the Ness folks, who regarded him as little less than a saint. Thus it was that, when the charge fell vacant, a petition was presented by the congregation with a view to securing his proper induction as a minister. Against this, in their capacity as elders, both MacDonald and MacKay had protested. Determined not to submit to MacBeth's demands, and distressed at the resentment shown them in consequence by their neighbours, they resolved to expiate their conduct by quitting Lewis and going into exile. On the morning of Monday, May, 20th, 1884, therefore, they sailed northward from Ness. Late that night they landed at North Rona. Men from Ness who visited them the following August, and again in September, endeavoured to persuade them to return to their homes and families. They steadfastly declined. The Ness-men reported on their return that both exiles were well, and that they appeared to be enjoying their seclusion, occupying their time in constructing sheep-fanks, in fishing, in sealing, and in reading the Gaelic Bible. Yet, though removed from the hostility of men, they now had to contend against the enmity of Nature, and with diminishing resources at their command.

On April, 22nd, 1885, eleven months after their departure from

Lewis, seamen from Ness landed on Rona. On this occasion no one on the island greeted their arrival. Just inside the door of the half-underground dwelling which the two men had rehabilitated, the seamen discovered the lifeless body of Malcolm MacDonald, in a sitting posture beside an improvised fire-place, as though he had fallen asleep and then quietly expired. On the floor near at hand lay the corpse of Murdoch MacKay, his tartan plaid neatly placed over and under him, indicating that the loving hands of his companion had performed the last rites to his cold, earthly frame. How soon thereafter MacDonald himself expired, we do not know.

The bodies, wrapped in canvas by the seamen, were interred in the primitive burying-place by St. Ronan's Chapel, and at the spot marked by the stone accordingly inscribed.

Rumour had it that the exiles had met their fate as the result of foul play. The matter was raised in Parliament, in consequence of which the Crown authorities ordered an inquiry. The procurator-fiscal at Stornoway, accompanied by two medical men, now proceeded to Rona aboard the fishery-cutter, *Vigilant*. The bodies were exhumed, and a post-mortem was carried out on each of them. But no evidence was found that either of the exiles had met his death by violence. It was seen, on the contrary, that Murdoch MacKay had died of acute inflammation of the right lung and of the left kidney, and that Malcolm MacDonald had succumbed to exposure and exhaustion. The view taken at the time was that, night and day, the latter had attended faithfully to the needs of his dying companion, and that in the end he himself became too weak to bury the body. Unable to remain any longer in the lonely dwelling with the dead, he crept out to sit and die by the fire he had improvised there. On its cold embers stood a small pot suggesting that Malcolm MacDonald was on the point of cooking food he did not survive to consume. The post-mortem revealed nothing in his stomach but a few grains of meal, and a small quantity of brown liquid which, in all probability, was tea. The exiles' bodies were re-interred side by side after they had been placed in the coffins brought to the scene aboard the *Vigilant* by Malcolm MacDonald's son.

How these lonely men spent the long, dark, winter hours, no one knows. It is almost too terrible to contemplate. Neither could write; and, in any case, it is questionable whether they possessed any of the requisites. But they could read the Gaelic Testaments, in which they were known to have been well versed. On a bar of symmetrically and accurately dressed pinewood 2 feet in length and 1⅛ inches in the side, they recorded the days, the weeks, the weary months. A looped cord placed through a hole in the end of this ingenious calendar enabled them to suspend it in their lowly dwelling. Every day of the week a neat notch was cut in the corner of the bar: every Sabbath was indicated by a deeper notch: the end of each month was marked by a deep incision made from side to side of the bar. The notches commence with Friday, June, 21st, 1884. They cease with Tuesday, February, 17th, 1885. That the hand keeping this register was beginning to lose its power is seen in the fact that, toward the close of the exiles' lives, the notches are less neat and less accurate. Owing to failing strength, the deft fingers which had fashioned this calendar and had kept it so faithfully during the first seven months could make, during the eighth, but a diminishing impression on the hard wood.

We know not whether, like Saul and Jonathan, Malcolm MacDonald and Murdoch MacKay were lovely and pleasant in their lives. What we *do* know is that, in their death, they were not divided. So this explains the incongruous tombstone on Rona. And, perhaps, those whose artistic susceptibilities are offended by it will feel more generous toward the people who placed it there, when they recall the story that lies a-mouldering beneath it.

Associated with the death of these lonely men is a curious instance of what is known in the Highlands and Hebrides as the Second-Sight. On the 17th of February, 1885, an old woman named Flora MacDonald, living at Ness, had a strange presentiment concerning the exiles. They were in a terribly bad way, she declared. It was in answer to her earnest entreaties that their kinsmen felt obliged to make for North Rona. Owing to storms, however, two attempts to do so had failed. The third attempt, made on April, 22nd, 1885, succeeded; but the Ness seamen were alarmed at finding no one within sight to welcome their arrival at the island. "It is singular, if nothing more," concludes Dr. Alexander Carmichael's version of this tragedy, "that it was about the very time that Flora MacDonald began to see her 'warnings' that the last notch in the stick records the cessation of the last life. These 'warnings' became so all-absorbing to her that she walked fifteen miles to tell the friends of the exiled men about them."

Carmichael relates, further, that he himself also interviewed in Edinburgh a young man named Donald Morrison, who was on his way home from Canada on a visit to his kinsfolk at Ness. Morrison told Carmichael that, a couple of weeks earlier, he had received a letter from Ness, mentioning that the relatives and friends of the two men on Rona were exceedingly anxious about the wellbeing of the latter, because of Flora MacDonald's 'warnings'. When he arrived at Liverpool, he learned that in the meanwhile a visit to the island had proved Flora to have been gifted with 'The Sight'.

In the late summer of 1885 a number of sheep, oil barrels, and the humble plenishings of the dwelling in which the dead men had lived, consisting of tea, sugar, soap, a grinding-stone, *et cetera,* were stolen by Grimsby trawlermen. Since all these commodities were there in June, but a few weeks previously, feeling ran high in regard to this interference with the property of the dead. The culprits were arrested in their homes at Grimsby, and brought for trial before the sheriff at Stornoway. The master of the trawler was sentenced to eight months' imprisonment, and members of the crew to a couple of months'.

*   *   *

Some years ago I visited Rona in company with Alasdair MacFarquhar, his shepherds and their dogs, and those supernumeraries from Ness who are only too eager to accompany this annual expedition out into the North Atlantic in order to lend a hand with the gathering, shearing, and transportation of that island's semi-wild sheep. A summer's nightfall of fog and small rain found me alone by the storm-rent breakwater at Port of Ness, waiting there for the arrival of the motor fishing-vessel, *Provider,* owned by a Lewis crew, and due at any moment from Stornoway, thirty-six miles or thereby to the suthard. Against the cliffs everywhere around me, heavy seas were striking with an air of defiance. The swell, visibly increasing in determination every moment, gave little hope of anything but a rough passage that night—if, indeed, a passage were to be attempted at all! I felt a little chilled and disconsolate at the prospect when wandering in solitude about the deserted harbour, doubtful whether the *Provider* would turn up that evening. About 10 p.m., however, a transient lane in the fog disclosed a craft of one kind or another, roughly half a mile distant, making for the Port. Could this be the *Provider* at last? My pulse seemed to quicken as the vessel neared sufficiently to enable me, not to read her name in the falling light, but to identify Calum Beag MacLeod, her skipper, a neighbour at

Sùla Sgeir from the south-east (*Page 69*)

Lunndastoth, Sùla Sgeir's southern extremity

A few gannets and their *gugas* on Sùla Sgeir

A corner of the guillemot colony located roughly halfway down Sùla Sgeir's west side

my own village of Sandwick, a seaman of great acumen. There was no longer any doubt that this was the vessel for which I had been waiting, and that in all probability would make the forty-six mile trip out into the North Atlantic that night, intent on finding herself off Rona at daybreak.

A scene of loneliness and desolation suddenly was transformed into one of bustle and activity. The storm, the heavy ground-swell, the darkness falling ominously, now appeared of little consequence. As if from nowhere, men in groups of twos and threes began to descend by the cliff footpaths, carrying all manner of things—provisions, pots and pans and kettles, coal in a sack, chunks of firewood, a gun or two, picks and spades, hammers, nails and staples, wooden posts of varying dimensions, fencing-wire, wire-netting, together with all the other paraphernalia requisite to penning and shearing in the primitive setting for which we were bound.

Offshore the *Provider* dropped anchor, the swell and an onshore gale rendering her coming alongside the pier an undertaking too hazardous. In three or four relays with the small boat, men and dogs, provisions and implements, were transferred aboard her. As we weighed anchor, a crowd of some fifty Ness people assembled to witness our departure, despite the fog and chill rain. Standing in sharp silhouette on the skyline above the cliffs, they waved us adieu after the fashion that has been observed in northern Lewis all down the centuries during which men have sailed out once a year from Port of Ness to the sparse and lonely pastures of Rona.

Night had fallen now. Angrier grew the seas. A powerful head-wind whistled through the rigging and through much gear tightly roped down on deck. I felt as though we were voyaging away into an Outer Dark, out to a mysterious Unknown, out into an immeasurable welter of storm and troubled water, to a horizon dim and foreboding, and eternally land-less—voyaging, as it were, out of the world altogether. As soon as we had cleared the Butt of Lewis and had its lighthouse flashing on our stern, we steered on a nor'-nor'-easterly course along which, hour after hour, we pitched and rolled. On deck the rains began to beat more persistently, with the result that before long most of us had crept away to sleep either in a bunk, or in a corner of the warm cabin.

It was about 4 a.m. when one of the crew woke me with a mug of the strongest tea ever brewed by sailorman. The vessel was still rolling heavily. Every now and then one heard the lolloping and slithering of loose objects gravitating temporarily to a new place of rest. Shortly afterwards, still half asleep, I came on deck to find that the night rains had ceased and the winds had abated. Seated on deck by the hatchway were the two older members of the crew who had been on watch throughout the night. "Rona ahead!" said one of them to me. Brushing the sleep from my eyes, I peered through the first glimmer of dawn to envisage a long, dark, seal-like mass stretching across our bows. We were off the eastern side of the island of our quest, still about a mile distant. Not until half an hour or so later did the *Provider* anchor a couple of hundred yards off the lee shore. Here, amid the noise of barking seals and flighting seafowl, we awaited sufficient daylight to enable us to transfer our selves, our dogs, and our equipment by small boat to a perilous landing-ledge among the sheering cliffs. At no time is embarkation or disembarkation at Rona devoid of risk. A swell or a breaking wave of any magnitude whatsoever renders either wellnigh impossible.

Meanwhile the island's cliffs seemed to become alive with hurrying, scurrying, crying seabirds. Winging about the rocks at its south-east end were groups of inquisitive puffins—sea-parrots, as the sailors call them. Now and again one of them would wing out over our craft, as if curious to ascertain the object of our visit to their sanc-tuary. A year had passed since they had seen the form of man. Everywhere around us now, the creeks were hotching with seals—truly, an ocular demonstration of the appropriateness of this setting, since Rona, when viewed from the sea at a distance, looks for all the world like a huge bull-seal.

No sooner did the sheep-dogs sight land than they became restive to be put ashore. Most of them had been here on previous summers, and were quite familiar, therefore, with the procedure to be adopted. With the first contingent of shepherds and dogs, I landed, hanging on tenaciously to my camera and its appurtenances. Since there was still too little daylight for photography, I spent the next hour in assisting with the unloading of various materials on the perilous rocks, and in carrying them a little inland to the dry-stone sheep-fank. By this time one or two of the Ness shepherds had set off for the other side of the island to locate the sheep, and to drive them down toward and into the fank. The gathering of this semi-wild flock was no simple affair. At times a few of its members would break away from the main body, and dash off at terrific speed to some inaccessible haunt among the sea-cliffs.

While this gathering was in progress, the remainder of the party was engaged either in preparing breakfast on the coal fire kindled in the shelter of the fank, or in erecting the temporary funnel of fencing designed to facilitate the converging of the sheep at the entrance to the fank. It was like a scene from some primeval land when, a little later, men and dogs and sheep were observed moving in silhouette down the sloping skyline toward our improvised fences. The wind had gone completely, though even at our inland scene of operations one still could hear the distant strains of sea-music created by the previous night's storm. Smoke from the coal fire now rose in a tall, straight column to the windless heavens—a queer reminder of the ages when men lived and moved and had their being in the village, now derelict and half-buried in green turf, on the other side of the island. When all seemed to be going well, and there were prospects of our completing in record time the agrestic duties that primarily had brought us here, out of the world as it were, a section of our fencing collapsed before the pressure placed upon it by the converging flock. Some twenty sheep escaped to the hills again; and more than an hour elapsed ere a detachment of shepherds and dogs was able to retrieve the most elusive of them. Meantime, the shearing of those already penned proceeded apace.

The day was heavy and oppressive, though visibility was extraordinarily good. Twelve miles away to the west, Sùla Sgeir and its gannetry stood out upon the sea with a sharpness indicating that further bursts of rain still had to fall on the North Atlantic before one could expect to see much of the sun. As I climbed to the summit of Rona's highest hill with my camera, and looked forth across its sombre acres of rough grass and sedge to the flat, barren territory of Fianuis, at its northern extremity, and to the leagueless ocean beyond, I felt something of that eerie loneliness—stillness—lifelessness—pervading the remoter reaches of Hirta whilst, barefoot, I hurried over them for the last time in the autumn of 1930, an hour or two before it was evacuated. Anxious to use my camera while the lighting seemed at its best, I now proceeded to the deserted village and to the overgrown places where a people long vanished had tilled and sown and garnered in ancient fashion a meagre area of lazy-beds. As I wandered along the thrift-covered walls of Rona's desolate habitations, there came upon me a feeling of the utter purposelessness and futility of man's presence on the face of the earth.

Soon it was obvious that, as in previous years, there had been a good deal of nesting among the island's ruins. Young, fluffy fulmars squatted in deep burrows everywhere around me, often betraying their whereabouts, noisily and unnecessarily, by spitting out their oil at me as I passed along in an endeavour to find suitable spots from which to photograph these eerie ruins. Year after year the fulmar nests in a recess in the walls of Rona's manse. As the time of our arrival was July, I knew that in all probability a visit to this particular ruin would provide me with an excellent photograph of a baby fulmar. And it certainly did, as is seen in the lower illustration facing page 40. Another baby fulmar, ensconsed amid the ruins of St. Ronan's Chapel, near at hand, also presented itself to the camera, but not before it had exhausted its internal oil supply, and had landed one huge ejaculation on my camera front, within a fraction of an inch of the lens.

I now lingered through the old burying-ground, among the shapeless mounds and sunken stones marking the mools of an ancient and almost forgotten race. As one momentarily stilled, I gazed at the inscription on the tilted stone erected over the bodies of those exiles who, in 1885, perished on Rona in such solitude. Close at hand stood the shell of the village, a place apart, a place literally out of the world—so much so that, nearly a century earlier than the evacuation of St. Kilda, men were constrained to abandon it to its ghosts.

*   *   *

By the time I returned to the scene of operations, the gathering, the driving, the shedding, and the shearing were almost completed. It seemed strange to reflect that the intense activity of the last few hours was all that Rona and its wild inhabitants—its birds and seals and sheep—would witness of the queer ways of mankind until a year later—unless, of course, a trawler happened to anchor offshore, and some of her crew landed to replenish the larder with one of Alick MacFarquhar's lambs!

In the late afternoon, the team-work that had characterised our disembarkation in the early hours of the morning was now renewed preparatory to embarking while conditions appeared most favourable. The swell had subsided considerably. The wind had fallen. A blink of sunshine made some of us loth to depart a moment sooner than was necessary. The task of transferring some fifty of Alick's sheep by small boat to the *Provider* at her anchorage demanded the closest coöperation of everyone ashore. Each animal had to be carried on shoulders to the very edge of the landing-ledge, and then handed down to the seamen manning the small boat. Immediately the sheep were aboard, the temporary fencing was thrown down, dismantled, and rolled up in somewhat clumsy fashion. In due course, it found its way to the deck of the *Provider,* along with the various culinary utensils and such of the coal as had not been used. The last man ashore, scattering by the sheep-fank the smouldering embers of the open fire, came away with such fleeces as had been left behind by those of us who already had carried down to the landing-ledge as much as we could. By this time the shorn sheep had returned to their haunts on the other side of the island, well out of sight.

As we weighed anchor, countless seabirds resumed their tenancy of the cliffs from which our arrival had disturbed them so early in the morning. Several seals now popped up their heads on every side of us, anxious to witness our departure for the peopled world. Apart from a score of seafowl shot by one or two of our company with the guns they had taken ashore, this day on Rona witnessed only one casualty. As a boat-load of sheep was being ferried over to the *Provider,* one of them leapt overboard and swam farther out to sea. Immediate attempts to retrieve it failed; and it therefore was drowned. For some time we lost sight of it entirely, owing to the restless nature of the water. Quitting our anchorage, we cruised about for a little, until one of our number located its floating carcass upon the tide. The small boat, being towed astern meanwhile, and occupied by two of our crew, was given considerably more rope. A minute or two later, a dead, limp, brine-saturated thing lay on the planks at our starboard bow. This sheep's drowning was treated in a very casual manner. It was regarded as one of the very minor episodes in an expedition of this nature. The crudeness, the primitiveness, of the whole setting became even more apparent when a young fellow aboard, having all the technique of butchery at his finger-tips, rolled up his sleeves, and set-to on the carcass. In the matter of a few minutes he had skinned and completely dismembered it, much to the admiration of the ship's passengers who stood round to witness what, to me at any rate, was a sickening sight savouring of a primitive barbarism. But seamen harbour no such squeamish feelings; and, so, in less than an hour they were visiting the cabin in relays to partake of the drowned sheep's corpse.

We now were steering a course for the Butt. At nightfall, six hours or so later, I disembarked at Port of Ness, leaving the shepherds and their dogs to proceed with their sheep to Stornoway. Thus ended a unique and memorable experience.

Except for the annual excursion from Ness of these shepherds and fowlers, North Rona remains but a grim reminder of the race that endured its indescribable solitude and desolation. Untended sheep now roam its lone hillsides. Grey seals sing unheeded in its caverns. Seabirds innumerable inhabit not merely every ledge of its cliffs, but also every nook of the old, primitive village and of St. Ronan's Chapel. The quern-stones that once crushed the grain of the ancient inhabitants lie buried deep in grassy turf. For weeks on end, and sometimes even for months, brooding fogs envelop this haunted isle. For more than half the year the Atlantic's unfettered storms reverberate through its ruined homesteads.

In recent years both naturalists and archaeologists have written and published a great deal about this isle, each in turn reviving one's own memories of it, none more enduring than that of the dawn arrival I mentioned, the still darkened air around one thronged with winged life prodigal in abundance, prodigious in clamour.

*   *   *

This chapter would be incomplete were it not to contain some allusion to the visits paid to North Rona by Rosemary Studdy and her ornithologist husband, Myles Smith, of whose island adventures I shall have much to relate in our *next* chapter. Where this particular island is concerned, their story begins in June, 1952, when, as Rosemary herself has written, they camped there primarily to pry into the private lives of Leach's fork-tailed petrels, which have their nesting-burrows in the nooks and crannies of its ruined, semi-underground village, now so overgrown with tufts of grass and thrift. Rosemary mentions in a memorable passage the fulmars occupying annually the shell of the old chapel, and their habit of spitting pungent oil at anyone whose approach disturbs them. "Through the day the whole village belongs to the fulmars nesting on the old walls and in the bothies; but at night the fork-tailers take over and whirl through the ruins with bat-like flight and eerie cries, which are answered by the birds in the burrows with such an intensity of trilling that the very ground seems to vibrate with the sound of it. We used to walk across from our camp to watch, fascinated, while high-speed petrels brushed our faces in passing, the musky smell of their feathers mingling with the smell of trodden chickweed, and the scent of clover drifting over from the 'lazy beds' nearby."

One night they followed with a torch the circling flight of a petrel which disappeared in a bothy. Peering inside with the aid of the torch, they noticed a human skull lying on its earthen floor. Examining this gruesome and somewhat soil-stained object, they came to the conclusion that it was of no great age. The lower jaw was gone. The upper jaw, however, still displayed a few good teeth. How did such a relic come to be lying there? And, in any case, whose skull was it? Rosemary records that she and her husband replaced the skull where they had found it. Next morning they buried it deep under the turf covering the graveyard wall. They left Rona a few days later.

Although the incident of the skull received wide publicity in the Scottish dailies at the time, they did not recall it until six years afterwards when, with a further visit to the island in prospect, they thought they might dis-inter the skull and have another look at it. Indeed, it now occurred to them that a thorough search of that particular bothy might reveal a skeleton and, perhaps, some clue as to whose skull it was. But they were disappointed to discover that in the meantime the wall in which they had enturfed it had collapsed, and that, in all probability, it lay buried thereunder.

This was not the last they were to hear about that skull. One evening the following winter, as they sat talking islands round the fire with the adventurous Dr. Morrison, he related a strange coincidence. "I gave a chap a lift in my car the other day," he said; "and he told me that he was one of an R.A.F. salvage party who went to get a crashed Whitley off North Rona in 1940. They camped in the village, and for a night or two everything went well. But grumbles began when a change of wind brought a smell like a very dead sheep's. The stench was too powerful to be ignored. So they hunted around for the source of it, and in one of the old bothies they found the body of a German naval officer in uniform, with hat on, sitting upright against a wall. But the odd thing was that he had no identity papers or disc, or anything to show he'd tried to live there—though, if he had been washed off a wreck, surely he wouldn't have had his hat on. Anyway, he was in such a state that they just shovelled him in, still upright, on the bothy floor."

Could this skull have been that of this German officer found on North Rona twelve years earlier by these R.A.F. men? "And what was he doing there anyhow?" asks Rosemary in her own account of this incident. How did he get there? Had he been landed surreptitiously to report by radio the movements of the Atlantic convoys in these northern waters? Had he been preparing to leave the island, destroying beforehand all evidence of his having been there? Had the U-boat which should have retrieved him failed to keep its rendezvous? Had he perished of starvation in consequence, just like those exiles in 1885? And where is the skull now? Has somebody carried it away as a trophy, or does it still lie buried beneath the turf and fallen stones of that bothy? Anyhow, Rosemary states that there was no trace of it when she and her husband paid a third visit to Rona in 1960.

Shortly afterwards, Rosemary was told a strange story by Dr. Pennie, of Dingwall. In 1949 Pennie and the noted ornithologist, James Fisher, spent a day on North Rona. While exploring its ruins together, they observed a desiccated hand poking out from a bothy floor! Since their formally reporting the matter would have necessitated a visit to the scene by some unfortunate police-officer from Stornoway, with instruction to exhume someone long past human aid, they sensibly agreed to 'forget' the episode.

"One of the fulmars seen by Rosemary Studdy sat incubating her egg among the heap of old, rubber boots discarded there from time to time"
(*Page 80*)

Interior of one of Sùla Sgeir's bothies showing its stone sleeping platform. The pot-hook and chain hang below the hole in the roof which served as a chimney. A fulmar finds for her chick a soft spot on an old mattress
(*Page 79*)

Monach Isles: A quiet, autumn evening at Port Roy, Ceann Ear

What remained of the crofting township on Ceann Ear just prior to its
evacuation in 1943. Note the schoolhouse to the left

Loch of the Virtues, Ceann Ear, haunt of the dreaded water-horse

CHAPTER THREE

Sùla Sgeir
The Solans' Skerry

IT MAY be recalled that in Ness, northernmost parish of Lewis and, indeed, of the Outer Hebrides, a particular aspect of the Birds' Protection Act of 1954 provoked violent opposition because its schedule, in enumerating such birds as may be taken lawfully at certain seasons, did not include the *guga*—the unfledged gannet, the baby solan goose. The framers of the Act had taken no cognisance of the peculiar position of the crofter-fishermen of Ness, who were prompt to urge that, where the taking of the young solans is concerned, they ought to be exempt from the heavy penalties its infringement entails, on the ground that for centuries they and their ancestors, almost without intermission, have made an annual expedition to remote Sùla Sgeir, the Solans' Skerry, solely for the purpose of collecting for human consumption as many young gannets as they could. They therefore entered a claim to special consideration.

The Act imposes a fine of £5 for each gannet killed; and anybody caught eating a *guga* is liable to be amerced in a like sum. The expedition to Sùla Sgeir in the autumn of 1954 returned to Port of Ness with a boat-load of roughly a thousand *gugas*. If the Nessmen had arrived home with that number the following autumn, they would have rendered themselves liable to fines totalling £5,000, had a singular exemption not been granted them in the interim. The previous autumn's harvest, as it happened, was a modest one in comparison with those of earlier years. In September, 1951, for instance, they landed on Sùla Sgeir from two boats and came back in due course with no fewer than 2,200 *gugas*.

In August, 1954, four months prior to the passing of the Act making illegal the killing, at any time of the year, of the gannet, eight Nessmen, in pursuance of the traditional slaughter of the *gugas* on Sùla Sgeir, voyaged thither in a borrowed boat. The boat, when it had landed them there, immediately returned to its anchorage at Ness. Three weeks later, as arranged, it revisited Sùla Sgeir to take them off, together with their harvest of a thousand young gannets. In response to representation made on behalf of the people of Ness by the County Council of Ross and Cromarty (the county of which the island of Lewis forms a part), the Secretary of State for Scotland, after consultation with the Advisory Committee on the Protection of Birds for Scotland set up under the Act, sanctioned the Nessmen's yearly killing of the *gugas* on Sùla Sgeir only, and after August, 31st, of each year, at the same time providing any objector to this concession with an opportunity of making representation to the Scottish Office.

In view of this concession, the Ness crofters, now Britain's only gannet-eaters, looked forward to August, 31st, 1955. That afternoon the *Star of Hope,* a small fishing-vessel appropriately named and adequately provisioned, skippered by John MacRitchie and having a crew of six, sailed from Port of Ness for Sùla Sgeir, precisely as at least one craft has done every autumn for centuries, 'just when the barley is ripe'. As *The Times* put it, those aboard had an eye on the calendar rather than on the crops then ripening on their croft-lands, since this was the first expedition ever authorised by a Secretary of State to set out for a boat-load of Sùla Sgeir's *gugas.*

Zero hour for the gannets was midnight, some eight hours after the vessel's departure from 'the Port'. However, the inclement weather delaying its arrival was to concede to the *gugas* a few additional hours of life. Soon it was discovered that the men of the *Star of Hope* were not the only Ness crew awaiting the dawn of August, 31st. Another from Skigersta, a crofting township by the sea a few miles to the south of 'the Port', likewise had been held up by un-favourable winds. In fixing this dead-line, the Secretary of State for Scotland has lent to the Nessmen's fowling custom in this region something of the character of a boat-race.

The crofters of Ness still look upon the *guga* as an agreeable article of diet—nay, as a historic and hallowed dish, as an integral item in their simple economy, and as a traditional delicacy which they would be loth to forego. When I left lone St. Kilda with the last of its inhabitants in the autumn of 1930, the gannet was still eaten there, although the natives' raids upon the gannetry of Boreray (incidentally, the largest in the world) had not been made for two or three years owing to insufficient man-power to sail the boat, and do the collecting and plucking.

*   *   *

Early Scottish records of the taking of the young gannet for food carry us back at least as far as the beginning of the 16th century. We know from these, for instance, that on three or four occasions during September, 1511, the solan geese on the Bass Rock were raided for the larder of King James the Fifth. The eating of young gannets at that time, as we learn from such writers as Hector Boece, was regarded as a cure for catarrh and gout. So profitable was the traffic in them a century and a half later that, when Thomas Pennant, in 1771, was conducted to the Bass, it had to be explained to him that the birds must not be shot, since the sum of twenty pence for each was obtainable in Edinburgh. There, when roasted, they were a popular and appetising preliminary to the robustious dinners of the better-to-do. That by 1885 the practice of eating these birds taken on the Bass had declined, if not indeed ceased, is shown by the fact that as many gannets' *eggs* were taken there that year as had been taken annually of the birds a few years earlier. The taking of Ailsa Craig's *gugas* for food continued until about 1875.

The Nessmen urged that so long had their forebears claimed anything Sùla Sgeir might offer as to have placed beyond all doubt their right to its *gugas*. Round the evening peatfire they still tell the story of the race between their Lewis ancestors and the men of Sutherland. Although the latter arrived off this skerry first, they were unable to land because of the swell. That was the occasion, they say, when their ancestors' foresight established for them a prescriptive title to it. Having approached as close to it as was thought safe, in order to fling ashore a live peat from the fire already kindled in the bottom of their boat, they made good their title in accordance with ancient custom.

The Sutherlanders had abandoned the eating of the gannet long before the Nessmen ceased to supplement their Sùla Sgeir harvest by a perennial visit to Sule Stack, a well-nigh inaccessible, suboceanic rock situated roughly thirty miles north of Loch Eriboll, in Sutherland, and forty from Cape Wrath. Often for two or three consecutive weeks they camped in the north of Sutherland, fishing for cod while waiting conditions suitable for landing on precipitous and perilous Sule Stack. Their last visit to it for its *gugas* was made in 1932.

The gannet is as much bound up with the name of Sùla Sgeir as the skerry itself is with the ancient economy of the northernmost parish of Lewis; and one recalls that this remote skerry of the North Atlantic was accorded some publicity when, in 1938, the killing of its *gugas* by the men from Ness was the subject of vigorous controversy. At that time the gannets on Sùla Sgeir came within the jurisdiction of the Ross-shire County Council, to whom several bird-protection societies already had made representation with a view to saving their young from the Nessmen's annual ravages. The Council, fortified in its inactivity during the controversy by the pronouncements of one or two well-known ornithologists that such *gugas* as were taken influenced but little the total gannet population, that this population was actually on the increase, and that the removal of these young birds, while admittedly involving the slaughter of great numbers of them, was no more cruel than other long-established methods of obtaining birds for food, declined to move in the matter. On the latter aspect—the humanitarian aspect, as we might term it—the ornithologist, R. M. Lockley, expressed the wholly logical view that the taking of these gannets could not be regarded as being any more objectionable than the modern methods of killing farmyard animals and fowls, and was, indeed, much less objectionable than such blood-sports as pheasant-shooting.

*   *   *

Sùla Sgeir is the most north-westerly and one of the most inhospitable of the oceanic isles of Britain lying off the Hebridean coasts. Though there would appear to be no definite pre-requisite for an isle to be considered oceanic, biologists, I understand, use the term to denote an island or a group of islands, such as the Azores or the Canaries, situated far from continental land masses, where, for a considerable period of time, faunal and floral evolution would seem to have proceeded largely on its own. To islands such as Sùla Sgeir, Fraser Darling, perhaps a little loosely, applied the term, sub-oceanic, describing thus small islands washed by uninterrupted ocean seas, and generally uninhabited, if not actually uninhabitable, by man. These islands, he reminds us, are important in the lives of migrant or semi-migrant fauna. Their significance to the naturalist is appreciated when one recalls that the Boreray of St. Kilda is the world's largest gannetry, and that the Atlantic seal, rarest of the world's twenty-five species, congregates on North Rona in larger numbers than anywhere else. Indeed, it has been estimated that roughly half the world's population of this species gathers there in the breeding season. It is necessary to bear in mind that an oceanic island, as Fraser Darling remarks, is a metropolis in the animal world, and usually a significant port of call in the systems of communications which animals establish.[1]

But we hasten to revert to Sùla Sgeir, with which we are primarily concerned at the moment. This isle, situated roughly 39 miles north of the Butt of Lewis and 12 west of Rona, lies in latitude 59° 6′ north, and in longitude 6° 10′ west. As the most north-westerly fragment of the British Isles, it must not be confused with Sule Skerry, that seal-haunted outlier of the Orkney parish of Stromness, lying some 40 miles to the west of Orkney Mainland, its 88-foot lighthouse tower, after that on Fair Isle, the oldest in Scotland's northern and western seas.

Sùla Sgeir's maximum length, measured roughly from north-east to south-west, is about half a mile. Its maximum width is but a quarter of that—little more than 200 yards. At Creag Trithaiga and Lunndastoth, respectively its southern and northern extremities, it reaches its highest points. That at the former, distinguished by a cairn of loose stones, is 229 feet, only a few feet higher than that at the latter. The narrow, low-lying neck occurring at the skerry's centre tends to divide it into two parts almost equal in extent. At this neck the altitude drops to about twenty feet, with the result that, even during a moderate Atlantic swell, and with little wind to speak of, this isthmus is often awash throughout its entire width. On tempestuous days the seas break over it to form an uninterrupted channel of frothy, yeasty, streaming brine.

Sùla Sgeir is composed of gneiss—Lewisian gneiss, the world's oldest rock. Of this skerry's geology, as also of much else concerning it, I first learnt from an old Edinburgh friend, the late John Wilson Dougal who, in the course of his flinty-crush and kindred researches, landed there from a motor-boat in September, 1930, and afterwards recorded his adventures in *Island Memories,* a volume prefaced and edited posthumously by myself, and published in Edinburgh in 1937. Apart from the Nessmen when on their seasonal raid upon the *gugas,*

[1] *Natural History in the Highlands & Islands,* first published by Collins in 1947.

Dr. Dougal would appear to have been the only person of whose landing there exists any record for 43 years. That is to say, since the remarkably fine summer of 1887, when that earnest ornithologist, J. A. Harvie-Brown, succeeded in landing from the *Shiantelle* on this desolate isle 'forever fixed in the solitary sea'. Harvie-Brown found himself in neighbouring waters in June of that year when, in company with Professor Heddle and William Norris (the latter in the capacity of photographer), he paid his second visit to North Rona. To his description of the birds he saw on Sùla Sgeir, we shall turn in a moment.

Sùla Sgeir, along its entire perimeter, rises steeply from the ocean. In other words, it is shore-less—and harbour-less. Its forbidding flanks are pierced by innumerable gullies and caverns. Indeed, the southern peninsula of the island, at its isthmus, has been tunnelled right through in a north-westerly and south-easterly direction by the eroding seas. In the course of a few millenia, the roof of this tunnel will have fallen in to create two quite separate islands. A landing is possible only in conditions in which, from a heaving boat, the most agile members of human society can leap on to a ledge of rock but a few inches wide. Dougal relates how he landed from the Ness scow, *Pride of Lionel*, brought as close to the cliff's face as was safe. "A jump was made to a six-inch ledge," he writes.

When in olden times the Nessmen sailed thither in their large, open lugger—their *sgoth*, as it was called—they leaped ashore and immediately dragged it up fifty or sixty feet of cliff to batten it down against the wind, out of the reach of all but the most unexpected wave, just as the St. Kildans did when, for the same purpose, they visited Boreray. So little foothold is there on the steep rock-face at Sùla Sgeir up which these seamen hauled their *sgoth* that, as they still say of such landing-places, a bottle could not be made to stand on it, even on the calmest day. Once the craft was secured, the Nessmen proceeded to rehabilitate the rude and ancient, drystone bothies of stone slabs which, for two or three weeks each year, had sheltered them and their intrepid ancestors while bludgeoning, plucking, singeing, and salting as many young gannets as circumstances of weather and the capacity of their craft would permit. These bothies still exist, of course, albeit they would soon fall completely into ruin if to some extent the disrepair wrought by the North Atlantic's winter storms were not made good by members of each successive expedition.

Fulmars occupy them throughout the year, even while the Nessmen are using them. In the same way fulmars, as we have seen, dwell in the nooks and crannies of the old, ruined, half-buried homesteads on North Rona.

Sùla Sgeir's bothies are situated in the southern part of the isle, just where it attains its maximum width. There are five of them, each roughly 12 feet in breadth and 5 in height. They are built of enormous slabs of rock readily obtainable there because of the nature of the rock bedding and of epigene weathering. Their walls are very substantial. According to Malcolm Stewart, who took their dimensions, they are four feet thick. Each has a door. A second aperture possessed by one or two of them may have functioned as a window. The roofs of all but one were complete a few years ago. Some of them have a sheltering wall just outside the door. Each has a stone bench within. *When* they were erected, no one can say. That they are ancient seems probable, not because anybody ever lived there for any length of time, but because they have been the temporary abodes down the centuries of successive generations of Ness fowlers.

A sixth building, lying to the east of the five bothies, is known as the *Teampull,* or Temple, ever since the visit in 1860 of T. S. Muir, the archaeologist and ecclesiologist. Muir assigned to it a name signifying the House of Blessing, imagining it to have been an early Christian hermit's cell; but with what historic justification, one does not know. Though in olden times anchorites did live in isolation well-nigh incredible, there exists no record that one did so on Sùla Sgeir. Muir gives the internal measurements of this particular structure as 14 feet long and 8 feet at its widest. At the eastern end was its small and only window, under which lay what he fancied to have been an altar stone. That this building was used for sacred purposes, rather than as an ordinary shelter, seems not improbable. The Nessmen, isolated on Sùla Sgeir for several consecutive weeks, may well have used it as a chapel. Beyond that, it possesses little of interest.

Muir landed on Sùla Sgeir under ideal conditions and, in his own words, took his full of the island "very deliberately". It presented to him an appearance naked and repulsive. "What can be said of it," he asks, "more than [that] it is a high, horrent, and nearly herbless strip of gneiss or other such adamantine matter . . . so narrow in many places that, in the winter-time, the strepent wave must be

evermore lashing over from side to side, and cutting up the whole
mass into so many of the merest particles?"

*   *   *

Though from time immemorial crews of Ness seamen have made
excursions to Sùla Sgeir in order to obtain boat-loads of its baby solan
geese, it has never been visited as frequently as Rona. The Ness
fowlers' annual stay on it, when weather permits a landing at all,
usually lasts from seven to ten days. Storms have been known to
detain them there for several weeks; and this is why they always
embark for it well provisioned in the matter of food, drinking water,
and fuel.

Although Sùla Sgeir is deeply indented by three small bays and
several caves, it possesses no beach. Like Rona, it is shoreless. Thus,
when the seamen disembark on the landing-cliff where a ledge affords
foothold of about six inches in width, they haul their craft, weighing
roughly a ton, up the precipitous cliffs to a height of fifty or sixty
feet, as we have seen, and secure it there with strong ropes against
storms. At this altitude the boat remains until the crew is ready to
return. These fowling parties have been known to reach 'the Port'
with as many as 2,800 solans. Though they slay these young geese in
such numbers, they profess a traditional affection for the species,
known among them as Brenhilda's Bird.

During the fowlers' visit to Sùla Sgeir a few years ago, the water
supply gave out. In order to ward off unnecessary thirst, they ab-
stained from taking salt in any form with their food. Their potatoes
they boiled in their jackets in the green, slimy, brackish water found
in small pools among the rocks' crevices. Drinking water was obtained from such as lay in rock depressions situated at some distance
from that part of the skerry densely populated with bird-life. So
limited was it, however, that thirsty fowlers had to sup it from such
crevices with a spoon.

During their stay on Sùla Sgeir the Nessmen have always occupied
the five rude, beehive-shaped bothies mentioned earlier. In the
largest of them they sleep. In the four lesser they not only store
their food, salt, fuel, oil, *et cetera*, but also pluck, salt, and singe
the ensnared solans over a fire of the peats brought by them from
their Ness peat-mosses. Although T. S. Muir believed the most
easterly of these structures to have been a chapel, and for this reason
gave to it the name of *Teampull Sùla Sgeir*, the view generally

Ceann Iar from Ceann Ear, with the Shillay lighthouse on the horizon

Ceann Ear from Ceann Iar

Low tide at the landing-place on the Sound of Shillay below the Shillay lighthouse, now disused

Lobster-fishermen and their summer dwellings among the Monach Isles
(*Page 94*)

The Shiant Isles: Razorbills flying out to sea as shags stand on the rocks
of Garbh Eilean's huge bird warren

accepted is that all these quite primitive structures were erected by men from Lewis who, for so many centuries, have been voyaging thither in September for the young gannets.

Of vegetation Sùla Sgeir is entirely devoid except in the vicinity of the bothies. Malcolm Stewart, in his book, *Ronay*,[1] mentions the five species he collected during his visit in the summer of 1932— thrift, scentless mayweed, scurvy grass, orach, and chickweed. Lunndastoth, the northern part, is as wanting in vegetation as it is in birdlife. The birds confine themselves almost entirely to the island's southern parts.

To Stewart's brief botanical list, Robert Atkinson adds seaspurrey and the little weed grass, *Poa annua*.[2] Away from the site of the bothies the plant-cover thins out until only orach and sea-pink remain, and finally only sea-pink. The abundance of the latter in 1887 is commented upon by Harvie-Brown, who mentions that it then grew to the very edge of the precipice in wonderful, tree-like tussocks, "often developing single stems like tree-ferns, and their roots and gathered earth binding together the great, loose, weathered slabs and boulders, which strew the whole upper surface, and rattle beneath our footsteps as we pass along".

The extent to which thrift (evidently the first plant to colonise Sùla Sgeir's gannet guano) had increased by 1936 is noted by Robert Atkinson. Along the ridge of Creag Trithaiga, in the southern part of the island, "it grew fantastically . . . The columns of thrift . . . were mushroom-shaped and nearly touching each other, a nitrogenous overgrowth which hardly flowered. It was a fearful job getting about in this area; you had either to frisk on the wobbly stilts, or plough along the stony bottom with your feet out of sight. Like the first sight of the gannetry, the tree-fern thrift did not look native. It covered patches of the slab-strewn top of Creag Trithaiga, which we [Atkinson and his friend, John Ainslie] called the badlands."[3]

*   *   *

Probably the earliest record of the annual excursion from Ness to Sùla Sgeir for its summer crop of *gugas* is that contained in Dean Monro's description of the Hebrides, through most of which he travelled in 1549. The Dean's account is worth giving in full, since

---

[1] Oxford University Press, 1933.
[2] *Island Going*, published by William Collins in 1949.
[3] *Ibidem*.

it shows how little the practice of obtaining these birds has varied down the centuries:

"Be sexteen myle of sea to this ile [of North Rona], towards the west, lyes ane ile callit Suilskeray, ane myle lang, without grasse or hedder, with highe blacke craigs, and black fouge thereupon part of thame. This ile is full of wylde foulis, and quhen foulis hes ther birdes, men out of the parochin of Nesse in Lewis use to sail ther, and to stay ther seven or aught dayes, and to fetch hame with thame their boitt full of dray wild foulis, with wyld foulis fedders. In this ile ther haunts ane kynd of foule callit the colk, little less nor a guise, quha comes in the *ver* to the land to lay hir eggis, and to clecke hir birdes quhill she bring thame to perfytness, and at that time hir fleiche of fedderis falleth of hir all hailly, and she sayles to the mayne sea againe, and comes never to land quhyll the zeir end againe, and then she comes with her new fleiche of fedderis. This fleiche that she leaves zeirly upon her nest hes nae pens in the fedderis, nor nae kynd of hard thinge in thame that may be felt or graipit, bot utter fyne downes."

Doubtless, the Nessmen already had been making their annual trip to Sùla Sgeir centuries before Dean Monro's time; and it is worth recalling that, not until the wars of our own century reduced, if only temporarily, the number of able-bodied men in Ness available for a voyage so fraught with hardship and hazard, was there any break in their visiting this desolate isle.

What is this "kynd of foule callit the colk" to which the Dean refers? A century and a half after his journeyings, it turns up in Martin Martin's account of Sùla Sgeir. The colk, Martin tells us, is a little smaller than a goose, has feathers of divers colours, and is beautiful to the eye. Furthermore, "it hath a Tuft on the Crown of its Head like that of a Peacock, and a Train longer than that of House-Cock, but the hen has not so much ornament and beauty. This Fowl looseth its Feathers in time of Hatching, and lives mostly in the remotest Islands . . ."

What is the colk, then? This question I could not have answered, had I not learned from Robert Atkinson, who travelled with me to remote North Rona some years ago, that it is the eider-duck. "Unfortunately," writes Atkinson in that admirable book of his, "the colk was no fabulous rarity, but merely the common eider, the drake showy and parti-coloured, the duck drab, and lining her nest with her own 'utter fyne downes'."

In June, 1844, there went ashore on Sùla Sgeir from his yacht, *Medina,* John Swinburne, the naturalist—probably the first serious naturalist ever to set foot either on the Gannets' Skerry, or on North Rona, the Seals' Isle. Swinburne had been piloted there from the latter by a certain Norman MacLeod. Doubtless, Norman, at one time shepherd on Rona, had visited Sùla Sgeir before, and therefore would have been able to tell Swinburne all about the Nessmen's annual excursion for its *gugas.* Ornithologically, Swinburne does not seem to have benefited much from his visit. This was due in some degree to the attitude of a pilot who tended to regard the bird-life there, and especially the gannets, as the peculiar property of his Lewis kinsmen. So the *Medina* soon returned to Rona, though not before its owner had investigated those "curious looking erections," the bothies.

An account of a visit to Sùla Sgeir one cannot but enjoy is Harvie-Brown's. He and Professor Heddle, having landed with perfect ease on the evening of June, 19th, 1887, scrambled up Sùla Sgeir's tilted strata of gneiss to find its slopes populated with razorbills, puffins, and guillemots. The rocks nearer the cliff, white with, and deep in, gannets' excrement, were covered with their big, clumsy nests. Some of these contained fresh or rotten egg: some had young in varying stages of development. The stench was overpowering. What it must have been in wet weather cannot be imagined. Everywhere around lay evidence that the Nessmen recently had paid their annual visit. Innumerable gannets' heads were strewn about the bothies. A few unused peats lay in a dry crevice nearby. The top of the island was sticky with guano, "most assertive in its smell, if stirred up in foetid hollows and dark green spray-pools, which later are usually covered with green slime and feathers, and surrounded by dead young birds, rotten or highly incubated eggs, and old saturated nests from six to eight or more inches in depth".

Close to the landing-place Harvie-Brown saw a starved and wretched sheep. Elsewhere Heddle found the piled bones of another. Harvie-Brown thought they might mercifully have carried the surviving sheep away to more succulent pastures, for on Sùla Sgeir it had nothing to feed upon but tufts of sea-thrift and cast seaweed. By every second gannet's nest lay a herring or two, fished from the deep.

Harvie-Brown, reviewing retrospectively his visit to Sùla Sgeir, with its "ghastly lonesomeness" and the "geologically disintegrated nature of the place," assessed it as the most memorable and remarkable of all the Hebrides he had visited. A place pathetically sad in its rude stone huts, in its wretched and solitary sheep, in the bleached bones of another of its kind, in "the heads of defunct Gannets strewn all over the surface".

One of the most readable accounts of a visit to Sùla Sgeir is to be found in Robert Atkinson's *Island Going*. Early in 1939, he spent an enchanting night there, among burrow-calls and flight-calls, among gannets and crying petrels. This account has endeared itself to me ever since I read in it his reference to John Wilson Dougal—how my old friend, within ten minutes of his landing, found on the isle an abundance of his beloved Flinty Crush—how his elation at reaching this remote skerry, his objective for so many years, compensated for the rains that drenched him as he ranged over its rough rocks, hammer in hand. Atkinson epitomises exquisitely Dougal's triumph: "Gentle Dougal came tapping with his geologist's hammer in the streaming rain, and found the Flinty Crush!" That brief sentence fills me with something akin to pain.

*   *   *

Owing to the North Atlantic's vagaries and the hazardous nature of landing and disembarking, not to mention the risk of being unable to locate so small an isle in thick weather, the voyages from Ness to Sùla Sgeir have seldom been devoid of danger, and the voyagers' families never wholly free from anxiety. In the days before speedy communication, when the Nessmen set out with the intention of remaining on the rock for three or four weeks, their failure to return promptly thereafter, owing to stormy weather, always occasioned alarm. In Lewis one may hear tales of tragedy connected with the age-long custom of visiting this gannetry. The Ness people tell of the disappearance of those who left for Sùla Sgeir in 1830, believing them to have been intercepted by pirates, and sold into slavery. According to at least one account of what happened, a Lewisman, arriving in Morocco by sailing-ship, discovered there a number of men with whom he was able to converse in Gaelic, and from whom he thus was to learn that they had been shanghaied when halfway between Rona and Sùla Sgeir.

Swinburne refers to an occasion when, in the month of June, the Nessmen's boat was wrecked as they landed. This must have been sometime prior to 1844, and for a reason apparent in a moment or two. For several weeks the islanders subsisted on the birds. In August the revenue-cutter, *Prince of Wales,* commanded by Captain Oliver, reached Sùla Sgeir when searching for them. Not a trace of the men was to be seen. That they had been taken off by some passing vessel seemed probable, however, since the wreck of their *sgoth* was found, and also an oar propped up on end, with a pair of canvas trousers hoisted upon it. A pot containing birds' flesh stood on a fire long extinguished. Not until the month of October was anything heard of the missing Nessmen. A Russian vessel, homeward bound, met in the Orkneys a Stornoway boat, and informed its crew that, in response to the dangling trousers, it had taken the men off Sùla Sgeir and had landed them on Rona. Captain Oliver thereupon proceeded to Rona to find the marooned men in a sorry plight. They were reduced to the last barrel of potatoes belonging to Donald MacLeod, Rona's last resident. Donald and his family evacuated Rona in 1844. Since then, Rona has been uninhabited except for the brief period of ten or twelve hours each year when, weather permitting, the Ness shepherds land to cull its semi-wild sheep.

In the autumn of 1912, the Nessmen were so long overdue that their relatives and friends had gone into mourning for them. They were thought to have perished in a tremendous gale which had swept these lone waters. H.M.S. *Phoenix* was sent north to look for them. She cruised close inshore round Sùla Sgeir and Rona, sounding her siren in the hope of attracting attention. The vessel returned with the distressing news that she had received no response of any kind, and had found on neither isle any sign of human life. When, weeks later, the Nessmen returned to Lewis with a record harvest of *gugas,* the relief was as great as was the criticism of the *Phoenix's* commander and crew. The islanders rode out the storm on Rona, twelve miles to the east-nor'-east.

The most recent expedition to occasion apprehension was that made in the autumn of 1949. The men had but sailed in their open fishing-boat when a violent storm arose, preventing their returning immedi-ately. It was very doubtful whether, under such conditions, they would even *sight* Sùla Sgeir, far less be able to land on it. However, they did manage to land; and, having done so, they killed some hundreds of gannets. A fishery cruiser and a couple of aeroplanes went to search for them. By good fortune their distress signals were seen by the *Panco,* a Norwegian vessel driven somewhat off her course through bad weather. The *Panco* took them in tow and, amid much rejoicing, landed them at Skigersta. Before the Second World War, as many as three boats from this crofting township sailed yearly to Sùla Sgeir for its *gugas*.

My ornithological friends inform me that the gannet population of our Northern and Western Isles is increasing rapidly. In some degree this must be due to the birds' freedom from human depredations on such isles as Boreray. The census of Sùla Sgeir's gannets in 1939 showed nearly 4,000 nests. That taken ten years later disclosed an increase of over 2,000. Meanwhile, the gannet is founding new colonies everywhere, seeking in this way to resolve the problem of over-population at its home stations, as it were. One might add that, but for the evacuation of St. Kilda in 1930, the North Atlantic's gannet population certainly would have been smaller than it is. Were the St. Kildans still making their historic excursions to the enormous gannetry of Boreray and its mighty stacks, Stac Lee and Stac an Armuinn, they would have had a claim to special treatment identical with that statutorily conceded to the people of Ness in respect of Sùla Sgeir's *gugas*.

*   *   *

No isle with soil as sparse and thin as Sùla Sgeir's, and with scarcely a drop of drinkable water, can sustain even a minimum of human life. For this reason comparatively few landings, apart from the Nessmen's, are made there. One of the most rewarding visits in recent years was that made possible by Dr. Robert Morrison. In July, 1959, he put ashore on it, from his 32-foot yacht, *Mary Rose o' Morar*, the island-going ornithologists, Rosemary Studdy, and her husband, Myles Smith, who remained there for five days, observing and photographing its breeding gannets with the most commendable results. "Humping our gear up the steep path from the landing-place," Rosemary afterwards wrote, "we came into a clamorous, strong-smelling metropolis of sea birds. We passed young shags chattering in the extremity of fear, ledges packed with raucous guillemots, and fulmars which spat oil at us from their nesting-places among the giant-size clumps of guano-nourished scurvy-grass; while overhead there flowed an endless stream of birds which never ceased in daylight, and only slackened during the short nights. Arrived on the saddle of ground between the main block of the island and the northern point of Lunndastoth, which forms one arm of the landing bay, we found space among the fulmars to pitch our tent on the thrift near one of the old bothies grouped at this part of the island."[1] Rosemary Studdy's detailed description of what they observed on Sùla Sgeir in the summer of 1959—the avian slum of seaweed nests built on an accumulation of reeking guano, the restless solans everywhere around them, the fulmar nesting in a burst flock mattress found in one of the bothies, the rusting iron bedstead in the *teampull*—makes fascinating reading. Their primary object in visiting Sùla Sgeir that summer was to have a closer look at the blue fulmar they had seen there, by the *teampull*, during a brief visit at nesting-time the previous summer. To be sure, they found the same bird sitting precisely at the same spot.

Until the late 1880s nesting colonies of the fulmar were found nowhere in Britain except on the St. Kilda group of islands. By the close of that decade, however, it was breeding on Foula, that enchanting isle of the Shetlands lying 16 miles south-west of the nearest point of Mainland. Since 1922, when this bird founded a colony on the splendid sea-cliffs at Bempton, not far from Bridlington, it has gradually established itself at varying intervals along the entire cliffy coast of the British Isles. I learn from Seton Gordon that in quite recent years it began paying some attention to coastal stretches of the Isle of Wight. Whether by now it nests there, I am not sufficiently informed to be able to say. It certainly has obtained a firm footing on the coasts of Devon and Cornwall, where it now nests in increasing numbers. The first fulmar egg known in those parts is that believed to have been taken from a nest on Lundy, in the Bristol Channel. Whether these comparatively recent colonisers in south-west England came from St. Kilda or, perhaps, from the Faeroes, one does not know. If the fulmar were a great layer, this increase might have been expected. But the bird lays a single egg a year. If by some mischance she should lose that egg, she does not lay another until the following nesting-season. A pair of fulmars, therefore, rears one solitary chick a year. This species's great increase in recent years is thought to have been due in some degree to the fact that, since the evacuation of St. Kilda in 1930, the taking of the fulmar for oil and for food has virtually ceased. On the other hand, it should be remembered that, some years prior to the St. Kildans' quitting their lone outpost for more congenial surroundings on the Scottish mainland, they had left the fulmar almost undisturbed.

[1] *Scotland's Magazine,* June, 1960.

The increase both in the numbers and range of this bird of powerful flight is, today, one of immense ornithological interest.

Only in the immediate vicinity of Sùla Sgeir's bothies is there any green vegetation in the usual sense of the term. This embraces, in varying proportions, mayweed, orach, sea-thrift, meadow-grass, scurvy-grass, sea-spurrey, and chickweed—the skerry's seven species of flowering plants listed by the observant Rosemary. Thrift thrives on the springy tussocks composed largely of its own humus, built up over the centuries to cover the slope above the wildfowlers' temporary abodes. Leach's fork-tailed petrels breed in such numbers in the burrows they have made in this tussocky area as to render it what may well be the densest of their Hebridean habitats. One of the fulmars seen by Rosemary Studdy sat incubating her egg among the heap of old, rubber boots discarded there from time to time by the Nessmen when on the point of embarking for home, at the conclusion of their annual raid on the *gugas*. Rosemary's photograph of it faces page 64.

CHAPTER FOUR

The Monach Isles

BEYOND THE Sound of Monach, in the Outer Hebrides, roughly $4\frac{1}{2}$ miles to the south-west of the Rudha Mòr, a headland in the Paible district of North Uist (of which Inverness-shire parish it forms a part), lies that cluster of five islands known as the Monach Isles, identified as Heiskeir by M. Martin, Gent., in his unrivalled account of the Western Isles, based upon such personal observations and investigations as he made during his memorable tour of them in 1695. Indeed, the natives of these parts—of the Uists and Benbecula —usually refer to them collectively as Heiskeir, which explains why this alternative name is also entered against them on most maps of this region.

According to more than one place-names authority, Heiskeir is derived from the Norse, *hellu-sker*, denoting a flat reef or skerry. This origin seems more akin to the name by which the group was known in the 16th century than to the word, Heiskeir, as usually spelt nowadays. Dean Monro, in his *Descriptione of the Westerne Isles of Scotland callit Hybrides*—the outcome of his having travelled through most of them in 1549—refers to the group as Helsker Nagaillon. Various modifications of this spelling are to be found in a number of subsequent works containing references to the Outer Hebrides.

One must be careful, of course, not to confuse Heiskeir with Haskeir, the name applied to two clusters of skerries lying roughly a mile apart and in the same locality. The venerable Dean alludes to these as Haysker, "quherin infinit slauchter of selchis [seals] is. This ile perteins to Donald Gormsone." Blaeu's Atlas (1654) marks these skerries as Helskyr Egach and Hayelskyr na Meul, and indicates that they were inhabited. They say in the Hebrides that, centuries ago, a certain recluse named MacCrimmon, desirous of meditating where he might be removed entirely from the intrusions of mankind, pre-

81

vailed upon some North Uist fishermen to land him on Haskeir with a considerable consignment of food. Half a year later the fishermen returned to Haskeir to find no trace of MacCrimmon, whose fate to this day remains a mystery. There are some rude ruins on Haskeir believed to have formed part of MacCrimmon's habitation, and to which the natives of North Uist still refer as MacCrimmon's Dyke.

The sea between the Monach Isles and North Uist is uniformly shallow. From a small boat crossing leisurely on a calm day the sound separating them, one can follow its floor with ease throughout the entire distance. At intervals during the last five centuries the sea has made serious inroads in this neighbourhood. How far the Monachs themselves have actually been affected in this respect, geological investigation reveals. Many official documents show clearly that the sea has made several encroachments upon the land on the west of North Uist, immediately opposite the Monach Isles. It is probable, therefore, that the same marine denudation has also been in operation in the case of these off-lying islands, though perhaps more gradually and imperceptibly. References to the Lost Continent believed to have linked St. Kilda and the Monachs and the Seven Hunters with the main belt of the Outer Hebrides are frequent in Hebridean folk-lore and folk-tales. Allusions to the hunting-ground that intervened between North Uist and St. Kilda, for instance, are common to the legendary of St. Kilda and of Harris. When I was living on St. Kilda in the autumn of 1930, immediately prior to its evacuation, the St. Kildans on more than one occasion entertained me with their versions of the warrior-woman who hunted between Hirta and Harris before the sea separated them. In confirmation of those they assured me, although not entirely relevantly, that stags' antlers had been found on the summit of Oiseval.

Owing to the sea's encroachments, the valued rental of North Uist was reduced in 1542 by about three merk-lands. This is borne out by that year's entries in the *Exchequer Rolls* with reference to devastation wrought by the sea somewhere about 1540. That similar encroachments were taking place approximately two centuries later is shown by the following document, dated 1721, and addressed from North Uist to the Forfeited Estates Commissioners:

"We, the wadsetters, tacksmen, and possessors undersubcrivers attest and deliver—That in regarde of the extreme povertie reigning amongst the haill tennants and possesors within the Barony of

North Uist occasioned by a murain in our cattle first in 1717 but more especially this year by a second murain whereby a great many of our cattle have perished to the number of seven hundred and fourtie five cows, five hundred and seventy three horse, eight hundred an twentie sheep ... And moreover we attest and deliver that about Candlemass last the sea overflow'd severall pairts of the countrie breaking down many houses to the hazard of some lives which hase impaired the lands to such a degree as its possible it may happen more and more that they cannot answer to the worst sett in former tymes."

The signatures to this attestation prove that the devastation alluded to in 1721 occurred along the west and north-west shores of North Uist.

* * *

The Monach Isles, named from east to west, comprise Stockay, Ceann Ear (East Head), Shivinish, Ceann Iar (West Head), and Shillay. Their aggregate area is under 1,600 acres. Measured from the easternmost tip of the barren skerry of Stockay to the westernmost of Shillay, they cover a distance of just under $4\frac{1}{2}$ miles. Except for Stockay and Shillay, they differ from the other detached groups of islands with which this volume deals in that, when approached from whichever direction, they present themselves to the eye, not as islands rock-bound and precipitous in the pattern familiar to those of us who know the North Atlantic's islands, but with a *terra* low-lying and not too *firma,* consisting of sand-dunes and machars, and of a number of offshore skerries, many of them little more than awash when not actually exposed.

Between Stockay and Shillay are the three low-lying islands already mentioned—Ceann Ear, Shivinish, and Ceann Iar. At low water these are accessible from one another on foot. Shivinish, the islet situated between, is really a partially detached portion of Ceann Iar. It is fordable from Ceann Ear at half-tide. At ordinary high tides it still forms part of Ceann Iar, but not during the high *spring* tides. In other words, the Monach group consists of four islands during high-water or low-water, whereas during the high spring tides it consists of five.

Ceann Ear is by far the largest. Its greatest length is roughly $2\frac{3}{4}$ miles: its greatest breadth $1\frac{3}{4}$. Its area is almost double that of Ceann Iar, easily the next in order of size. After the abandonment in 1942 of the lighthouse on Shillay, the Monachs' remaining population of two, or perhaps three, resided in what stood habitable of the village on Ceann Ear, already so deserted and largely tumbledown. The village, which included a small, Presbyterian mission-hall cum school, consisted of stone buildings roofed with tarred felt. A resident missionary fulfilled the functions of teacher and pastor. Thatched roofs had been replaced on Ceann Ear several years previously; and there remained no more than a vestige or two of the 'black houses' of earlier generations.

Weather permitting, mails were conveyed regularly between the post-office at Bayhead, in North Uist, and Ceann Ear in a boat owned and sailed by John and Alick MacDonald, crofter brothers then living together as smallholders on Ceann Ear, pasturing black cattle there and on Ceann Iar, and cultivating a portion of the soil in the immediate neighbourhood of their home. The Monachs became uninhabited when, in September, 1943, the MacDonald brothers retired to the North Uist mainland.

*   *   *

Except where sandy bays and coves give way to rocks and storm-beaches, the main islands, so flat in places, have a sandy soil largely in the form of bent-covered sand-dunes curved and crested by the winds, and much given over to rabbits. Until about half a century ago, they were renowned for the tough bent-grass from which were made such articles as mats, ropes, horse-collars, small poaching-nets, and the heavy baskets and sacks in which both the natives and their North Uist neighbours conveyed their cereals and meal to and from the mills on North Uist. So thickly pleated were the sacks of Heiskeir bent that the weavers of them boasted of their having been virtually impervious to rain or sea-spray. While sheltering in a barn on Kirkibost, an island on the west of North Uist, Erskine Beveridge, of Dunfermline, the archaeologist who purchased the Vallay property in North Uist at the beginning of this century, watched bent ropes in process of manufacture. At that time Heiskeir was supplying most of the raw material, although the inhabitants of North Uist were then beginning to show a partiality for the bent growing on Kirkibost itself.

On Ceann Ear are two freshwater lochans. That situated in the vicinity of the village is known in the Gaelic as *Loch nam Buaidh*, Loch of the Virtues. Why virtues, one asks, recalling that for centuries is was believed by the natives to be the haunt of the fearsome water-horse! Much of the folk-lore of the Monachs is devoted to the dreaded activities of this supernatural creature. Ceann Ear's other lochan usually dries out entirely during a summer drought. On Ceann Ear, moreover, are spots which the natives regarded as the very special province of the faery folk.

On Ceann Iar is the Monachs' only noticeable hillock. Albeit attaining an altitude of no more than about 60 feet above sea-level, it is called the *Cnoc Mòr*, the Great Hillock—great, of course, when compared with the low-lying aspect of the rest of the group.

Nobody has lived on Ceann Iar in any permanent way for many, many years, although the crofters living on Ceann Ear resorted to rude dwellings on it in the summertime. Nevertheless, there still may be seen on Ceann Iar, at a spot called Croic, a tottering stone building doubtlessly once occupied. Erskine Beveridge, in the stupendous work on the archaeology and topography of North Uist he published in 1911, refers to a large cattle-fold on Ceann Iar "with a range of seven adjoining huts, these latter serving as temporary accommodation for the crofters of Ceann Ear". This shows that, as recently as the opening years of the present century, the inhabitants of Ceann Ear had their summer shielings on Ceann Iar.

Shivinish's area is small. This islet is joined to Ceann Iar by the elevated spit of sand and the storm-beach which, as already mentioned, are fordable except during the high spring-tides. The rock-bound channel between Ceann Iar and Shillay is roughly a third of a mile at its narrowest. It is fairly deep as Monach waters go—sufficiently so at all events to permit of the passage of small craft, and to have enabled the *Pharos* to anchor close at hand when effecting reliefs, or when replenishing coal and other supplies at Shillay's lighthouse.

* * *

The name, Monach, is said to have originated with Shillay. In olden times Shillay was known by the Gaelic name, *Eilean nam Manach*, Island of the Monks. On Blaeu's map the group is marked Hekskyr na Monach. The lighthouse on Shillay is believed to occupy the site of an ancient monastic settlement. Moreover, it is held that on this very spot the monks of old maintained throughout the night a red beacon to warn the tall sailing ships and the chieftains' birlinns of danger, just as the lighthouse warned their powered successors.

One or two references to the Monach Isles suggest their association with nuns, as well as with monks. George Buchanan, in his history
of Scotland, refers to the group as *Helsher Vetularum*, "so called,
as I suppose, because it belongs to the Nuns of the Island of Icolum-
kill" (Iona). The Monachs' connection with Iona is mentioned in
Dean Monro's *Descriptione* and elsewhere. "Be aught myle of sea
frae this isle," writes the Dean, "towarts the west, lyes ane ile four
myle and haff myle braid, laiche maine land, callit Hesker Nagaillon.
It has abundance of corne, and elding for fire, it perteins to the
Nuns of Columnkill."

In an obligation dated 17th March, 1575–1576, allusion is made
to an annual payment for a proportion of the farms of Heiskeir. In
this document Heiskeir is called Halskienagallechie, obviously an
attempt at spelling the Gaelic, *Heiskeir nan Cailleach*, denoting
Heiskeir of the Nuns. The payment actually was in respect of "the
third of the fermes of Halskienagallechie"; and the assessment was
"tuentie males grane, and the third pairt of ane maill". Payment
of the same was due yearly by James McDonuill Growemych of
Castle Camus, in Sleat, to the Bishop of the Isles, "in tyme cuming
to be yerlie maid in Ycolmkyll [Iona] betwixt Petersmess and
Beltane". The *male* or *maill* was a measure of grain believed to
have been of Norse origin, and once extensively adopted in the
Orkney Islands.

The date of the earliest record of the lands of Monach is doubtful.
Sometime during the 13th century, Donald, son of Reginald, grandson
of Somerled of the Isles, mortified "the Island of Heiskeir to the
Nuns".[1] However, for genealogical and chronological reasons too
complicated to justify our inquiring into them here, Erskine Beveridge
thought one would be safe in ascribing this mortification to the
14th rather than to the 13th century. A later reference in the
publication just cited, probably dated about 1500, occurs in the
passage describing the sister of Donald Gallda of Lochalsh as having
been "such an idiot that she was sent to Heiskeir, a remote island,
lest she should be seen by strangers, to the care of a gentleman
living there, a Macdonald called Donald Du Maclauchlane". Donald
Gallda's sister was 'sequestrated' on Heiskeir, as was the unhappy
Lady Grange 232 years later, prior to her removal to St. Kilda.
Lady Grange was sent there in the autumn of 1734. From a letter
written by her in 1738, it would seem that, much as she hated

[1] *Collectanea de Rebus Albanicis.*

Heiskeir, she preferred it to St. Kilda. "I was in great misery in the Husker;" she wrote; "but I am ten times worse and worse here."

Another reference to Heiskeir's associations with Iona occurs in an Elizabethan document entitled *The Isles of Scotland and the Division thereof, with the Names of the Chieftains,* dated Edinburgh, March, 1595. It mentions "Helsker pertaining to the Nunnery of Icolmkill 20 men".

In 1692, the year after the Massacre of Glen Coe, Alexander MacDonald (*Alasdair Ban Mac Iain 'ic Uisdein,* to give this gentleman the name by which he was known to his own generation, and by which he still lives in the traditions of the Outer Isles) despatched his galley from Heiskeir to Ballachulish with a cargo of barley-meal to relieve destitution among that remnant of the MacIans which, having escaped the vengeance of Robert Campbell of Glen Lyon and his felonious accomplices, had returned to its charred glen from the refuge of the hills. MacDonald was tacksman of Heiskeir at the time. His promptitude in rendering this assistance to his clans-people, said to have saved them from starvation, is still remembered at the telling of tales in seannachie fashion on winter evenings. That he was able to send forth such a cargo testifies to the fertility of the Monach Isles.

MacDonald must have been a man of some substance: in 1694, a couple of years after his generosity to the MacIans, he advanced three thousand merks to Sir Donald MacDonald of Sleat upon a wadset of "the 10 penny lands of Heiskeir, the penny lands of Peinmore and Peinnie Trynoid, and the 10 penny lands of Balranald". During the 16th and 17th centuries the wadset occupied a prominent position in the tenancy of North Uist and the islands adjacent thereto.

*　　*　　*

On the question of Heiskeir's fertility annotators appear to be somewhat at variance. Dean Monro, in the passage already quoted, speaks of its having an abundance of corn. Martin Martin, referring toward the close of the 17th century to its sandy soil, says that it is "very fruitfull in Corne and Grass, Black Cattle, and the Inhabitants labour under the want of fuel of all sorts, which obliges them to burn Cows Dung, barley straw, and dry'd Sea-ware". *The Old Statistical Account,* mentioning Heiskeir merely in passing, describes it as possessing a sandy soil, as yielding very little grass at any time, and as being of no value except in respect of the small quantity of grain raised there, and of the kelp-burning carried on along its shores.

Another appropriate reference is Captain Otter's, published about 1885. "About seventy years ago," he writes, "the islands were covered with good pasturage, with machirs or sandhills of considerable height. At half-tide all the islands, except Shillay and Stockay, were connected, as at present, by a sandy beach, and they were inhabited by eighteen families, besides cottars, who were able to keep 1,000 head of cattle, sheep, Etc." If this account be accurate, Heiskeir's population in or about 1810 must have been over a hundred. The number of livestock he gives seems incredible for such an area, so much of which consists of sand-dunes covered with bent. "About ten years after" [*circa* 1820], continues Otter's report, "without any apparent cause, the whole of the surface of the islands was denuded of soil and grass, except two very small portions on each end."[1] As a result of this, he tells us, the natives, with the exception of one family, were obliged to quit Heiskeir, which was now to remain uninhabited for close on fifteen years, during which time a channel 6 to 8 feet in width was scoured out on each side of Shivinish.

About 1846, according to Samuel Lewis,[2] when the population had fallen to 39, the soil yielded a very scanty pasturage, and but a small quantity of grain. Whether Lewis actually visited the Monachs, I cannot say. His references to a scanty pasturage and a paucity of grain would seem to indicate that he obtained his information from *The Old Statistical Account,* rather than by personal observation and inquiry. The suspicion that at any rate he was familiar with that publication is strengthened by his concluding remark on Heiskeir: "The isle has hitherto derived its chief value from its kelp shores."

Be this as it may, the Monach Isles are still noted for their fertility, as fertility goes in the Outer Hebrides. Their last farm was one of the last to be worked in accordance with the old runrig system. From a letter I have by me, written some thirty years ago by Hector MacKenzie, then factor for North Uist, I see that this farm, at the time of his writing me, was divided into six full shares. The souming of each was eight cows with followers, two horses, and twenty-four

---

[1] *Sailing Directions for the West Coast of Scotland* (1885).
[2] *Topographical Dictionary of Scotland with Historical & Statistical Descriptions.*

The Shiant Isles: The Anchorage on the east side, between Garbh Eilean (left) and Eilean an Tighe. Note the columnar basalts at the left, and the great bird-infested screes beyond, the nesting-place of myriads of puffins

The finest columnar basalt cliffs in Britain are on Garbh Eilean, where they plunge like giant organ-pipes

The Shiant Isles: Garbh Eilean from Eilean an Tighe. Immediately beyond the house in the middle-distance is the shingly isthmus connecting these two islands

The house on Eilean an Tighe built for Compton Mackenzie (*Page 101*)

sheep. For souming purposes two cows were reckoned to be equal to one horse.

*   *   *

On Ceann Ear in 1886 there were eight crofter and six cottar families, and a teacher. Its population was 75; and fine specimens of manhood its male members were, I have been told by those who knew them—big-boned, deep-chested, alert, and intelligent, few of them under six feet. Their homes were the abode of the traditional Highland hospitality. Owing to emigration to Canada so soon after-wards, as also to simultaneous transference to holdings on North Uist, to which the islanders always referred as 'the mainland', popula-tion fell steadily. By the mid-1930s it had dropped to 17, made up of three crofter families, one cottar, a teacher-missionary, and the three keepers manning the lighthouse on Shillay.

Well into the 1930s the inhabitants' fuel was peat. A grand sight in olden times were the Monach smacks leisurely ferrying home the peats. During the month of August these smacks might have been seen lying off Dusary and Claddach Kyles, and at a place appropriately called Ardheiskeir. The peats were cast on the moor of Kyles Paible, on the west side of North Uist, and also on certain allotted bogs fringing both sides of the Committee Road. This is the name given to the road running a distance of four miles between Malacleit and the Vallay Strand, in the north, and Dusary, in the south, facilitating a shortcut across the north-west portion of North Uist. It was con-structed about 1846 with a view to providing a measure of employ-ment during the widespread distress consequent upon the Potato Famine.

Some years prior to the Second World War the inhabitants of the Monach Isles began to burn coal instead of peat. This reached them by the puffer arriving periodically with supplies for the lighthouse on Shillay. On Heiskeir as elsewhere, the use of coal soon led to the introduction of a convenient type of American stove.

Mention of fuel reminds one of the natives' having informed Martin that bread baked by the fuel of seaware relished better than bread baked by any other means. At that time they were in the habit of salting their cheeses with the ashes of barley straw "which they suffer not to ly on it above 12 hours time, because otherwise it would spoil it".

The Heiskeir crofters were always regarded as among the most prosperous in the Hebrides. In addition to lobster-fishing, kelp, and the making of tweed, they were renowned for their black cattle and sheep—from a butchery point of view, of course! Well into the present century, large quantities of tangle ash and also of kelp were produced. Owing to declining man-power, this lucrative home industry had to be abandoned. No kelp has been exported from Heiskeir since 1926.

*   *   *

Superficially at all events, the Monach Isles are almost entirely devoid of archaeological interest. In this respect they are very different from the Uists, which are so rich in ancient duns and castles, chambered cairns, barps, cells, chapels, earth-houses, standing-stones, stone-circles, ecclesiological remains, and the like. Martin, however, does mention a stone chest discovered there, "having an earthen Pitcher in it which was full of Bones, and so soon as touched they [   ] to Dust".

In July, 1906, Erskine Beveridge came upon a kitchen midden of shells and ashes near the north-west corner of Ceann Ear, hard by a cist with human bones exposed by the shifting sands, and also another large midden of limpet shells toward the north-east of the same island. Two hammer-stones were discovered about this time on Ceann Iar. Beveridge expressed the opinion that the Monachs' sand-drifts probably conceal much evidence of pre-historic occupation. One or two authorities speak of the existence of ancient crosses. *The New Statistical Account*, for example, refers to several crosses rudely cut in stone such as are found in burying-grounds, "particularly on the island of Husker".

*   *   *

Long ago there resided on Ceann Iar a couple of ravens that would not tolerate the approach of any of their species. Immediately a stray raven came in sight, this couple drove it off "with such a noise as is heard by all the inhabitants". It was said that, as soon as its own young were able to fend for themselves, they were driven forth in like manner. One of the couple, wounded by gun-shot, was forced to shelter for some weeks in a cleft among the rocks, during which time its mate daily brought it provisions. When eventually the female died, the surviving bird left Ceann Iar, returning a few days later, accompanied by about a dozen of his own feather. Subsequently, he selected from this number a new mate, after which the others departed, leaving Ceann Iar once again in the possession of a pair of their species. If at any time a carcass lay on the fields, or had been cast ashore on any of the Monachs, the natives declared that they were able to distinguish by the ravens' noise whether it was flesh or fish. When Martin told the islanders that he scarcely credited this 'nicety', they replied that they could vouch for the accuracy of this statement from personal observation, adding that the ravens were always noisiest when the carcass was flesh.

The channel in which the natives used to catch seals is undoubtedly that separating Ceann Iar and Shillay. In olden times they caught them in nets they themselves had made of several horse-hair ropes. The most famous place for sealing in this locality was, of course, Cousamul, that sprinkling of skerries lying roughly six miles due north of Ceann Ear. To the annual raid upon the seals at Cousamul, boats used to go from places as distant as the crofting townships near the Butt of Lewis.

In the days before the erection of the lighthouse on Shillay, the natives pastured sheep on that island. There came a day—so the story has it—when most of them, men and women, went over the sound to the shearing of the Shillay sheep. The men were not long at their task when they yielded to the temptation to raid the seals on a neighbouring skerry. But they had failed to secure their boat, with the result that it drifted well beyond reach by the time that a flowing tide began to encroach upon this skerry. Frantic with despair for the safety of their menfolk were the Monach women as they watched from Shillay the surging flood-tide encompassing the sealers. Their piteous cries at length were heard by a woman on the North Uist shore. Unaided, she launched the only boat available. Alas! her effort was in vain. The tide had swept Monach's men-folk to drowning long ere she could reach the skerry. Many in the Outer Hebrides were convinced that this fatality was a judgment upon the people of Monach, since they believed the seals to be human beings, under enchantment. The Seal-folk, one recalls, are emissaries from the Courts of the Kings of Lochlann, *under spell*.

*   *   *

When staying at Lochmaddy shortly before the outbreak of the Second World War, I set out for the West Side by way of West Ford Inn and Claddach Kyles and Claddach Kirkibost, arriving in due course at a tiny place called Bayhead. Diverting there from the main road, I lingered through the wild flowers about Balmore and Knockantorran until I reached the shore at Maskeir. Out in the Atlantic lay the Isles I was anxious to visit. As I sat a-dreaming among the waving marram and the grasshoppers, I suddenly noticed afar off the Monach boat, sailing toward the customary landing-place among the rocks at Maskeir. I could see that she was a boat with only one mast and a fairly large sail. Only one mast, I remark, because the Monach boats usually had two, each designed to carry a canvas somewhat smaller than that associated with a single-masted boat of similar draught and dimensions. The Monach seamen used to maintain that, in the event of a squall overtaking them during the passage between Port Roy and North Uist, they could always handle with confidence a boat having two masts and two smallish sails.

All the world this day seemed radiant with the sun's light and warmth. Mirrored in a still sea were the mountains of South Uist. Away to the right of them lay the Barra Isles, seen as if through a purple gauze separating faeryland from the full gaze of men. Barra itself and distant Mingulay dwarfed the other islands so closely associated with them. To the east of me lay Benbecula and the Great North Ford, the latter at this range appearing to run up to the base of the mountain called Eaval. Far beyond, and without the faintest vestige of a cloud upon them, were the Coolins of Skye. One picked out afar three islands of the St. Kilda group—Boreray, Hirta, and Dùn. The steep precipices of Conachair and the Bioda Mòr stood out with a clearness truly dramatic.

Despite a canvas virtually windless, the Heiskeir boat continued to approach at a steady pace. Every now and then she was completely obscured by the offshore reefs. I knew pretty well how long it would be ere she set sail again for Port Roy, aware from experience of such settings and conditions that the Monach men would have several matters to attend to, and cargo to take aboard. The prospect of my returning with them later in the day seemed reasonably good. In anticipation of so fortunate a contingency, I already had deposited at a spot easily found among the sand-dunes the few things I would require.

While the Monach men landed to wander leisurely through the fields to the post-office at Bayhead, I likewise took to wandering. In so doing I came upon a cart-track winding through the machar where, in places, wheel-ruts lay hidden by wild flowers at a depth of more than 18 inches: so overgrown is this track in the summer-time. It soon led me to a tiny homestead at Paiblesgarry, encircled by hayricks, and corn but half ripe. Here I asked for food, since hunger was now upon me, and I already had tramped many a good mile to reach the West Side and the Heiskeir ferrying-place. Soon I returned from Paiblesgarry to the shore. There I found a flat-bottomed dinghy drawn up among the rocks, waiting, as I hoped, to ferry me in due course to the Monach boat now anchored about fifty yards offshore, and shortly to return to Ceann Ear. By invitation I stepped aboard, and in less than an hour disembarked at the landing-stage among the rocks at Port Roy. When sailing in by Stockay, we overhauled a small craft containing three Uist fishermen engaged in drawing in flounders on lines with greater rapidity than the disciples ever did on the Sea of Galilee in the days of miracles. The sandy sea-floor off the Monach Isles, especially that stretch of it between Ceann Ear and North Uist, abounds in flounders. A native informed me a day or two later that, on a line of 400 hooks, he often had caught as many as 360 within a couple of hours. Seals innumerable were now swimming off the skerries on every side of us, heedless of our proximity.

The day was calm and warm. Lobster-fishermen from Grimsay and Benbecula, just returned from visiting their pots, lay sleepily on the scented grass above the shore, their boats meanwhile riding at anchor or attached to moorings in Port Roy's sunlit harbour. Grimsay, an isle approximately 20 miles from Port Roy, is renowned for its boat-building. Indeed, all the Monach boats at that time, and also those from which lobster-men still exploit these waters, were built there. The boat in which the natives passed to and fro between Heiskeir and West Ford Inn or Maskeir was built at Kallin, on Grimsay.

I walked along the path leading through Ceann Ear's fields to the house of the MacDonalds, with whom I now had been invited to sojourn. And I must confess that not in all my experience of the Outer Hebrides had I seen better corn and barley and potato crops than here. Small wonder Heiskeir, when inhabited, had a reputation for fertility! From its rewarding tilth I lingered thigh-deep through its acres of wild flowers and clover, among bees and butterflies and purple moths, all of them enjoying the profusion of this Hebrid isle in time of blooming and ripening. Ceann Ear in ways reminded me strangely of Vatersay, one of the Barra Isles. Here, as on Vatersay, one finds buttercup and daisy, ragged robin and wild thyme, bedstraw and clover, vetch and orchid and lady's smock, knapweed and silverweed, harebell and bird's-foot trefoil, and the tiniest heart's-ease, each and all striving for a place in the sun.

*   *   *

There is about these lone fragments of the Hebrides a soothing air of antiquity, an atmosphere ancient and mellow. On Ceann Ear, at the sun's downgoing, you might have seen an old woman with a shawl wrapped round her head, her cheeks weather-tanned; and she lingering in her footless stockings through the island's pastures toward the west shore, carrying a couple of pails. Had you watched her closely for a moment or two, you would have noticed her sudden disappearance among the shoreland rocks, since the islanders' well lay hidden by boulders just within a few feet of highwater mark. The problem of good, fresh water had been a difficult one on Ceann Ear in a dry season. Yet the island, judging by its many marshy and mossy spots, is by no means deficient in springs. It ought to have been possible to find a plenteous and reliable supply of drinking water on Ceann Ear.

The Benbecula and Grimsay lobster-fishermen erect for themselves on the Monach Isles turf and stone hutments. These they inhabit from the end of April till late in September. In floating crates moored at no distance offshore, they keep their lobster catches in readiness for the market. One of their number told me that during the summer months they despatched to an agent at Lochmaddy as many as 30 dozen lobsters at a time, and that in winter they sent them direct to London.

While strolling through the trefoil and the orchids, I chanced to fall in with the island missionary. He informed me that the population stood at 22, and that this number would dwindle. All the inhabitants were MacDonalds, all of whom were related to one another. One felt tempted to inquire whether any of them would have admitted descent from Neil MacDonald, the 17th-century native who was subject to the falling of his tonsils at every change of the moon, a condition that lasted only throughout its first quarter. "This infirmity," says Martin, "hath continued with him all his days, yet he is now [1695] 72 years of age." Neil had at Paible, in the person of John Fake, a contemporary who was always afflicted with a fit of sneezing a day or two before rain. The greater the sneezing, the greater the rainfall it prognosticated. So reliable a forecast had his sneezing been over a period of nine years that the islesfolk nicknamed him the Rain-Almanac.

At the time of this visit of mine, eight or ten children attended the village school, there to be taught by the missionary himself. Only five of the village's houses were inhabited: several were quite derelict. "There's ample room for a much greater population," the missionary naively maintained. "Even another couple of families," he urged, "would make things easier for the rest." He had in mind coöperative tasks such as the unloading of Cunningham's puffer when she lay off Port Roy with a consignment of coal.

Some years earlier, a small jetty had been constructed among the rocks at Port Roy. At high water this jetty is completely submerged. What, then, was the use of it? one might ask. It was built to facilitate the shipment of cattle destined for North Uist by the Monach boat. The cattle were driven aboard a couple of hours before high water so that, when the boat reached the other side, either at Maskeir or at the West Ford Inn, the tide was full. The same procedure was followed when bringing cattle over to Heiskeir. Shipped at high water, they arrived at Port Roy with the ebb, just as the jetty was beginning to show above water.

*   *   *

The Monach folks knew everything about the Elements. Indeed, some of them adapted their lives to the calculable behaviour of sun, moon, and tide. They held that, if a new moon were visible within three days of her birth, the Hebrides would soon be visited by a spell of truly bad weather. Sometimes two visits to North Uist were possible in a day, depending upon the state of the tides. This the natives always endeavoured to achieve when transporting livestock of any kind. In winter the sheep on Ceann Iar were driven over to Ceann Ear; while the cattle grazing throughout the summer and autumn on Ceann Ear were transferred to Ceann Iar. Although, as we have seen, the ford is passable at a low tide, the cattle found no inducement to wander back until the spring, when water begins to run short on Ceann Iar, and its grass tends to lose its succulence. The Heiskeir folks told me that their calves would drink anything, although the rearing of calves on the Monachs not long before had been regarded as unprofitable, if not impossible, owing to what they

believed to have been the unsuitability of the islands' water. By way
of showing how the calves had adapted themselves to their environment, they now boasted that those then being reared on Heiskeir
would drink even a pailful o' broth!

Sea-spoil is often cast ashore on Ceann Ear, though not so frequently as on the strands of Baleshare and Kirkibost, which are more
favourably situated for driftwood and the like washed up by wind
and tide. Some years ago a timber-carrying vessel came to grief
in the Sound of Harris. Great quantities of the yellow pine she
carried were cast ashore at Ceann Ear, to the delight of its inhabitants.

With the exception of the schoolhouse, which faces north, the houses
in Ceann Ear, all of them now derelict, were built to face east.
They look out toward North Uist and Benbecula. Likewise was
the small mission-hall, with its red, corrugated roof. This meant that
little sunlight entered by doors and windows. On my asking the
reason for this uniform orientation, I was told that it afforded the
best protection from the prevailing winds. "The winter won't be so
strong on the door" was the explanation given me by my host, Alick
MacDonald.

Not infrequently are the Monachs swept by gales and high seas.
A few years before the last inhabitants left, the tempest's violence
brought the waves so far inland that they took fright and forsook
their homes for the island's few elevated spots. It was this experience
that engendered among them a desire to evacuate the Monach group
in favour of crofts situated on the North Uist mainland. One can
appreciate their anxiety in such circumstances, for, as we have seen,
these islands are very low-lying, and there was neither telephonic
nor telegraphic communication between them and the outer world
when the Atlantic rapped ominously at their doors.

*   *   *

When at ebb-tide on the morrow I crossed to Shivinish and Ceann
Iar, the sun beating on the tall dunes gave one the impression of
having wandered far into a desert country. In the Sound of Shillay,
the channel separating me from the island on which stands the lighthouse, a couple of Grimsay's lobster-fishermen pursued at low water
their calling from a boat scarcely visible among the dulsen reefs.
Eager to have them ferry me across, I hailed them. In a moment
they rowed clear of the skerries, hoisted sail, and made for the rock
on which I stood with a tide swirling round my ankles, my toes

The Shiant Isles: The seal-haunted Galtachean, or Galtas, from Garbh Eilean

St Kilda: A Soay ram

St Kilda: Where the cliffs of Conachair, loftiest in the British Isles, sheer 1,300 feet to the North Atlantic

gripping the glistening seawrack for fear of slipping. Three activities make me feel very particularly the meaning of freedom. One of these is the act of squeezing through a fence. Louping a dyke is another. The third is the getting of my feet on wet wrack. I find all three remarkably pleasureful.

Before long, I was to find myself on Shillay's jetty. In scanning the narrows I so recently had crossed, I pictured to myself the manner in which the puffer bringing fuel to the lightkeepers was allowed to drift gently broadside-on, with a rope at stem and at stern, each passed through a ring inserted in the rocks by the shore. The lighthouse relief boat lay off here at varying intervals when unloading supplies, or when the Northern Lighthouse Commissioners visited Shillay by the *Pharos*, on their biennial tour of inspection of Scotland's western lights.

On the afternoon of Sunday, November, 15th, 1936, there disappeared from Shillay two of its three lightkeepers—J. W. Milne, the principal keeper, and M. W. Black, one of his assistants. The missing men were last seen on land about 4.40 p.m., when they were assumed to have been returning from Ceann Ear with mails and provisions. The afternoon had been squally; and there had fallen a violent deluge. As time passed and the men failed to turn up, their relatives at the lighthouse-station became anxious. From the top of the lantern-tower, with the aid of binoculars, they observed them, huddled together, already waist-deep on a tidal rock. Drifting away from them was their boat, upturned. The tide was rising rapidly with the rising gale. A huge wave was seen to wash them from their perilous foothold.

This fatality left the operating of the Monach light to Archibald MacMillan, the third keeper, who was now to keep lonely vigil until aid could reach him. The Northern Lighthouse Board, on learning of the occurrence at its historic offices at 84, George Street, Edinburgh, directed that temporary assistance be sent to Archie from Barra, whence the Barra Head reliefs are carried out, and that meantime the Board's vessel, *Pole Star*, then at Stromness, her base, should proceed with all speed to the spot with a relief keeper from the lighthouse station at the Butt of Lewis. An exhaustive but fruitless search of the Monach shores and the adjacent shores of North Uist was immediately organised. But not until a month later were the lightkeepers' bodies recovered.

This was the first tragedy to have befallen any of the staff at the

D

Monach Light since its installation in 1864. The previous serious mishap in its vicinity occurred in 1903 when the barque, *Vanstabel*, registered at Dunkirk, was wrecked on the Duraborocks, and its total crew of 21 perished. Early in the eighteen-nineties a local boat was lost in the Monach Sound with three men on their way to attend a communion service at Paible. Some years before this, a Grimsay fishing-boat went down with its three occupants, having struck one of the many skerries awash off the Monachs.

The tragic loss of Milne and Black in 1936 drew attention to this cluster of isles, the existence of which hitherto was scarcely known but to the diminishing number of families inhabiting it, to the West Highland lobster-fishermen residing on them in rude huts of stone and turf during the summer months, to straying units of the Scottish Herring Fleet, to those in the service of the Northern Lighthouse Board, and to the farers of sundry nations constantly traversing these dangerous seas.

Rumour that the light, discontinued in August, 1942, because of the war, was to be manned again gained currency when in 1947 the Board was advertising lightkeeper vacancies. This inspired a fulsome letter to *The Oban Times* from a native of Uist, welcoming the prospect that this "beautiful light may shine out on the crofters' houses, and be a landmark for the locals". Promptly and understandably, realistic relatives of lightkeepers at remote stations like Shillay joined in letters of protest. "As a lightkeeper's wife who suffered there for 3½ years," ran one such letter, "I sincerely hope it will never be reopened." It never has been. Established at the request of the Board of Trade and the Admiralty for the benefit of sailing-ships bound for America and passing outside Shillay, and also to assist local shipping, the Northern Lighthouse Board sanctioned its permanent discontinuance in 1948, when it was found that it had ceased to be of any value to general navigation. Although the lighthouse is disused, the buildings are kept secure, and are inspected regularly.

CHAPTER FIVE

The Shiant Isles

WELL DOWN the fickle *manche* or sleeve of seaway intervening between the Outer Hebrides and much of the rest of Scotland lie the Shiant Isles, the rocky, remote, and now uninhabited trio known colloquially as 'the Shants', their name ascribed to their having been *sianed* or 'charmed' by priestly hands in olden times. Referred to by early Gaelic writers as the *Eileanan Seunta,* or Enchanted Isles, they certainly bore an air of enchantment when, in August, 1936, Robert Atkinson arrived to have a look at their birds. "Even at the edge of Scottish autumn," he wrote several years afterwards in his truly rewarding *Island Going,*[1] "the Shiant soil burgeoned with flowers. Earlier in the summer, when day was hardly divided from day, the place must surely have been Eileanan Seunta, the Enchanted Isles. There were roots of primroses and violets and kingcups, bushes of wild roses, the willow withies. Meadow sweet grew in the bog and forget-me-not by the stream; there was water-mint enough to make the lovely river reek. The highlands of Garbh were deep in heather, and one or two sheltered hollows up there were a yellow blaze of gorse from ancient twisted stems, very ligneous. Weedy composites spread their sunny discs, pink and white campion trained down the cliffs, where perched creaky great clumps of roseroot. Starry stonecrop and rockrose and milkwort, blue or pink, were summer bright; yarrow and sneeze-wort, mauve-blue scabious with the wine-coloured stamens, pink lousewort with its blown-up calyx, calamint and yellow rattle, buttercups and daisies. The wiry knapweeds topped with knobs—hardheads—had yet to break out into bright purple autumnal tufts. The clovers red and white grew best on the faint square which must once have been potato patch. Little field gentians grew among the west-facing crags above the

[1] Published by Collins in 1949.

house, where the soil was warm in afternoon sun." A more delectable passage on Hebridean flora would be difficult to find.

The Shiants, situated 5 miles or thereby off the south-east coast of Lewis, beyond the legend-haunted Sound of Shiant with its Blue Men of sinister repute, constitute the only isolated group of islands occurring on the east, or Minch, side of the Long Island. Included in the Lochs parish of the Isle of Lewis and, therefore, part of the county of Ross and Cromarty, the Shiants comprise Eilean Garbh (Rough Island), Eilean an Tighe (House Island), and Eilean Mhuire (Mary's Island), together with a distended string of eight or ten barren, much fretted, and usually seal-haunted skerries of varying sizes, the heavily eroded remnants of a dolerite sill stretching west toward the Lewis coast, and known as the Galtachean, or Galtas, their steep, north-facing cliffs showing as distinctly their columnar origin as do the major cliffs of the principal islands, particularly those of Garbh Eilean.

With an aggregate area of 3/4ths of a square mile, or 475 acres, the entire group fits a radius of 1½ miles, its three islands largely enclosing a lagoon swarming with all manner of seafowl nesting in due season on the ledges of the encircling cliffs or, as in the case of the puffins, in countless burrows among the screes of detritus and tumbled boulders beneath them. Garbh Eilean, largest and grandest, has an area of 9 square miles. Immediately to the south of it, and connected to it by an isthmus in the nature of a short, steep, and firmly packed shingle-beach which the highest tides all but submerge, lie Eilean an Tighe's 7 gentler square miles. But a mile north-east of them are the 5 square miles of Eilean Mhuire, the least rugged and, consequently, most luxuriant in the matter of natural pasturage. This is the isle referred to by Martin Martin (*circa* 1695) as fruitful in corn and grass, and as having upon it the chapel dedicated to the Virgin Mary, remembered in its Gaelic name.

Geologically, the shiants, although situated comparatively close to the main chain of the *Outer* Hebrides, have kinship rather with the *Inner*, as it were—with the basalts of Skye, rather than with the gneisses of Lewis and Harris. Indeed, as forming one large, intrusive sill more than 500 feet thick, Garbh Eilean and Eilean an Tighe may well be considered as the most northerly of those Inner Hebrides of which Tertiary igneous rocks are the principal ingredient. In their dipping to south and west, they present bold sea-cliffs on their northern and eastern sides. Garbh Eilean's almost vertical northern cliff-face, showing, as it does, a section of a great crinanite sill with regular columnar jointing on a grand scale, is one of the most dramatic in the Hebrides. Its columns, 5 or 6 feet in diameter, are generally hexagonal. At the base emerge Upper Lias shales. For the most part these shales, like the sill itself, lie concealed beneath a talus of large blocks. A lower sill under these shales, comprising the rocks at tide-marks, extends eastward as a low promontory which an interesting tunnel penetrates throughout its entire width.

All three islands have caves, some of them quite beautiful; and it should be mentioned that, whereas Staffa's celebrated basalt columns stand less than 20 feet, those of Garbh Eilean rise to a height of at least 350 in the face of cliffs soaring 500, curving near their summits as do the Bending Columns on Staffa. If, as Dr. John MacCulloch put it, the Shiants' columns lack the regularity of Staffa's, they certainly exceed them in simplicity, in grandeur, in depth of shadow, "and in that repose which is essential to the great style in landscape".[1]

The Shiants possess nothing in the nature of a harbour or of a pier. Indeed, they provide not even the simplest of jetties. Nevertheless, quiet haven may be found in the east bay of Garbh Eilean oftener than might be supposed by those taking literally that brief sentence in the Admiralty publication, *West Coast of Scotland Pilot* (1934): "Temporary anchorage can be obtained during the summer, if necessary only." One lands, as circumstances allow, at the shingly isthmus mentioned. On Eilean an Tighe, at a distance of no more than a hundred yards from this isthmus, and on the site of an earlier and quite primitive homestead, stands the cottage erected for Compton Mackenzie when, following upon Viscount Leverhulme's death the previous year, the Shiants were sold to him for £500. For half his purchase price, he erected this new house, incorporating in it the ruins of the old. In it he occasionally spent a night or two, the frequency and duration of his stays curtailed by his wife's very natural refusal to stay there with him. The Shiants remained Compton Mackenzie's property until 1936, when he disposed of them for £1,500 to Colonel MacDonald of Skeabost, who thought they might be suitable for breeding racehorses, members of a species of quadruped that, through no fault of its own, has done so much to degrade and deprave the human biped. The following year Mac-Donald, abandoning this foolish notion of his, sold them at roughly

[1] *A Description of the Western Isles of Scotland*, London, 1819.

the price he had paid for them to Nigel Nicolson. Nigel, now of the publishing-house of Weidenfeld & Nicolson, was then an undergraduate at Balliol. The Shiants have been Nigel's ever since. The manner in which he came into possession of them is related in a letter written at Sissinghurst by his mother, the late V. Sackville-West, in December 1936, to her husband, Harold Nicolson. "And oh, darling, I've got another activity in view: three tiny Hebridean islands for sale, advertised in the *Daily Telegraph* today. 600 acres in all. 'Very early lambs. Cliffs of columnar basalt. Wonderful caves. Probably the largest bird-colony in the British Isles. Two-roomed cottage.' Do you wonder, I have written to the agents for full particulars and photographs? ... They cost only £1,750."[1]

Nigel's tenant there at the present time is Donald MacLeod of Scalpay, a nephew of old Malcolm MacSween. Donald has some 400 sheep on the Shiants.

Contemporaneous records and, likewise, an examination of the ground show the Shiants to have supported about half a dozen crofting families throughout the 17th and 18th centuries, though probably in the most straitened way. In 1850, when, as part of Lewis, they had been six years in the possession of Sir James Matheson, they were abandoned by their four remaining crofters, two of whom went to adjacent Scalpay, and two to the Lewis mainland. Dykes, fallen and turf-sunken, still demarcate their humble homesteads. Traces of low-walled enclosures and of ancient lazybeds in their immediate vicinity are not difficult to find. The Blue Lias covering superficially so much of these islands and the absence of rabbits account for the rich pasture supporting for so many years now a flock of four to five hundred sheep.

On the Shiants, as in so many similar situations, the community dwindled until only one family remained. That family, named Campbell, occupied until 1910 the house built by Matheson's tenant —a man named Seller—on the site of the present house on Eilean an Tighe. A hundred yards to the south of it lies the well, the island's sole natural source of drinking water. Though clearly marked on the six-inch map, this well is now a little difficult to locate, being largely silted and overgrown. In the year mentioned, the Campbells left the Shiants when the father of the family went as a shepherd to one of the Falkland Islands—which explains how the Gaelic

---

[1] The late Sir Harold Nicolson's *Diaries & Letters*, 1930–1939, edited by his son, Nigel, and published in 1966 by Collins.

language can now be heard away down there. In 1946 Nigel Nicolson had a conversation with that shepherd's daughter, Marion, then an old woman living in Harris. Taken to Eilean an Tighe in 1862, when only two, she told Nigel that she never had quitted its shores until she was 19. Since the Campbells' day, the Shiants have had no permanent resident, albeit they have known a variety of absentee tenants in the interim, and occasionally have been visited by geologists and by naturalists, particularly by ornithologists and by those interested in whales, porpoises, basking sharks, and seals. Whereas whales are not common hereabouts, porpoises, basking sharks, and seals are moderately so. Seals in considerable numbers frequent Eilean Mhuire's southern reefs, and also the reefs below Garbh Eilean's northern cliffs. They are unusually tame. Nigel assures me that, if the visitor care to sing to them, they will gather round the enchanter's rowing-boat in consternation, if not also in admiration, to respond with their own seal-music, their heads meanwhile bobbing like black, shining footballs afloat on every hand.

Not infrequently Shiant waters are profitably exploited by a lobster-boat from Kyle of Lochalsh or from Mallaig. Lobster-fishing in Hebrid seas has been highly remunerative in recent years.

Marion Campbell and her family occupied on Eilean an Tighe the house which Seller had built; and she was indeed sorrowful the day they left, for all the solitude and poverty of their circumstances. The house had two rooms and two garrets. No other spot on the Shiants, she used to say, had been inhabited within living memory. Her family cultivated the lazybeds lying beyond the well, kept a cow, and shepherded the tenant's flock of some 300 sheep. It had sufficient butter and milk to be able to export small quantities of these commodities to the Isle of Scalpay. A few of the barest necessities it received in modest measure at odd times from visiting fishermen. The Campbell children never attended school. The Shiants were then the popular resort of affluent snipe-shooters who arrived in their yachts, and regularly purchased from the family a length or two of the tweed it spun during the long, dark, winter evenings. The Campbells snared puffins for food, and ate their eggs. With puffins' feathers they stuffed pillows and mattresses. During their lonely years there, two shipwrecks enlivened things for them. One of these occurred at the north-west extremity of Garbh Eilean, the other on Damhag, smallest and westernmost of the Galtachean rocks. Rats swam ashore in great numbers from the former. The crew of each vessel got ashore without loss, and lived with the Campbells for some weeks before being taken off.

When Donald Campbell's wife, Katherina, died on the Shiants in 1910, she was interred in a coffin made there by her deaf and dumb son, John, who survived her by 27 years. Katherina's body was carried for burial to Harris as soon as her family was able to attract outside attention by the fire it maintained on a conspicuous knoll near its home. Soon afterwards, and not without some reluctance, the family left the Shiants.

From 1900 until 1914 these islands were tenanted by a certain Roderick Martin, remembered because of his having destroyed the Campbells' old home when a ghost at his bedside asked, "Do you realise you're sleeping on my grave?". In 1914 the tenancy passed to Angus MacKenzie, a Stornoway butcher, who made the most of their suitability for sheep. These islands became Lord Leverhulme's when, in 1917, he purchased Lewis from my father's old friend, Colonel Duncan Matheson, installed himself in Lewis Castle, at Stornoway, and began to spend vast sums on vast enterprises which local intrigue and official stupidity obliged him to abandon. In 1921 Leverhulme, who thrice visited the Shiants, installed Malcolm MacSween there as his tenant. Malcolm remained their tenant throughout the remainder of Leverhulme's proprietorship, which terminated with the disposal of his Lewis properties by gift in 1923.

The future of the Shiant Isles at the time of Leverhulme's withdrawal from Lewis was clearly indicated by him. They were to be one of five modest exceptions from his gift. The other four were the Flannan Isles; Seaforth Island, which lay half in Lewis and half in Harris, and which he now proposed to attach wholly to the latter; North Rona and Sùla Sgeir; and the salmon-fishing in Loch Erisort. The Shiants, he stated, "are of the greatest interest to me, and are occupied by a tenant living in Harris; and really both they and the Flannan Isles can just as well be attached to Harris as to Lewis".

The tenant was, of course, Malcolm MacSween, whom we already have mentioned. It was Malcolm who persuaded Leverhulme to give up his idea of rearing on the Shiants silver foxes, goats, and rabbits, declaring that they would all devour each other. Today, as we have seen, these islands are tenanted by Malcolm's nephew, Donald MacLeod, who has sheep stock upon them. Consequently, shepherds spend about three weeks each year on them at lambing and clipping

times. The lambs are transported by fishing-boat to market at
Stornoway.

"One summer's day," writes Nigel Nicolson in his *Lord of the
Isles*,[1] "Leverhulme set out in a fishing-boat for the Shiants, and,
as he looked up at the great cliffs of columnar basalts rising like
organ-pipes from the deep sea, he remarked that it would be a fine
place for breeding silver foxes. Often when I have been there on a
sunlit day . . . I have rejoiced that Leverhulme's visions did not always
materialise . . . A farm for silver-foxes!" As Compton Mackenzie
commented, even the Shiants had to be 'developed'.

*   *   *

In the autumn of 1958, with Nigel's approval and with the generous
help of many, including the Goldsmiths' Company, the Westminster
School Society, and a number of private, commercial firms which,
among them, contributed a wide variety of food, essential supplies,
and equipment, a group of eight young persons from London, styling
themselves the Westminster Shiant Isles Expedition, spent a month
on these islands, surveying them and exploring and recording every
aspect of them, subsequently publishing an informative Report on
them, printed in Kent, at the Westerham Press. "All the food was
consistently satisfying and popular," ran an interim statement. "The
only items missed were fresh eggs, fresh bread, and potatoes. Appetites
and meals were equally immense; and we are grateful to all the
firms whose generosity made it possible to eat so well." Although
there already existed a six-inch Ordnance Survey map of the Shiants,
it was regarded as incomplete in so far as only one or two spot
heights were entered, and no contours at all. The Westminster boys
thought that, if only in some small degree, they might rectify such
shortcomings. Put ashore from the trawler, *Isa,* and having established close to the house on Eilean an Tighe a base-camp, they
erected an aerial for purposes of radio communication, and selected
a number of meteorological sites. The house was used as a kitchen
and as a store-room for scientific equipment. Thirty yards from it
lay the well of olden days, still providing ample water of a remarkable
purity.

The boys arranged a bi-weekly parachute drop of mails, provisions, and newspapers by an R.A.F. Shackleton bomber based on
Northern Ireland. Furthermore, they were successful where Nigel

[1] Published by Weidenfeld & Nicolson in 1960.

Nicolson had failed: they had managed to persuade the Postmaster-General to allow them, throughout their temporary isolation, the use of a small transmitting set, whereas he had informed Nigel that he would permit him to tee-in a telephone line to the main cable running between the Scottish mainland and the Outer Hebrides and passing within a few yards of the southernmost tip of the Shiants, adding that this would cost him £78,000 because it would necessitate the despatch to the scene from Southampton of a special cable-ship! Nigel thought he would try carrier-pigeons instead, with the result that today they are the usual means of swift communication between the Shiant Isles and the Outer Hebrides when the former, if only very temporarily, are inhabited.

Despite the fact that some peculiar magnetic influence on Eilean an Tighe rendered largely impracticable the expedition's use of the compass, all three islands were contoured and their principal heights accurately determined with the aid of an Abney level, a 10-foot folding staff, some 5-foot poles, prismatic compasses, and a couple of chains; and, although nothing professional was claimed, the completed contour-map proved sufficiently satisfactory to enable the expedition's botanists to classify with an acceptable degree of precision much of the islands' flora.

Regular meteorological readings were taken, as were also observations on raindrop sizes and on the development of hooked cirrus cloud, commonly called Mare's Tails. Indeed, the Meteorological Office had invited the boys to measure the relative sizes of orographic raindrops in an exposed and hitherto uninvestigated site, recent research having shown that raindrops actually do more damage to the exposed surfaces of aeroplanes than do hailstones of the same size. Experiments were hampered, however, because the type of rain suitable for them very rarely occurred—to the delight of all but the meteorological members of the expedition. With regard to Mare's Tails, there recently had been some controversy among meteorologists as to whether the 'blob' of this cloud formation developed from the 'tail', or the 'tail' from the 'blob'. The boys, though committed to no more than observing the clouds and recording their development, declared *both* processes to be true.

Meanwhile, the ornithological members, while taking a census of the islands' breeding species, carried out a large ringing programme on precipitous cliffs' edges reached by rope appropriately donated for the purpose by the Belfast Rope Company, and found exceedingly serviceable when ringing fulmar chicks otherwise out of reach. Most of the seabird counts were made from a boat enabling all three islands and the off-lying Galtachean to be circumnavigated leisurely. By far the commonest species was, of course, the puffin. There were thought to have been a million pairs. Unfortunately, the puffins departed while census work was still in progress, with the result that no puffin-ringing was possible at what may be regarded as the most populous puffinery in Europe. When the puffins are at their densest on the Shiants, they darken the sky with their fitful flight, before settling so thickly on the sea below the cliffs as to leave clear not the narrowest lane along which even a small boat could proceed without colliding with countless thousands of them. The shags ringed by the boys were caught mainly at their night roosts by dazzling them there. This method of capture, not previously tried with that species, proved highly successful on the Shiants.

The biological section of the boys' Report states that fulmars and kittiwakes followed the puffins numerically with nearly 1,500 pairs each. Flocks of meadow pipit, white wagtail, and twite were seen fairly frequently, usually after periods of easterly winds. Waders were observed more often, and ravens, buzzards, and kestrels occasionally.

Brown rats were common on all the islands, especially about the strand-line and in the vicinity of the seabirds' colonies where, doubtless, they destroy many of the young. From time to time some black rats were seen near the house on Eilean an Tighe. Rat skins were taken, and external parasites collected for identification by experts.

Of the 276 birds ringed, 99 were shags, and 105 were fulmar chicks on the cliffs' edges, reached by rope. No fewer than 45 species of migrants were noted. A representative collection was made of the islands' grasses, lichens, mosses, seaweed, shells, and barnacle. Despite the time occupied in precise scientific pursuit, opportunities were provided for exploring the islands thoroughly. This was rendered practicable by the small boat which members had brought with them. It enabled them to reach several caves, to sail through rock tunnels, and frequently to visit Eilean Mhuire, in some ways the most interesting of the Shiants.

A touch of drama was added when a Dakota circling overhead one foggy day reported that a large, German timber-ship lay aground and holed off the end of the Galtachean. Members of the expedition hurried to the scene to find the stranded vessel with the Stornoway lifeboat standing by. Floated by the next high tide, she proceeded cautiously to Stornoway, listing badly, taking with her, nevertheless, the boys' letters for posting there. This was but one of a number of unexpected visitors during their month on the Shiants. While breakfasting one morning, they were surprised to hear an unfamiliar voice inquire of them whether they were enjoying themselves. It was the voice of Finlay Morrison, the factor. Finlay had just landed with a party of shepherds to remove some lambs. Late that evening, three lobster-fishermen from Mallaig came ashore from a small boat at the shingly beach. For some nights they operated in neighbouring waters, giving the boys crabs and lobsters in exchange for modest supplies of petrol, tea, and margarine.

*   *   *

Numerous works published throughout the last century and a half have extolled the grandeur and exceeding beauty of Scotland. The first to embrace scientifically the entire country was Sir Archibald Geikie's *The Scenery of Scotland,* which Macmillan issued in 1856; and, although so much on this subject has been published since the appearance in 1901 of the third edition of this classic, one is constantly returning to it with an appreciation indistinguishable from reverence. My merely catching sight of its spine on my bookshelves sends me away into distant and delectable reverie.

The next really important work devoted to this kind of thing is *The Evolution of Scotland's Scenery,* a truly thrilling work which Oliver & Boyd published for J. B. Sissons as recently as 1967. But there is a substantial work which preceded these by many years, and to which allusion should be made if only because of the pleasing manner in which it treats of the Shiant Isles. I refer to *A Voyage Round Great Britain,* written by Richard Ayton, illustrated with a series of 308 aquatint views drawn and engraved by William Daniell, and published in eight volumes between 1814 and 1825. During several successive summers, these two persevering men travelled together to the scenes they depict, completing their work in London during the winter months, hoping that, as Ayton put it, "many who would not venture in pursuit of amusement out of the latitude of good inns and level roads, to make paths for themselves over rocks and crags, may still be pleased to become acquainted, at a cheaper rate, with the character of their own shores, where they are most conspicuous for boldness and picturesque beauty". Although Sir

Walter Scott's *Rob Roy* and *The Lady of the Lake* instantly were
to bring tens of thousands by stage-coach and boat to the romantic
Trossachs which these works so faithfully depicted, very few were
ever likely to visit remote and almost inaccessible scenes such as the
Shiants, so interestingly described in Ayton's text (Volume IV., 1820),
so dramatically portrayed in Daniell's two aquatints entitled 'Part of
the Northern Face of one of the Shiant Isles,' and 'Near View of
one of the Shiant Isles'. These islands were then the property of
Mrs. Stewart MacKenzie, formerly Lady Hood, a member of the
Seaforth family.

With these aquatints I have been familiar since childhood. Unob-
trusively framed, they have been for at least a century among the
favourites chosen from Daniell's great number to hang in private
homes and public collections, exhibiting, as they certainly do, the
Shiants' most striking feature, namely, a mighty precipice of columnar
basalt haunted by seafowl inconceivably numerous; "and the eye,"
wrote Ayton, "might form an imaginary scale for calculating its
magnitude on viewing them, as they seemed to be diminished to the
size of bees." So unaccustomed to human intrusion were the puffins
that they exhibited not the least apprehension at the approach of the
boat from which Ayton and Daniell landed, which explains how
several were taken by the boatmen with the greatest ease. Incidentally,
while this group of islands has been referred to as the greatest
puffinery in Europe, it has, of course, several other bird species—St.
Kilda wrens, kittiwakes, guillemots, cormorants, gulls of every kind,
and literally thousands of gannets. Its puffin population remains
enormous, despite a decline in comparatively recent years, attributable
to an invasion of rats.

A setting for a schoolboys' expedition more rewarding than the
Shiant Isles would be hard to imagine. It offers enough of everything, including just that essential touch of remoteness.

When we gaze at the basalt columns of the Giant's Causeway,
when we behold similar formations at Staffa and Ulva and kindred
Hebridean scenes, do we realise that they constitute the most readily
visible evidence of the volcanic matter that, 20,000,000 years ago,
poured over these regions and the seas amid which they now lie,
long since cooled and solidified, long since worn down to the merest
shadow of their former terrifying splendour? The first formations
of the kind I ever beheld, and with such memorable rapture and
wonderment, were not at any of the comparatively accessible scenes

I have mentioned, but at the Shiants. For this, all through my life, I have been immensely grateful to William Daniell for the curiosity his aquatints kindled in me in my boyhood. My first contact with the Shiants, however, might well have been tangible in a truly disastrous sense, since the fishing-boat taking me on my first trip from Stornoway to Tarbert was driven off her course, dangerously close to them. The Blue Men of the Minch, those storm-kelpies tormenting the unwary in this fitful tideway of theirs, all but encompassed us, obliging our running for shelter to the nearest creek of Scalpay, some miles short of our intended destination. These storm-kelpies haunt this tideway as the Merry Men o' Mey haunt the spectacular tiderace on the Caithness side of the Pentland Firth.[1]

Anything more inspiring than the Shiants' basalts, soaring hundreds of feet in unbroken sweeps from sea-level to cliff-top, I have yet to see.

---

[1] The Blue Men are dealt with at greater length in Chapter IX of my book, *The Peat-fire Flame: Folk-tales and Traditions of the Highlands & Islands* (Edinburgh, 1937 & 1947).

CHAPTER SIX

St. Kilda
A General Survey

IN 1899 there was published in London by Cassell & Co. a book entitled *With Nature and a Camera*. Its pages, recording the observations of a field naturalist and of an animal photographer, illustrated by no fewer than 160 photographs, were the first I ever read voluntarily. The naturalist was Richard Kearton: the photographer was his younger brother, Cherry. In the Highland home of boyhood, this book of theirs was accorded a place among its household gods. It occupied in our family library a position inferior only to *The Scriptures* and *Chambers's Twentieth-Century Dictionary*. Its first chapters dealt with St. Kilda and its no less precipitous satellites. And who, reared in the Scottish Highlands or Islands, did not hear in boyhood, if not indeed in childhood, *something* of that remote group of isles? On a clear day many natives of the Outer Hebrides have seen St. Kilda afar, although few have ever set foot upon what, until the autumn of 1930, shared with Foula the distinction of being one of the two remotest of Britain's inhabited fragments.

I was about six when my didactic father, anxious that I should be instructed in matters of wholesome report, carried me triumphantly through the Keartons' book; and so vividly did I remember many of its illustrations that when, eventually, I landed at St. Kilda, I found the island strangely familiar.

In the summer of 1896, a year or two before I was born, the *Dunara Castle* dropped down the Firth of Clyde from Glasgow with the Keartons aboard. Brimful of excitement and expectation, they were on their pioneering way with notebook and camera to St. Kilda, where they hoped to observe much, especially in regard to the amazing bird-life populating its stupendous sea-cliffs. Few people in the world have witnessed anything half as awesome as these mighty precipices with their myriads of seafowl. Even on the brightest day they darken the very heavens when, in deafening alarm, they take to the wing.

As the *Dunara Castle* approached Village Bay, the only place among these shoreless isles where mariners can find shelter and effect a landing without tackle and undue hazard, the captain expressed doubt as to whether it would be possible for the Keartons to disembark: a fresh wind was blowing from the south-east, worst of all directions so far as Village Bay, the Bay of Hirta, is concerned. In due course, however, the brothers, together with their belongings, were got ashore. The story of their prolonged stay with the St. Kildans is enshrined in the volume in which they coöperated so memorably.

Through a happy circumstance to be related later, it was with Neil Ferguson and his family that I resided during my sojourn among the St. Kildans in 1930. From Neil I heard much about the Keartons and their exploits together when Neil and they were comparatively young men. All that had happened while the brothers were on St. Kilda was as clear in Neil's memory as though he had just refreshed it by reading again *With Nature and a Camera*. The copy which the brothers had sent him on publication reposed on the kitchen dresser, carefully wrapped in an abundance of old newspaper, to be brought into the daylight only on very special occasions. This book was one of Neil's few cherished possessions. Its pages set forth, for all the world to see, the names of himself and his neighbours, with all of whom the Kearton brothers had had so much to do. Richard by this time was dead; while Cherry had attained world celebrity. Neil felt in his heart that, perhaps, without his being too immodest, he had had a little to do with their first venture, with their initial contribution to literature, and with Cherry's fame. Recalling the occasion when that hurtling stone threatened Cherry, he actually escorted me to the scene where fatality so nearly befell. Although busy with preparations for Hirta's impending evacuation, he did make time to wander afield with me over the island, pausing here and pointing there when some incident relating to the Keartons came to mind. On our reaching the Lover's Stone, he told me what, indeed, I already knew from my perusal of the Keartons' book, namely, that an accident had robbed them of the photograph Cherry had taken of this perilous platform protruding seaward at an altitude of 850 feet above the seething sea.

Throughout my days on St. Kilda, the Keartons were never far from my mind: so deep was the impression their book had made upon me in early life. If, during the day-time, I were not abroad with my own camera amid the scenes they had explored together, I was seated by Neil Ferguson's fireside, round which, of an evening, the Keartons and their doings always supplied the topic of conversation after everyone was tired of discussing matters concerning the island's sheep stock and its impending transshipment.

The evening before we all left St. Kilda, Neil gave me a keepsake —one of the puffin-gins he himself had fashioned for Richard Kearton, but which Richard carelessly had left behind him. I still have that gin, though it is not the sort of thing *I* should ever use. I value it as an intimate reminder of those last days on St. Kilda, and of the volume that inspired in me my earliest desire to reach that oceanic outpost.

Richard Kearton died in 1928, at the age of 66. In the early winter of 1930, a month or two after the evacuation of St. Kilda, and 34 years after the Keartons' visit, I met Cherry for the first time, and was able to tell him how vividly the St. Kildans remembered them both. Cherry enquired for old friends and helpers about whom I was now in a position to tell him much. The islanders by this time had been settled on the Scottish mainland. Some were at Lochaline, in Argyll: Neil Ferguson and his family were now at Kincardine-on-Forth, in Fifeshire. It was soul-stirring to learn from Cherry's own lips of Finlay MacQueen's feats on Boreray and of Neil Ferguson's daring on Conachair, where the cliffs, loftiest in Britain, tower nigh 1,300 feet over the Atlantic. (See photograph facing page 97.)

In 1940, at the age of 69, Cherry Kearton died in London while returning home after a broadcast during an air-raid. What a wealth of literature, so richly illustrated, this pioneer of animal photography left behind him! His books are too well-known to necessitate one's mentioning any of them in particular. It was fitting that the folks of Swaledale should have erected on the walls of Muker School, near Thwaite, where Richard and Cherry were born, tablets commemorating the achievements in later life of its two most illustrious pupils. At a party shortly after my first meeting with Cherry, I made the acquaintance of Richard's son, Cherry Kearton—Cherry the Second—a publisher.

So much, then, by way of prologue.

*   *   *

The remote and precipitously rock-bound cluster of islands known as St. Kilda lies roughly 40 miles off North Uist and Harris, about as far to the west of the main chain of the Outer Hebrides as North Rona and Sùla Sgeir lie to the north-north-east of the Butt of Lewis. Situated, moreover, 110 miles west of the Scottish mainland and in the same latitude as Inverness and the southernmost tip of Greenland, it comprises the most westerly of the British Isles with the exception of Rockall, the subject of our final chapter. As David Mallet, unaware of the existence of Rockall, put it two centuries ago,

> *Aloft to heaven remotest Kilda lifts,*
> *Last of the sea-girt Hebrides that guard,*
> *In filial train, Britannia's coast.*

By deep-sea fishermen pursuing their calling in Rockall and St. Kilda waters, this cluster is referred to simply as The Kildas. In ancient times this truly dramatic group, for its size and in so many respects the most remarkable in the world's seas, was called Hirt, or Hirta, the name by which it still is known to the Gaelic-speaking communities of the Scottish Highlands and Islands, the name moreover which the natives themselves applied throughout the centuries to the largest of them—to that upon which they and their forebears had lived a thousand years when, in the autumn of 1930, their declining remnant was evacuated to accessible homes on the Scottish mainland.

Hirt is an old name appearing as *Hirtir* in an Icelandic saga of the 13th century. So far as one knows, its first published appearance as applicable to St. Kilda is in Dean Monro's account of his Hebridean travels undertaken about 1549. There he states that "out in the mayne ocean seas, be threescore myle of sea, layes an ile callit Hirta, ane maine laiche [low-lying] ile, sa far as is manurit of it, aboundant in corne and gressing, namelie for sheipe, for ther ar fairer and greiter sheip ther, and larger tailled, then ther is in ony uther isle about". The Dean then mentions its natives and their condition. "The inhabitants therof ar simple, poor people, scarce learnit in ony religioun, bot M'Cloyd of Herray [MacLeod of Harris], his stewart, or he quhom he deputs in sic office, sailes ance in the zeir ther at midsummer, with some chaplaine to baptize bairnes ther, and if they want a chaplaine, thay baptize ther bairnes thamselfes."

It was from the descendant of the MacLeod mentioned by the Dean four centuries ago that in 1934, four years after St. Kilda's evacuation, the Earl of Dumfries (to be mentioned again later) purchased St. Kilda.

*   *   *

Although nobody as yet has traced a saint known as Kilda, the name, St. Kilda, or a variant of it, has been applied consistently to this remote group of islands ever since the publication in London in 1698 of Martin Martin's *Voyage to St. Kilda*. Precisely where Martin found the name, one cannot say. It is not improbable that a man of his inquiring disposition spotted *S. Kilda* and *S. Kilder*, or something very like them, on those 16th- and 17th-century Dutch charts, since no Scottish cartographers used it at that period. These Dutch charts, as Dr. A. B. Taylor pointed out in his contribution to the Scottish National Trust's *Newsletter* of October, 1957, owe much to Willem Blaeu's *Licht der Zeevaert (The light of Navigation)*, that rare collection of charts and sailing instructions he published at Amsterdam in 1608, the British Museum's copy of which I studied a few years ago. As Dr. Taylor remarked, Blaeu's outline of the St. Kilda group, so excellent, must have been based on accurate reports received from mariners. Etymologically, however, we are still without anything satisfactory about the name, St. Kilda.

The group's principal islands, in order of size, are Hirta, Soay, Boreray, and Dùn. They embrace in addition a number of isolated stacks. In the channel separating Hirta and Soay, for instance, lie three—Soay Stac, Stac Biorach, and Stac Dona. That situated off the entrance to Village Bay is called Levenish. The two most famous, and deservedly so, lie off Boreray. They are the prodigious Stac an Armin and Stac Lee, with their fantastic wealth of resident seabirds at nesting-time. The former, at 625 feet, stands 200 feet higher than Orkney's celebrated Old Man of Hoy. That is to say, about as high as is the summit of Arthur Seat above the Queen's Park of Edinburgh. It is Britain's loftiest stack, rising 173 feet higher than Stac Lee which, nevertheless, may well be regarded as the most majestic and awe-inspiring of the world's oceanic rocks. Besides these, there are several lesser stacks and reefs, most of them fringing the western cliffs of Hirta itself.

The dimensions of St. Kilda's islands and principal stacks tabled below are those which my father's Gaelic friend, the late John Mathieson, geographer, prepared during the summer of 1927, and published the following spring in the *Scottish Geographical Magazine*, together with notes on their geology by the late Dr. A. M. Cockburn, on their flora by John Gladstone, and on their birds by Seton Gordon:

Name	Length of Sea Coast Miles	Highest Point Feet	Area Acres
St. Kilda	8¾	1396.8	1575
Soay	2¼	1225	224
Boreray	1¾	1245	189
Dùn	2	576	79
Stac an Armin ...	–	627	13
Stac Lee	–	544	6
Stac Levenish ...	–	185	6

Total Area: 2092

Conachair, the highest hill, and the neighbouring peak of Oiseval, both on Hirta, are composed of a cream-coloured granophyre. The remaining two-thirds of Hirta, along with St. Kilda's other islands, are built up for the most part of dark-coloured masses of gabbro, dolerite, and basalt deeply weathered along the coastline and in the sea-cliffs above, giving those weird, fantastic skyline effects familiar to climbers of the Coolins. Working along lines of weakness, along joint lines, and at places where dykes reach sea-level, the sea has excavated deep caves and natural arches, and is in process of cutting these islands into a series of isolated stacks. But for the weathering which has produced innumerable ledges and chimneys among the dyke rocks, most of St. Kilda's cliffs would have been so absolutely inaccessible that much of the fowling upon them would have been impossible. It is doubtful whether Hirta could have carried its population down the centuries had it not been for the extent to which the natives were able to pursue their fowling among these perilous cliffs.

In striking contrast with the rugged grandeur of Hirta's coast-line is the smooth, rounded topography of its interior. The perfect cone of Conachair and the gentle slopes of Oiseval are reminiscent of the Red Hills of Skye. The Great River and the River of the Glen (*Amhuinn Mhòr* and *Amhuinn a' Ghlinne Mhòir*), Hirta's only streams of any size, are too insignificant to account for the valleys through which they run. Both valleys therefore must be relics of a greater drainage system, modified perhaps by glacial action. Yet, there is no definite proof that St. Kilda was ever under an ice-sheet, although the smoothness of its inland topography strongly suggests glacial action.

So far as we know, Hirta is the only member of the group to have been inhabited in a permanent way. Its maximum length is 2½ miles: its maximum breadth 1¾. At a distance of about 4 miles to the north-east of it lies Boreray. With the exception of the landing-place on Soay, that on Boreray presents the greatest hazards. Here a wall of cliff ranging in height from 300 to 1,200 feet encloses an area of 189 acres. In places these cliffs have weathered into the weirdest shapes. Only when a small boat, deftly handled, rises on the swell is it possible to leap from it on to Boreray. Each person upon landing is obliged to scramble immediately up some 300 feet of sheer cliff, with a rope round his waist for safety. Boreray, besides possessing Britain's largest fulmar colony, is the world's largest gannetry. Between a fourth and a fifth of the world's gannets nest there and on the two colossal, oceanic stacks adjacent thereto. Furthermore its grassy slopes are riddled with the burrows of puffins. The island possesses several stone and turf hutments (cleits) in which the St. Kildans used to live for about a week at a time when fowling, or when taking the fleeces from the hundreds of sheep pastured there.

Caves and caverns and deep fissures characterise the cliffs forming the coast-line of all these islands. Some of the caves extend subterraneously for distances exceeding 200 feet. When overtaken by storms while absent from Hirta on fowling or sheep-shearing expeditions at Boreray, the natives often spent the night in one or other of its many caves or *geos*. A glance at John Mathieson's map shows that the St. Kildans had supplied him with a name for every *geo* in the intricate coast of Hirta and its adjacent islands and stacks. Here it should be observed that, whereas elsewhere on the coasts of north-western Scotland a *geo* denotes a creek, in the case of St. Kilda the term was applied strictly to a cave or tunnel scooped out by the sea. There is not a single *gob* or promontory wanting a name. Among St. Kilda's place-names are literally hundreds of *geos* and *gobs*.

There lies immediately below the altar on Dùn the entrance to one of the most wonderful caves in Scotland. The light striking the golden sand upon its floor on a sunny day sends up bright rays in green and gold. From the dome of this cave is re-echoed the sound of the tiniest wave. A friend of mine was quite overcome when he found this subterranean surprise awaiting him on Dùn. Another cave, situated near the Landing-place of the Strangers, runs a hundred yards through cliff.

Among the sea-cliffs below the Carn Mòr, on the south of Hirta, is the Cave of the Irishman, with which is associated the following tale. An Irishman in the act of crossing in a small boat to an islet with a keg of whisky to celebrate some festival or other with his people, who lived there, was carried off in a squall. Eventually he was driven ashore at the entrance to this cave. There he remained for two or three days until the natives, having by this time perceived a wrecked boat in its vicinity, lowered a rope and rescued him, just as he was on the verge of collapsing from exposure and want of food. The St. Kildans used to say that more than a year elapsed between the time of his rescue and the opportunity of transferring him to his home in Ireland.

North of Conachair, and no more than fifty yards from the shore, lies an isolated rock named Mina Stac, 212 feet in height. The St. Kildans believed that a few centuries ago a natural archway concealed the channel between the present stack and the cliffs of Conachair, and that the archway caved in when the tip of the topmast of one of the Spanish Armada's vessels, driven before a gale, struck it. According to a tradition still current among the natives at the time of their leaving St. Kilda in 1930, this mishap resulted not only in isolating Mina Stac from Hirta, but also in the foundering of the vessel beneath tons of falling rock.

The vast majority of St. Kilda's place-names is of Norse origin. Among the few of Gaelic origin may be noted the following:

Gob na h-Airde, Beak of the Heights.
Cambir, crooked or bent.
Dùn, a fort.
Sgeir Mhic Righ Lochlainn, Skerry of the Son of the King of Norway.
An Torc, the Boar.
Sgeir Mhòr, the Big Rock.
Laimhrig nan Gall, Landing-place of the Strangers.
Airidh Mhòr, the Great Shieling.
Cnoc Glas, the Grey Hillock.
Tobar nam Buaidh, Well of Virtues.
Tigh an Triar, House of the Fold.

Although historical documents mentioning the ownership of St. Kilda are puzzling and contradictory, there is little doubt that for a very long time it remained the property of MacLeod of MacLeod. In the Western Highlands there is a tradition that long, long ago there arose a dispute between MacLeod and MacDonald of Clan Ranald as to the ownership of St. Kilda. Eventually it was decided that two galleys should make for it simultaneously, one rowed by MacLeods, the other by MacDonalds, and that the clansman whose hand first touched St. Kilda should be regarded as having won it for his chief. The contest was a close one. When at the very last moment there seemed a danger that the MacDonalds were going to win, one of the MacLeods chopped off his hand and cast it ashore, and thus was regarded as having touched St. Kilda. Be this as it may, the connection between the MacLeods of MacLeod and St. Kilda is centuries old. The late John MacKenzie, factor to MacLeod of MacLeod at Dunvegan, was of opinion that St. Kilda had been a MacLeod possession from time immemorial, and that it formed part of the extensive territories ceded by Norway to the Scottish Crown following upon Haco's defeat at Largs in 1263.

As I already have said, the mountains of Hirta bear a strong resemblance to the Red Hills of Skye, more especially, perhaps, when the latter are viewed from a boat a few miles off Broadford. But the greenness of their smooth, symmetrical slopes also reminds one of Scotland's Southern Uplands. Etched against a clean sky when visibility is good, the perfect cones of Oiseval and Conachair are in themselves an inspiration. Towering Conachair, attaining an altitude of 1,396 feet, dominates the scene. In a succession of broken granite cliffs, its seaward side sheers perpendicularly to the Atlantic, more than 1,200 feet below, to form the greatest perpendicular precipice in the British Isles.

At least three other peaks are worthy of note—to wit, the Mullach Mòr, the Mullach Bì, and Oiseval, which are 1,172, 1,164 and 948 feet, respectively. At that part of Hirta known as the Cambir, one may review the cliffs of the Mullach Bì rising out of the sea to over 1,100 feet, populated by myriads of birds. A tremendous rock on this side of the island, jutting seaward at a height of some hundreds of feet to the south of the Mullach Bì, is called the Lover's Stone. It is said that in olden times a prospective bridegroom, seeking the heart and hand of a St. Kildan bride, was expected to demonstrate his prowess by standing on the very edge of the Lover's Stone on one leg, as if he were on the point of leaping from it into the Atlantic surge.

Hirta, as might be expected from its limited area, possesses no river in the ordinary sense of the term. Several streams and streamlets, however, drain its higher ground. Among its wells and springs, all of them noted in olden times for their excellent water, is *Tobar nam Buaidh*, Well of the Virtues. This is the *Tou-bir-nimbeuy* mentioned by Martin as the finest of Hirta's fountains. Its water was considered efficacious against all manner of ailments. Referring to it in 1745, the Rev. Kenneth MacAulay noted that "the water here was a sovereign cure for a great variety of distempers, deafness particularly, and every nervous disease". The Well of Virtues lies by the shieling in the Great Glen. On an altar hard by, the ancients who came to drink of it left votive offerings. So famed was this well that the more nimble tourists landing on Hirta during the summer months from the *Hebrides*, or from her sister-ship, the *Dunara Castle*, dashed over the col between the Mullach Sgar and the Mullach Geal to drink of it during the few hours either of these efficient, little ships lay at anchor in the Bay of Hirta.

The well from which some believe these islands to have received their name is Tobar Childa. When in olden days the natives were delayed by contrary winds, they resorted to this spring and to St. Brendan's Well. The direction of the wind altered in their favour, it was said, when each man waiting to put out to sea stood astride the water of either of them for a few seconds. Then, somewhere on the slopes of Conachair lies the spring to which the natives referred as the Lost Well of Youth. Up to the time of their leaving, they recounted folk-tales of how it suddenly appeared, and as suddenly vanished.

*   *   *

Heavy rains, damp mists, and frequent gales are characteristic of St. Kilda. Tempestuous winds and heavy seas were the portion of its inhabitants for the greater part of the year. These islands are also subjected to keen frost and severe snowstorms.

Except for a few dwarf willows, St. Kilda has neither tree nor shrub. So little conception did the natives have of a tree that, when the architect, Alexander Ross, who reached Hirta from Inverness in the winter of 1884, drew the likeness of a tree for their edification, they were unanimous in their conclusion that he had reproduced for them the Tree of the Knowledge of Good and Evil![1]

Only within the walls of the ancient burying-place behind the village is the common nettle to be found. Nettles seem to have a distinct partiality for corpses! Ferns grow in a few sheltered clefts. The tiniest honeysuckle flowers luxuriantly even on the exposed cliffs of Oiseval, at an altitude of 500 feet. Alick Cockburn informed me that he saw a cluster of honeysuckle growing under the Mullach Bì, on the west side of Hirta. It may well have been brought there by birds. He noted matricary, sea-pinks, and scurvy-grass on Levenish during the few courageous hours he spent on it in 1927. Indeed, the summit of Levenish is covered with matricary—wild marguerites. Dockens galore are to be found on Hirta and Boreray; while purple vetch flourishes on the sheltered side of Soay. Also found on these islands are purple mountain saxifrage, the moss campion, ragged robin, midsummer-men, and primroses. The last mentioned grow in tremendous profusion among the cliffs. Iris plants thrive in the marshy places; and the creeping thistle may now be found in the vicinity of what was the factor's house. The grasses of St. Kilda are abundant and nutritious. There are no fewer than 130 species of grasses, sedges, and rushes.

*   *   *

St. Kilda has a fauna of its own. Its bird-life, of course, is stupendous. According to Seton Gordon, who has written so much about the Hebrides, the solan goose does not nest on Hirta itself, but on the cliffs of Boreray, and at a height above the Atlantic of more than a thousand feet. It also nests on the smaller islands and on Boreray's mighty stacks. The two birds most in evidence are the fulmar petrel and the puffin, though seldom is either seen crossing over that part of Hirta where lies the village, now in ruins. Where Conachair's cliffs fall so terrifyingly to the sea from an altitude of between 1,200 and 1,300 feet, myriads of puffins inhabit them. These cliffs are also the habitat of guillemots, kittiwakes, and razorbills. Puffins are to be found in their greatest numbers on Boreray and Soay, where they burrow into the grassy and peaty slopes above the cliffs. As St. Kilda is devoid of anything in the nature of a rabbit, the puffin may be regarded as its only burrowing animal. Oyster-

[1] An account of Ross's visit to St. Kilda appears in the *Transactions of the Inverness Scientific Society and Field Club*, 1884, vol. iii, pp. 72–91.

catchers, ducks, scarts, and gulls of all kinds frequent Hirta in great numbers; but land-birds are comparatively few. Seton Gordon and others have noted migrating swifts; and I myself have seen some sparrows. Richard Kearton, on the other hand, listed several land-birds.

Ornithologists believe Hirta to have been the last nesting-place of the gare-fowl, or great auk. The occasional visit of the cuckoo was said to presage the death either of MacLeod of MacLeod or of his steward; whereas the arrival of the heron was regarded by the more superstitious inhabitants as the visit of a witch from Lewis. In the loneliness of the Great Glen of Hirta in 1927, Alick Cockburn heard the cuckoo. Aware of the natives' superstition, he at first did not tell them. When in the end he did so, he was a little disappointed that they exhibited nothing of the alarm he had anticipated. Neither MacLeod nor his steward (factor) died that year. The former did not die until two years later.

The fulmar and the gannet formed two of the main articles of diet in the days before the regular sailings of the *Hebrides* and the *Dunara Castle* made the St. Kildans largely dependent upon imported supplies. Not only did they use these birds for food, but they also extracted from them the oil they burned in their cruses—their old-world lamps. In addition, the feathers were used for pillows and mattresses. "Can the world exhibit a more valuable commodity?" wrote the missionary, the Rev. Kenneth MacAulay, when referring to the indispensability of the fulmar. "The fulmar furnishes oil for the lamp, down for the bed, the most salubrious food, the most efficacious ointment for healing wounds, besides a thousand other virtues of which he is possessed, which I have not time to enumerate. But to say all in one word, deprive us of the fulmar, and St. Kilda is no more." MacAulay, whose *History of St. Kilda* appeared in 1764, mentions that great quantities of fulmars were salted in casks each year to supplement the islanders' winter provision.

Hardly less important was the gannet, or solan goose. Martin Martin (1697) refers as follows to this fowl in relation to the St. Kildans: "The solan geese are very numerous here, insomuch that the natives commonly keep yearly above twenty thousand young and old in their little stone houses, of which there are some hundreds for preserving their fowls' eggs, etc. They use no salt for preserving their fowl; the eggs of the sea wild-fowl are preserved some months in the ashes of peats, and are astringent to such as be not accustomed to eat them." In Martin's time—toward the close of the 17th century—when the population of St. Kilda was 180 souls, the natives must have been particularly fond of gannets!

In the autumn of 1841, James Wilson, the ornithologist, brother of Christopher North (Professor John Wilson), visited Hirta. He put the number of St. Kilda's solans at 200,000, and came to the conclusion that this species devoured no fewer than 214,000,000 fish—the equivalent of more than 300,000 barrels.[1]

Since the St. Kildans ceased to use for food such great quantities of fulmars, many authorities on bird-life have noted the marked increase in their number. It was about the year, 1877—the year that the *Dunara Castle* began her regular summer sailings—that the change in the dietary of the natives commenced. The increase in the fulmar population was noted also by the late John MacKenzie, factor to MacLeod of MacLeod, who, for over roughly half a century, paid an annual visit to St. Kilda. Up till about the middle of the 19th century, the inhabitants existed entirely on what their own islands and the surrounding sea produced—birds and their eggs, mutton from the much over-rated St. Kilda or Soay sheep, a little beef, milk, butter, cheese, crowdie, oat-meal, barley-meal, and fish. They ground the meal with the ancient quern-stones. It was in their pursuit of seafowl on the cliffs, as also the frequency with which the sheep evaded capture on virtually inaccessible rocks, that the St. Kildans became such a wonderful race of cragsmen.

Lizards, frogs, toads, snakes, and their amphibian kind are totally unknown on St. Kilda. So too are rabbits, as we have seen. Furthermore, there are neither hares nor rats. However, about the beginning of the 18th century an annotator remarked that, while Hirta could boast neither tree nor bee, "the Awphibia seen here are ottars and seales".

Hirta had—and may still have—its own species of mice, the St. Kilda long-tailed variety, and a particular house-mouse, the celebrated *mus muralis,* which confined himself to the island's post-office building, and consequently became known to naturalists as the post-office mouse.

Quite early in Neil Ferguson's career as postmaster (dealt with at length in subsequent chapters), the post-office mouse took up

[1] *A Voyage round the Coasts of Scotland and the Isles,* 1842, vol. ii, pp. 1–113.

residence at his premises, among the groceries it contained. What has befallen him, now that the post-office building lies in ruin and there are no stores for his sustenance—no sacks of flour and sugar and the like—and the cats left behind by the natives have had to fend for themselves, we do not know as yet. Naturalists writing to the London newspapers at the time of the evacuation showed concern for his future. Regarding his fate as one of the minor tragedies associated with man's relinquishing his hold on St. Kilda, one of them wrote:

> O what will become of the Post-Office mouse,
>   When the Post-Office posts no more?
> It will mope, it will mope in the Post-Office house,
>   And die on the Post-Office floor!

Naturalists have expressed anxiety also for the St. Kilda wren, a bird enjoying the distinction of having had a special Act of Parliament passed for its protection. Professional ornithologists and egg-collectors threatened it with extinction; and so, in the 1880s, Sir Herbert Maxwell introduced a measure to protect it.

St. Kilda was the only part of Great Britain specially exempted from the provisions of the Wild Birds' Protection Act (1880) and of subsequent Acts, because of the extent to which the natives relied both upon eggs and birds for food.

*   *   *

Turning to domestic mammals, one finds that the St. Kildans kept neither goats nor pigs. Nor did they possess a horse at the time of their leaving. They appear to have had goats, however, when Dr. John MacCulloch landed in 1815. James Wilson, aforenamed, mentions that, not very long before he visited St. Kilda in 1841, goats were so numerous that they had to be disposed of, mainly because they disturbed the remunerative seafowl at nesting-time.

In Martin's time Hirta had eighteen horses, "all of a red colour, very low and smooth skinned". By 1841 the number had fallen considerably. There were one or two small horses on Hirta when, in August of that year, Wilson visited St. Kilda in company with Sir Thomas Dick Lauder, who at the time was Secretary to the Board of Fisheries. According to tradition, the few remaining horses were taken off the island by a former lessee on the ground that they were injuring pasturage he wanted to reserve for sheep. The absence of the horse meant the absence of the plough. "Thay use na pleuchis, bot delvis thair corne land with spaiddis. Ther is na horse nor meire in this Isle", according to a description of the Western Isles believed by William Skene to have been written between 1577 and 1595. Until about 1835, tillage on St. Kilda was done with the ancient *cas-chrom*, or bent-foot plough, worked by hand and foot. In times more recent, the little delving in which the St. Kildans engaged was done with the ordinary spade.

The dogs on St. Kilda at the time of the evacuation were a mongrel type of collie. For rounding up a flock of sheep they were no use whatever, although excellent at catching an individual sheep, and holding it fast until its owner could lay hands on it. Many years ago the factor offered to equip the natives with nets in the hope of inducing them to adopt a more humane and less wasteful method of catching their sheep. In declining his offer, they expressed a preference for their own method because of the danger and excitement it entailed! The loss occasioned at various times by sheep leaping over the cliffs in endeavouring to escape from the dogs must have been considerable.

St. Kilda was famous for its sheep. With Soay, as already mentioned, was associated the Soay sheep. Soay means Sheep Island. Its particular sheep has been described as a domestic breed derived from the Moufflon so thoroughly domesticated and improved by breeding that the wool-coat has become a fleece quite obscuring the original coat of hair. The sheep on Soay belonged to MacLeod of MacLeod. Their wool, not clipped in the usual way, was simply plucked off when it became loose. Shearing, it was argued, would have removed both the fleece and the undercoating of short hair. The latter was said by the St. Kildans to have been necessary for the protection of the animal against the severities of their winter. The plucking of the wool in this fashion was known as *rueing*, or *rooing*.

The sheep population of the St. Kilda group, toward the end of the 17th century, was estimated at two thousand. Toward the close of the 19th, the number had fallen to roughly twelve hundred, though at this period it was believed that the natives were particularly averse from making accurate returns lest MacLeod, the proprietor, fixed his rent in proportion to their sheep stock.

*　　*　　*

The earliest mention of St. Kilda is probably that embodied in the charter granted to Reginald by his father, John, Lord of the Isles. This charter must date back to about 1360, since it was confirmed by King Robert II. The first really authentic information we have of St. Kilda is that supplied by Dean Monro. On one occasion, according to the Dean, the steward took with him to the island a quantity of malt with a view to brewing liquor for his own consumption. But the natives, discovering that they quite liked his concoction, fell to consuming it until "baith men, weemen, and bairnes were deid drunken".

Unquestionably the most valuable account of olden St. Kilda is Martin's. It relates, among so much, that the horses and cows on Hirta in 1697 were smaller than those on the other Hebridean islands he had visited, and that the sheep differed only in respect of their very long horns. Except at the annual cavalcade at All-Saints', when the St. Kildans without either bridle or saddle, rode them along the sands below the village, Hirta's horses, then 18 in number, were employed solely in carrying home peat and turf for fuel.

As no ornithologist would deny, Martin supplies much useful information about St. Kilda's bird-life. At the time of his visit, and indeed well into the present century, the natives burned in their lamps—in their cruses—the oil they obtained from the fulmar petrel when they managed to secure that bird before he had had time to squirt it, as he does when approached or molested. This oil, Martin tells us, was also used for rheumatic pains and aching in the joints. In Edinburgh and in London it had proved itself an excellent remedy in cases of toothache and sprained ankles. In fact, fulmar oil was the St. Kildans' panacea.

At this time Hirta's population was roughly 180. The natives, Martin adds, were well proportioned. When a certain islander went to Glasgow, he felt as though he had dropped out of the clouds. When he saw a pair of horses drawing a coach, which he took to be a tiny house with two men seated inside, he was of opinion that the horses actually were hauling the coach with their tails. Greatly surprised was this native by the movement of the coach's wheels; but he came to the conclusion that only a coachman who was mad would sit on the roof of the little house, when he could have been safer and more comfortable on the back of one of the horses!

*　　　*　　　*

In 1773 was printed the description of St. Kilda written by the Rev. Alexander Buchan, missionary there from 1705 until 1729. A preface to the first edition by Buchan's second daughter, Jean, shows that her deceased father considered Martin Martin's book both dear and out-of-date, and therefore felt it incumbent upon himself to write an account based upon his own observations, as well as upon information he had derived from accredited persons during his long residence on St. Kilda. Buchan was Hirta's first settled minister. He was ordained and sent there by the Church of Scotland in 1705. His stipend was £16. 13s. 4d. "And he being master of the Irish tongue," runs a passage in his daughter's preface, "and qualified with ministerial gifts suitable to his office, did labour amongst them during the foresaid time with great success in the word of the gospel, having found them most ignorant, and much given to idolatry."

*   *   *

One of the most illuminating authorities on St. Kilda is the Rev. Neil MacKenzie, who ministered there from 1829 till 1843. *Episode in the Life of the Rev. Neil MacKenzie at St. Kilda,* published privately in 1911, was edited by his son, the Rev. J. B. MacKenzie, minister at Kenmore. From it we learn that his father, on his arrival at St. Kilda, found the natives so ignorant of what he referred to as the leading truths of Christianity that he instituted practical methods of teaching them. To test what progress they had made, if any, he arranged meetings at which he catechized them. Notwithstanding his arduous labours and ardent prayers, he confessed to his having seen no spiritual improvement.

There is much of interest in MacKenzie's *Episode* on Hirta's domestic and agricultural routine. He writes of the particular attention the natives devoted to the barley crop, and describes how it was manured by the old thatch stripped off the roofs of dwellings when the blades were showing about a couple of inches above ground. He mentions the shieling in the North Glen, where cattle and sheep were retained for the period during which they were most liable to injure crops in the vicinity of the village. He shows how, since peat cut seldom lasted as long as was expected, the natives resorted to the turf covering the rocks and hillsides, thus destroying yearly a considerable extent of good pasturage. Twentieth-century writers likewise noted the St. Kildans' preference for cutting green sods, instead of going farther afield for really good peats, with a consequent diminution of the area available for cultivation. At one time they tilled more than twenty acres: at the time of the evacuation they tilled about three, after a fashion, and sowed them in spring-time with oats, barley, and potatoes. The implements used were spade, wooden rake, scythe, and sickle.

With the exception of the cotton cloth for the women's caps, a few kerchiefs, and the cravats worn by the men, the islanders' clothing in MacKenzie's day consisted almost entirely of woollen goods made by the natives themselves, and dyed locally with crotal or indigo. MacKenzie informs us further that the inhabitants suffered much from indigestion, largely owing to their indifferent cooking and to the inordinate amount of animal flesh they consumed. For reasons more substantial than climatic, fresh vegetables never have formed a popular part of the dietary of the West Highlands and Islands. Yet MacKenzie, when dilating of longevity, tells us that the annual register for 1767 records the death of "Simon Gillivray at St. Kilda in the 113th year of his age, who never was out of the Island". The St. Kildans at this time paid their rent principally in feathers. Each year the proprietor sent a small boat to collect his dues, to convey to St. Kilda any goods ordered the previous year, and to take away and market, on behalf of the inhabitants, their surplus oil, feathers, and homespun tweeds.

The St. Kildans used to resent the arrival of strangers in their midst, largely because they believed that they brought with them what was termed the boat cold. They declared that, following upon the visit of a stranger, they became infected with colds. To such an epidemic they referred as 'the strangers' cold'—*cnatan nan gall*. For its introduction they invariably blamed visitors from Glasgow, although sometimes their Harris neighbours were held responsible. In fact, they often referred to it in a Gaelic phrase signifying the Harris Cough.[1]

Boswell, mentioning the boat cold in his *Life of Johnson*, states that the Rev. Kenneth MacAulay, when compiling his account of St. Kilda, set out for that island with a prejudice against prejudice,

---

[1] St. Kilda's boat cold has analogies in other isolated islands scattered throughout the world. The same susceptibility is found among the inhabitants of Tristan da Cunha and Pitcairn, for example. On every occasion on which ships have called at Tristan in recent years, reports have reached London to the effect that the natives have been the victims of epidemic colds.

Village of St Kilda at the time of the evacuation in 1930

Neil Ferguson, St Kilda's postmaster, entering the island's post-office in August, 1930, with the last incoming mail-bag (*Page 148*)

Finlay MacQueen, the oldest native on St Kilda at the time of the evacuation, holding a gannet caught and stuffed by himself

Granny Gillies knitting socks and gloves outside her cottage a day or two before the evacuation of St Kilda in 1930

and strove to give the impression that he was a smart, up-to-date thinker. "And yet he affirms for the truth," writes Boswell, "that, when a ship arrives there, all the inhabitants are seized with a cold." That the natives caught cold in the manner alleged was challenged by Dr. Johnson, although it had been proved that they complained annually of some malady when MacLeod's steward arrived. "The steward always comes to demand something of them," writes Johnson; "and so they fall to coughing."

*   *   *

As mentioned earlier, Hirta, in addition to its being the largest and most fertile, is the only island of the group which has been inhabited for any length of time. Its village, crescent in shape, consisted of sixteen felt-roofed houses, although at the time of the evacuation some of these stood empty owing to the rapid decline in population in the years immediately preceding the island's abandonment. About 1862 MacLeod of MacLeod built zinc-roofed cottages, consequent upon a tempest that had unroofed the earlier and more primitive dwellings, several of which, up to the very night before the islanders left, were used as byres. Between 1697, when the population was 180, and 1724, the island was sadly depopulated owing to an outbreak of smallpox. It appears to have been re-peopled thereafter from Harris. In the 1731 Minutes of the Directors of the Society in Scotland for the Propagation of Christian Knowledge occurs the following sentence: "That regard might be had to the people of Hirta, which Island, by the yearly transporting of people to it, will soon be populous again."

When the Rev. Kenneth MacAulay went as missionary to St. Kilda in 1758, the population was 88. By 1815 it had risen to 130. When the Rev. John MacDonald, minister of Urquhart, visited the island in 1822, at the instigation of the organisation mentioned, it stood at 108. In 1851 the first government census showed a population of 110. By 1861 this had fallen to 78, due to 36 natives' having emigrated to Australia in 1852. Until just prior to the outbreak of war in 1914, the population had stood for some years at approximately 74. When the evacuation took place 16 years later, it was 36.

Half a century ago the inhabitants were grouped under the same five surnames as embraced them all at the time of their leaving—Ferguson, Gillies, MacDonald, MacKinnon, and MacQueen. There

E

were some MacCrimmons toward the close of the 19th century, and
also, at an earlier date, a few Morrisons and MacLeods.

*   *   *

The 36 St. Kildans mentioned as having left for Australia in 1852
ran into disaster that was to mean premature death for nearly half
of them. By one means or another they got from St. Kilda to Liverpool, though at least one of their number is thought to have died on
the way there. At Liverpool they boarded the barque, *Priscilla,* a
sturdy, soft-wood vessel of 572 tons' burthen, built to the order
of one, L. W. Eaton, by John Nicholson of Pugwash, Nova Scotia.
Changing ownership before sailing for Australia, she was registered
at Liverpool (though not in Lloyd's Register) as being owned by
J. S. de Wolf & Co. On October, 13th, 1852, she took her departure.
The death that occurred aboard her on November, 6th, while at sea,
appears to have been the first indication of some infectious disease—
probably smallpox—among the passengers, 42 of whom, out of a
total of 261, died during the voyage. None of the crew was affected.
On January, 19th, 1853, after a sorrowful passage of 98 days' duration, the *Priscilla* reached Melbourne, there to undergo five weeks'
quarantine.

In 1967, with the aid of the librarian of the State Library of
Victoria, at Melbourne, and after a decade's diligent research, my
meticulous friend, Gavin Ferguson, of Cavendish Square, London,
most dedicated of the Clan Ferguson's seannachies (historians), was
able to pick out from the passengers' list those bearing any of St.
Kilda's six surnames recorded in the 1851 census—Ferguson, Gillies,
MacCrimmon, MacDonald, MacQueen, and Morrison. Furthermore,
Gavin, although primarily concerned with his own Ferguson clans-
folk, has succeeded in abstracting the names of all but 2 of the 36
St. Kildans who actually embarked for Australia, and has listed
separately those who perished on the voyage or in quarantine at
Melbourne, and the 16 who survived, later to send from Australia
small remittances to their relatives on St. Kilda.

While pursuing the subsequent career of this ill-fated barque, Gavin
recently obtained from Lloyd's the following:

> "St. John's, N.F. Jan. 10th, 1854. *Priscilla,*
> Master, Thomas, from Philadelphia to Liver-
> pool with grain and flour was dismasted on the

night of December, 29th, 1853 in Lat. 14 N.,
Long. 60 W., during a heavy gale, sprang a
leak, and the crew being unable to keep her
free, she was abandoned. Crew taken off by
Peerless, Master, Sharp, arrived here."

From the St. Kildan survivors of this sad 1852–3 voyage, the
St. Kilda district of the city of Melbourne, which I know intimately,
took its name.

*   *   *

My reference to 18th-century outbreaks of smallpox brings to mind
the terrible toll *tetanus infantum*—the disease known among the
St. Kildans as 'the eight-day sickness'—took of their newborn over
a considerable period. Records of this show it to have been recognised
long before the official appointment in 1856 of the Free Church
catechist, Duncan Kennedy, as the island's first registrar. Of the
total of 56 births there between 1855 and 1876, 41 infants died of
tetanus, the disease explaining the preponderance in the island's
walled burial-ground of small, unhewn stones marking the graves of
the very young. "I felt sad at the sight of so many infant graves,"
wrote George Murray, St. Kilda's schoolmaster from 1886 to 1887.
"One man, not yet fifty years, I should say, pointed the place to me
where he buried nine children. He is left with four of a family.
Another buried no less than a dozen infants and is left with two,
now grown up. Sad to think of the like."

It was because of this scourge and of the complete absence from
the island of medical and nursing aid that Miss Emily MacLeod,
the proprietor's sister, visited it in 1877. Emily, already over sixty,
felt she must do what she could to alleviate the islanders' lot in
this regard. I now quote from a revealing contribution to the Summer
issue of *The Countryman* in 1953 by her great-niece, Brenda
MacLeod, daughter of my old friend, the late Canon Roderic
MacLeod of MacLeod, that conscientious historian and splendid
photographer known to his generation as Canon Rory, who helped
me considerably when, in 1925, I was engaged on *Over the Sea to
Skye*:

"So, armed with a bed, cooking utensils, and crockery, as well
as with medical supplies, she [Great Aunt Emily] set out one
afternoon from Skye in a yacht belonging to friends. The only

regular means of communication with the island at that time was a vessel sent twice a year by the proprietor to take supplies and collect rents. The arrival of a yacht, therefore, was a great event for the St. Kildans, and the visitors received a tumultuous welcome.

"Soon after her arrival, Aunt Emily went to inspect the room she was to occupy during her stay. It was a four-roomed house partly used for stores, and her courage nearly failed her. However, she got six girls to clean and scrub it, and by evening the bed was up and the boxes in which the crockery had been packed were turned upside down and covered with tablecloths. She chose one of the girls to wait on her, but soon decided to do her own washing-up, as the St. Kildan method was to wipe plates with a corner of a shawl, and put the spoons in the mouth.

"The great excitement on the island was a newly born baby which was in a bad way. When the father asked Aunt Emily to go to see it, she found the small, stuffy room full of neighbours and the infant being fed on port-wine and milk. She was quite equal to the occasion, telling the father firmly to turn the women out, and persuading the mother to nurse the child herself. It eventually recovered and did well. The islanders never took whisky unless they were ill, yet they used to give it to the unfortunate babies, and it never occurred to anyone that this strong diet caused the deaths of many of them. One poor woman had had twelve children and succeeded in rearing only one.

"Sometimes the mothers went to the island of Harris for their confinements in the hope of returning with a living child, but this meant being away from home for months on end. The mortality rate was also high among mothers. Aunt Emily found that out of eight young couples four of the women had died when their first babies were born. She was worried, too, by the constant use of bleeding as a remedy; while she was in St. Kilda, one girl who was not very well underwent this drastic treatment and became really ill."

After a fortnight on St. Kilda, Great Aunt Emily, as Brenda usually calls her, left by the first passenger steamer ever to call. One of her life's ambitions was fulfilled when, some years later, a nurse was sent to look after the islanders. It must be remembered that at this time their idea of hygiene was still extremely low, despite the fact that Sir John MacPherson MacLeod, then the proprietor, had built for them early in the 1860s the new row of cottages known as Main Street, and had provided it throughout its entire length with the stone causeway I myself trod so often in 1930. Not many years before these cottages were built, the Rev. Dr. MacLachlan had sent the islanders a quantity of crockery. This included chamber-pots for which they found no use except as porridge bowls. Mounds of ash and refuse accumulated at each cottage's door. "It would not take long to scrub up everything they possess," wrote John Ross in 1889; "but they never think of such a thing." Ross, who succeeded George Murray as schoolmaster, went on to say that their homes' interiors were packed overhead "with unmentionables, from the stomachs of solan geese to the scythe blades". Visitors already arriving regularly during the summer months by the steamships mentioned were appalled at the natives' low standard of personal cleanliness.

Not until 1890, during the Rev. Angus Fiddes's incumbency, was St. Kilda's infantile mortality seriously tackled. Fiddes, St. Kilda's last ordained minister, attributed this infant death-rate to the islanders' practice of using on the severed umbilical cord a mixture of dung and fulmar oil, when islanders elsewhere used butter. That year, in response to his application to Glasgow for help, Nurse Chishall arrived. After two prolonged spells of duty, endeavouring throughout to overcome the natives' ignorance and superstitious practices, she went back to Glasgow, unwilling to undertake further duties on Hirta. Meantime Fiddes, amid mounting opposition to anything in the nature of cleanliness and antiseptics, went to Glasgow to take a midwifery course under Dr. Turner. With Turner's directions on the immediate and repeated application of iodoform to the stump of the umbilical cord until the umbilicus healed and the stump came away, he returned to St. Kilda to meet the stubborn opposition of the islanders and their *bean-ghluinne*, their knee-woman, or midwife. This recalcitrancy he overcame in the end. We now revert to matters less unpleasant.

*   *   *

Among the few historic ruins on Hirta are those of the humble abode occupied by the unfortunate Lady Grange who, from 1734 until 1742, was "sequestrated" (secretly abducted and secluded) there by her husband lest she might divulge certain Jacobite secrets. In latter years this dwelling of hers was used as a cleit in which turf and hay were stored. While staying at Dunvegan Castle several years ago, collecting material for *Over the Sea to Skye,* I was much interested in its relics associated with Lady Grange. At Dunvegan may be seen the yellow, time-seared accounts rendered in respect of her board while on St. Kilda, and of her funeral expenses in Skye.[1] Also preserved there is the lamp that dimly illumined the hovel in which she was detained for seven years. It is a low, iron receptacle resembling a flat cream-jug with a long, upright handle. In this, oil was placed. A wick floating in the oil produced a miserable light. The quern with which was ground the corn for Lady Grange's sustenance lies in the hall at Dunvegan, where also are preserved two wooden door-locks from St. Kilda, a number of puffin snares, and the box and bladder once used as "the St. Kilda Mail-boat", to be referred to later, and duly illustrated.

St. Kilda's association with Lady Grange was not its only connection with matters Jacobite. The Hanoverian authorities got the notion that Prince Charles Edward, after the defeat of his army at Culloden, had left the continent of Scotland for Hirta. So they directed General Campbell to proceed there to take him prisoner. When Campbell made his appearance off its coast, most of the inhabitants fled in panic to the hills, where they sought to conceal themselves. A force was landed, and inquiries prosecuted as to the whereabouts of the royal fugitive. The natives were utterly dumfounded by their interrogators. Never had they heard of the Young Pretender. All they truthfully could say was that they knew of a report to the effect that their laird, MacLeod of Dunvegan, had had some difference "with a great woman abroad, but that he had got the better of her, and that was all they knew of the disturbances in the world". Thereupon General Campbell and his men withdrew.

St. Kilda's isolation was proverbial. Not only had its inhabitants never heard of the campaign of Prince Charles Edward, but they knew nothing of Napoleon and Waterloo. They continued to pray for William IV. long after his death. "In 1837," wrote the Rev. Neil MacKenzie, "we heard of the death of William IV; and I was not a little horrified to find that I had been praying for him some months after his death. I consequently altered my style of praying, not for anyone by name, but for His Majesty the King. When the packet

---

[1] A facsimile of the account rendered to MacLeod of MacLeod by Rory MacNeill in respect of Lady Grange's funeral expenses faces page 206 of my book, *A Last Voyage to St. Kilda,* published by Cassell & Co. in 1931.

came in autumn, 1838, I found I was not yet right, and that I should have been praying for Her Majesty the Queen."

Again, when Dr. John MacCulloch and his party landed on St. Kilda in 1815, a matron-like figure advanced with an air of dignity and command to greet them with the words, "Friends or enemies?". The figure was the wife of the minister, who at that time received a stipend of £35. MacCulloch thought that this woman was the revived Amazon Warrior who persists in St. Kilda's folklore. Not aware that peace had been concluded with America, she suspected the strangers were Americans. The American war was very unpopular among the St. Kildans: they had been told it had raised the price of tobacco!

*   *   *

Remoteness has always lent to St. Kilda an especial interest. That the natives themselves realised how far they lived from the centre of things is shown by the fact that, when they wanted to refer to some great distance, such as separates Land's End from John o' Groat's, they resorted to their old adage, *A Hirt gu Peart:* From St. Kilda to Perth. Perth, owing to its proximity to Scone, where the Scottish Kings were crowned, they looked upon as the most important place in the Northern Kingdom.

Though isolation engendered in the St. Kildans an independence and a corresponding contempt for governmental intervention, by no means were they a lawless people. Crime and litigation were almost unknown among them. During the incumbency of the Rev. Neil MacKenzie—somewhere about 1840—there occurred a breach of promise case, however. It was heard in the open, by the end of the church, before minister and elders. The pursuer proved her case; and the defender was ordered to pay damages to the extent of a hundred fully grown fulmars, fifty gugas (young gannets), and a hair rope. Owing to the importance of a hair rope for fowling purposes, as also to the special status its possession conferred, it was by far the most valuable item included in the damages. In the crime-sheets of Inverness-shire (to which county St. Kilda belongs by a geographical fiction) the islanders never figured. Neither did they ever record a parliamentary vote. The franchise meant nothing to them. The only administrative council in which they exhibited the least interest was their own *Mòd* or Parliament. Weather permitting, this convened in the open, usually in front of the post-office, so that at least *some* of its members could seat themselves on its steps, while others huddled together on the wooden form placed against the wall of the postmaster's cottage. Gaelic was the official language of this assembly, which concerned itself with everything affecting the life of the community. Outside St. Kilda, its members had no interest excepting, perhaps, the welfare of any relatives who happened to live elsewhere than at home. Neighbouring Boreray was the limit of their foreign policy; and, even then, that policy was concerned solely with sheep, with seabirds and their eggs.

St. Kilda had a Queen, in addition to a Parliament. The first Queen of St. Kilda was a mainland woman named Betty Scott. She was the wife of a certain Malcolm MacDonald, and was a native of Lochinver, in Sutherland. Betty went to St. Kilda as a domestic servant to the Rev. Neil MacKenzie. With the exception of the minister himself, she was the only person there who had a word of English. So handsome, intelligent, and well educated was she that the St. Kildans could not conceive of the existence anywhere in the world of a woman more comely. Partly in jest, but chiefly because of the regard in which they held her, they called her Queen of Hirta. At her death the title passed to her daughter, and thereafter to the woman on Hirta adjudged the most beautiful.

The end of Hirta's first Queen was a tragic one. In 1861 a large and well-found boat named the *Dargavel*, costing some £60, was presented to the St. Kildans with the object of encouraging them to prosecute fishing. Two years later this boat left, presumably for Harris, with a quantity of cloth and salted fish. There were seven men aboard her, and one woman—Betty Scott. Nothing more was ever heard of the *Dargavel*. Clothing believed to have belonged to its occupants was washed ashore at Mealista, on the wild, western coast of Lewis. News of the disaster that had befallen the island boat reached St. Kilda about a month later, when three English smacks dropped anchor in Village Bay, and the skipper and crew went ashore to play quoits with the natives.

* * *

The St. Kildans' struggle to contend with the asperities of Nature had been unceasing. Declining man-power was making it increasingly difficult for so isolated a community to maintain itself. Latterly it became impossible to attend to the sheep on Boreray: there was no longer on Hirta a sufficient number of able-bodied men to handle

Village Bay, St Kilda, on evacuation day. At anchor (right) the *Harebell* and the Glasgow ship, the *Dunara Castle*. The former transferred the natives and their belongings to the Scottish mainland. The latter transported their livestock

Neil Ferguson, the island postmaster's son, carrying to the jetty the last sack of wool 'roo-ed' from the famous St Kilda sheep

The St Kilda Mail-boat launched by the author on the eve of the evacuation, and now on view at Dunvegan Castle, Isle of Skye

The St Kilda Mail-boat which Neil Ferguson launched at 11 a.m. on March 24th, 1897. It carried his well-known letter to Richard Kearton (*Page 167*)

the boat, and to capture and "roo" its wild sheep. The inclement weather of 1929 and an epidemic of wet eczema worsened considerably their situation. In January of the following year matters were brought to a head when a St. Kildan woman named Mary Gillies lay critically ill with an appendicitis, and the lighthouse vessel, *Hesperus,* owing to exceptionally heavy seas, was unable to reach Hirta. Mary's plight had been reported by the master of the *Caldew,* a Fleetwood trawler that had called at Village Bay on her way south. On February, 15th, 1930, Mary was got off on the fishery cruiser, *Norna,* which had sailed from Tarbert (Harris) with mails for the islanders, and had succeeded where the *Hesperus,* due to a raging tempest, had failed. But it was too late: Mary died very soon afterwards in Glasgow's Stobhill Hospital. When the *Henry Melling* visited St. Kilda a couple of months later, her crew found the islanders virtually starving and in a state of depression. By the time the *Hebrides* made her first call of the year on the last day of May, they were seriously thinking of leaving the island. The following month they formally invited the Scottish Office to render feasible their doing so. On August, 29th, at a cost of less than £1,000, and with a commendable measure of humanity, this was accomplished.

CHAPTER SEVEN

St. Kilda
Evacuation and Re-occupation

IN THE autumn of 1930, a week or two before the evacuation of St. Kilda was due to take place, *I* found myself dropping down this same Firth of Clyde aboard the *Hebrides* on my way to this island, just as Richard and Cherry Kearton had done aboard her sister-ship, the *Dunara Castle,* in 1896. The population of St. Kilda then was 73. This included the minister, or missionary, and his serving-maid. Thirty-four years later there were only 36 natives leaving their sea-girt outpost for re-settlement on the Scottish mainland. Five hours' steaming from Obbe, on the Sound of Harris, brought the *Hebrides* into the Bay of Hirta—into Village Bay—while the mists were clear-ing from Conachair and Oiseval and the Mullach Sgar. As she dropped anchor there, her siren echoed and re-echoed among the cliffs and mountain-crags, sending dense flocks of seabirds wheeling and screaming in every direction. The village itself now seemed to stir, if but reluctantly. All the dogs of this declining commonwealth could be seen racing through the sparse grasslands lying between the village and the shore. A ship's arrival seemed more of a novelty to them than to their owners. Most of these creatures had a front paw strung tightly up to the neck in that abominable fashion *still* so pre-valent in the Highlands and Islands and in Ireland, excused on the pretext that a dog can neither run away nor chase sheep when he is allowed the use of but three legs.

From this anchorage one could see how peppered with cleits were the valleys and the mountains above them. Those stone huts never failed to excite the wonder of the stranger approaching St. Kilda for the first time. A line of them, constructed at regular intervals on the skyline, stood out this day like the sentinel forts of an ancient race. At first they appeared as though they might have been the more primitive of the natives' dwellings, since at a distance they were so

138

much more conspicuous than was the village situated above Village
Bay. Close to the jetty one noticed the large fank in which were
gathered the islanders' sheep, awaiting shipment to Oban by the first
cargo vessel weather might favour. In preparation for her arrival,
these impounded wretches had been collected from the hills and cliffs
of Hirta some days earlier. So wild were they, so little accustomed
to the intrusions of men, that it had taken the more agile of the
natives several days to gather them. All St. Kilda's stirks, seven in
number, already had sailed aboard the *Hebrides* on her previous trip.

From an obscure creek the St. Kildans soon put out to us in two
rowing-boats. Against the strong head-wind then blowing, they took
a considerable time to reach us because this wind had necessitated
our anchoring farther offshore than usual. The mails were pitched
into the earlier of the boats to come alongside. It arrived under the
direction of Neil Ferguson with whom I was to reside until the
natives were taken off. Neil, by far the most forceful and intelligent
member of this isolated community, and the only elder of the island's
kirk, was Hirta's uncrowned king. When the missionary took ill or
was absent for a few days on the mainland, Neil superintended the
village school and preached the sermon on the Sabbath. As *maor*
or ground-officer for MacLeod of MacLeod, he regulated the dealings between tenant and tenant, between tenant and proprietor, and
resolved all questions relating to such matters as the grazings.
Furthermore, he was Mr. Speaker in the St. Kilda Parliament, often
convened at a moment's notice to discuss pressing problems affecting
the community. Through his brother, Alexander, then a prosperous
tweed merchant in Glasgow, he disposed profitably of the tweeds the
natives wove during the long, wintry evenings, and also of the woollen
garments the womenfolk were constantly knitting. Quantities of
tweed were also sold direct to the tourists in the summertime, along
with hand-knitted goods, and the blown birds' eggs sought by collectors. As late as 1928 the St. Kildans produced for export well
over a thousand yards of tweed, virtually their only article of
commerce.

With the second boat to return from the *Hebrides* half an hour
later, there reached the island several tourists with a couple of hours
to spare. Most of them soon had their feet on "Main Street" and
were making for its post-office. There Neil supplied them liberally
with postcards depicting local scenes and also with odd bits of information regarding the sheep and the folks who were about to

surrender their island to seabirds such as have nested on its cliffs almost since the dawn of time. Down to the jetty as these tourists arrived came the St. Kildan women with socks and gloves, tweeds and sheepskins, rugs and spinning-wheels. Sooner than had been expected, the *Hebrides* was sounding her siren for the tourists' speedy return. Weather conditions were altering: the wind was veering shorewards. Not long afterwards she weighed anchor and sailed out into an approaching storm, leaving me behind with Neil Ferguson. There were now 45 human beings on Hirta—36 natives, the nurse, the missionary, his wife and two children, three shepherds sent over by the government authorities to assist in the rounding up and trans- porting of the sheep, and myself. All the natives, of course, were living in "Main Street" which, as I already have said, consisted of 16 houses. This did not include the manse or schoolhouse, nor the factor's and the nurse's house. Since Mr. Munro, the missionary, attended both to the islanders' spiritual needs and to the education of their children, his abode was referred to either as the manse or as the schoolhouse. The entire village was served by a stone causeway run- ning up from the quay to the farthest house. I scarcely suppose there exists in the Highlands and Islands another village, along which one could pass so comfortably in wet weather. Never were its doorsteps the scene of rain-pools and quagmires, though earlier accounts of their insanitary condition are quite revolting.

After I had been introduced by Neil to his family, and had de- posited my belongings in the apartment they so tenderly had pre- pared for me, I lingered down to the schoolroom and the mission- hall. Nailed to the wall of the former was a blackboard still dimly showing characters chalked upon it by Mr. Munro—the faintest evidence of the last lesson he taught the St. Kildan children on their wave-girt isle.

Toward evening I went out to the cliffs over at the Mullach Sgar and Ruaival. There I sat awhile, hundreds of feet above the tide, among boulders cast down by Time, most irresistible of all the giants. Puffins and razor-bills and screaming gulls hovered near me as I peered through the hazy sunset toward *Tir-nan-Og*, bewildered by the raging sea that seemed to have no bourne this side of Eternity. At dusk I retraced my steps to the village, and entered Neil's home to be informed that I was to sleep, perhaps for the first time in my life, on a mattress of puffins' feathers. Before retiring for the night, I joined his household in the traditional reading of "The Books".

Thereafter I went to the door of the cottage to forecast the weather. Stars now hung above the bay; but the sea was still noisy, though the wind had fallen.

*   *   *

The following morning, which was Sunday, brought bright sunshine and a calm so wistful that the natives might have been tempted to change their minds about their impending removal to the Scottish mainland. Scarcely a wavelet invaded Village Bay. I broke fast at a small table placed in the window overlooking both the Bay of Hirta and the cliffy island of Dùn. The window was half open; and one or two hens, preening themselves on the sill, stepped inside to receive the few crumbs of soda scone I had cast in their direction. Soon I was off to the hills and the rocks with my camera. I climbed up the steep, stony glen behind the village, passing in Lag bho'n Tuath the sheepfanks that already had seen the last of the sheep. Soon I found myself in "the Gap" between the peaks of Conachair and Oiseval, viewing Boreray afar. The cliffs here defied description. Myriads of seabirds, perched in countless tiers above the swinging tide, and resentful of my intrusion upon their sanctuary, sent their fiery-cross of danger throughout the entire bird population. In the glen through which I just had climbed, the grass was long and luscious. Its greenness stood out in striking contrast with the delicate whiteness of the great cloud then drifting over Conachair and out toward Boreray and the Long Island and Scotland beyond. I now took to the ridge affording easiest access to the summit of Oiseval. From this height "Main Street" looked like a pigmy village inhabited by a people very tiny in stature. It resembled an illustration in a book on faeryland.

At a few minutes to 11 a.m., while seated on this mountain-top, I heard on the Atlantic breeze, and through the bright sunshine now bathing these wild islands, the sound of a distant bell. It was the ship's bell hanging from a wooden scaffold close to the little mission-hall, calling to those who might be wishing to attend the last English church service then about to begin. This bell bore the terse inscription, *Janet Cowan, 1861,* the vessel of 830 tons burthen, registered at Greenock, that went on the rocks at St. Kilda in April, 1864, while on a voyage from Calcutta to Dundee with a cargo of jute.

As the Gaelic service was due to commence an hour later, I speedily returned from the hills. When in the throes of face-washing and hair-brushing, the villagers living farthest from the mission-hall entered the house in passing to have a casual word or two with Neil Ferguson and with Annie, his comely wife. Discussion then ensued as to the whereabouts of Tulliallan, the place that had been suggested for Neil and his family when they quitted Hirta. No one appeared to have the vaguest idea where Tulliallan was: nor did Neil's post-office publications help to solve the problem. But someone thought—and correctly, as it happened—it might be in Fife.

With the pealing of the second bell, we all wandered down the causeway to the Gaelic service, the women wearing mutches almost concealed beneath their Turkey-red napkins. We entered the church; and there, in a little box under the pulpit, sat Norman MacKinnon, the precentor, who stared at me for all he was worth. My eyes in the meanwhile were scanning the walls, yellow with damp and mildew. Upon these walls crawled lazy creatures of the beetle tribe; while on ceiling and rafters profane spiders performed acrobatic tricks, regardless of the sanctity of the Sabbath. During the singing we remained seated; and only the menfolk stood at the praying, though some of the womenfolk stood stooping over the pews. Each time a psalm was announced, the precentor fixed his eyes on me, doubtless imagining that I did not know how to find the correct place in the Gaelic bible. When I felt myself in danger of catching his eye, however, I straightway began to sing lustily with the congregation in order to prove to him that not only could I find my way among the Gaelic psalms, but that I also could *sing* them. Though the St. Kildans were not a musical people, in church they sang vociferously. Nobody slept during the long, repetitive, Gaelic tirade, to which Mr. Munro subjected us. On the contrary, everyone seemed unusually wakeful, in deference, one imagined, to the last Gaelic service that may ever be held there.

After the benediction the men remained seated, so as to allow the women to make their exit first. This is a custom prominent in the Highlands and Islands. The service over, we lingered back to our respective firesides. With fragments of turf and coal, Neil's wife mended her fire. Turf, of course, was the island's only native fuel; but the islanders sometimes obtained chunks of coal from trawlermen anchoring in Village Bay during bad weather. The St. Kildans usually received from such trawlermen small quantities of coal in exchange for sheep-skin rugs and the like. During storms, as many as eight liners and Fleetwood trawlers may drop anchor in Village

Bay at a time. Trawlermen had a reputation for being good to the St. Kildans. Not only did they keep them in coal, but they also supplied them with fresh fish for less than the asking. And sometimes they gave them old nets to fasten over their wind-dishevelled hay-ricks.

By far the most interesting member of this dwindling community was my host, Neil Ferguson. This day he was overwhelmed with the correspondence that had arrived for him the day before by the *Hebrides*. Great numbers of people had sent him stamped, addressed envelopes in their anxiety to receive something bearing St. Kilda's postmark, and due to leave that island with its last outgoing mail. Others were worrying him for souvenirs and curios, inundating him with trifling postal-orders that fair bamboozled him, despite his attainments as St. Kilda's postmaster. There were requests for spinning-wheels, cruses, gannets' wings (which make splendid dusters), quern-stones, any quantity whatsoever of St. Kilda wool, and seabirds' eggs. Tourists who had come ashore from the *Hebrides* and the *Dunara Castle* during preceding weeks already had stripped Hirta of almost everything of a souvenir nature.

Neil and I were still studying various requests from folks on the mainland when there sailed into Village Bay a war-vessel flying the French flag. At first a number of the St. Kildans believed this to be the boat that had come to take them from the land on which they and their ancestors had toiled a thousand years. The vessel turned out to be the French cruiser, *Ancre*. The happy band of French sailors that came ashore told us that curiosity had prompted this visit: the French newspapers had published reports of the impending evacuation. In St. Kilda and its people, the sailors showed the greatest interest. Several of them, clad in white tunics, spent the afternoon in climbing Conachair and the Mullach Mòr, and in hilariously rolling huge boulders down the hillsides into the sea.

An hour or two after the arrival of the *Ancre* a trawler dropped anchor in the bay. She looked as though she had come in to mend her trawl in sheltered water; but she did not remain long enough for that. On quitting her anchorage, she sounded her siren. This drove all the village dogs into a state of temporary madness. The pandemonium of barking, as they raced through the croft-lands to the shore, was indescribable.

At tea-time there was not a drop of milk in the house for my tea; and so Annie Ferguson, Neil's wife, went out to a cow that happened to be passing by the door, and milked a cup-ful from her into a treacle tin.

*   *   *

Final days were busy days. Men, women, and Hirta's few children were engaged all day long in packing their belongings, or in setting out for the hills with the Uist shepherds and half a dozen dogs to bring in sheep that repeatedly had evaded capture by leaping to and from great heights inaccessible to man and dog. Even the high wall enclosing the cultivable lands was no obstacle to them. Several of those impounded down by the shore, preparatory to shipment, had escaped far into the hills, where circumstances now necessitated their being left to their own devices.

One day about noon I went out barefoot to the rocks over against Soay. Though my feet were sensitive to the screes, the grass in places was so short and slippery that bare toes gave one a better hold when approaching cliff edges and yawning chasms. I came down to the wonder caves by the shore below Ruaival, the Red Fell, passing by the site of St. Columba's Chapel to reach the site of St. Brendan's. Here I rested awhile, casting an eye over the bay to the village, where the islanders were now packing their wool, and generally getting ready for their departure in a few days' time. Soon I found myself on the slopes of Ruaival, making for the kyle between Hirta and Dùn, where the seawrack imparts to the tide a crimson hue.

On my returning to the village, I found the barefoot natives trailing through the grasslands to the jetty great planks of timber that, over the years, storms had cast ashore. The womenfolk were busy packing kists, supplying one another with the labels to be tacked on to boxes containing such household utensils as they were desirous of taking to their new homes in Argyll. Meanwhile, some of the men were sawing odd pieces of wood to dimensions such as would protect certain pieces of furniture from being damaged in transit. Men and women alike, moreover, were bearing heavy loads on their backs to the old store, hard by the jetty.

Later in the day yet another trawler dropped anchor in the Bay of Hirta. Her stay was of short duration. With the telescope left by the navy-men who had manned the St. Kilda gun toward the end of the First World War, we observed that members of its crew were mending the nets. By this time the shepherds were driving the sheep into the glebe enclosure for the night. Through the mists and the rains now beginning to fall upon us, they shouted and whistled. Soon Ruaival and the Dùn were obscured completely. The wind soughed; and half the flock took to bleating. Heard above all was the sobbing of the sea breaking on the ageless boulders of Village Bay before an onshore gale.

Over the turf-fire that evening Neil told me much about life on his native isle, and how altered climatic conditions had harassed the St. Kildans to an increasing extent during their final years. The winters had not changed much: the autumns, on the other hand, had been growing steadily worse. Because of wind and rain and the lack of sun, corn had not ripened for some years. Often after the harvest had been cut, rains had ruined it. Neil then proceeded to tell me how the natives used to go out at night in April, and lie among the rocks to kill the guillemots. By means of ropes they let themselves down the face of the cliffs, and then covered themselves with the white sheets on which the innocent guillemots landed and were caught, mistaking the sheets for guano-covered rocks. He then described how fulmars and puffins were caught with the snaring-rod. St. Kilda used to import horse-hair in quantities solely for the making of snares for these birds. When glancing up at the rafters of an old byre one day, I noticed quite a hantle designed for snares. As a memento of our conversation that evening, Neil then presented me with a typical St. Kildan snare which I still have. Weighing no more than a couple of drams, it is one of the neatest pieces of native workmanship I ever have handled. It must have taken hours and hours to pleat and to stiffen it up with birds' feathers.

*　　　*　　　*

On the morrow, as the curtain of mist rose from the peaks of Conachair and Oiseval, a blue window, so tiny in this width of sky, opened in the saddle between them. A giant seagull, followed by a raven, flapped lazily across Village Bay. Soon a glint of sun was warming the rocks, above which stood the sheep, weary of their close confinement, weary of waiting for the *Dunara Castle*. Within a few feet of me swam a seal, emissary, they say in the Hebrides, from the Courts of the Kings of Lochlann, in the Land of Sleep. Wistful were his eyes. I sang to him; but, contrary to the practice of his clan, he did not respond with his seal-music. Until the sands of Hirta Bay were completely inundated and I myself was surrounded by the incoming tide, I stood on a boulder awash, listening instead to the music of the sea, to the laughter of the waves. From boulder to boulder I picked my way back to the storm-beach, and felt, in treading upon them, the eloquence of their very muteness. Along the shore I lingered, among rocks and sea-anemones, until I reached the creek below Oiseval. There I discovered a sea-garden of tangle, fresh and multi-coloured, swaying gently in the tide as would a bed of flowers in fitful wind. On scanning the barren shoulder of Oiseval, one descried two or three of the sheep that preferred their freedom to the company of the acquiescent fold now awaiting transshipment to those frightful auction-marts at Oban. But there was work to be done; and I felt that again I should have been lending a hand with the heavy articles the villagers still were lugging to the jetty. So I proceeded down toward the store-house with a plank on my shoulder. Pausing at the door of old Finlay MacQueen, I persuaded him to pose for his photograph. No sooner was he seated before the camera than he insisted on rising for something he had left in the house. So he hurried in again, reappearing with a puffin and a gannet, both of which he himself had killed and stuffed fifty years before. Finlay was eager that the last photograph taken of him on his native island should depict him in the act of holding either a puffin or a gannet. Once again he seated himself near his threshold. He now held up the puffin in such a way as to ensure that, whatever happened, the puffin should appear in the photograph. He was quite unaware that he was holding the puffin the wrong way up. So I moved toward him to turn the limp, moth-eaten thing in his hand.

Finlay MacQueen was the most celebrated cliffsman of his day. Until a year or two of the St. Kildans' leaving, he used to venture to parts of the rocks to which no other man ever got within twenty yards. Richard and Cherry Kearton commemorated his skill as a rocker in their splendid work already alluded to. Cherry told me that Finlay had escorted them on every expedition they had undertaken, and had been, throughout, their most reliable informant. The naturalist, Norman Heathcote, in his book on St. Kilda published in 1900, likewise describes Finlay's agility and intrepidity when in 1898 he watched him leap to overhanging cliffs from a boat.

One day in the course of conversation Finlay, with great pride, showed me the great indentation in his head which he had received half a century earlier when a descending boulder struck him while fowling on the cliffs. His fellow-islanders assured me that he always despised the method of being let down the rocks by means of a rope held above by other cragsmen. So he usually wandered off alone with rope and stave in search of seafowl and their eggs.

With the trawlermen coming into the Bay of Hirta from time to time, Finlay was a great favourite. Seldom was a trawler long at anchor before Finlay was aboard, chatting amiably with the cook! The islanders declared that he always returned to the shore heavily laden with food of one kind or another.

Among the many topics Finlay and I discussed was the boat cold. He told me of a notable occasion on which all the St. Kildans caught it. Early in the spring of 1877 the *Peti Dubrovacki,* an Austrian vessel of some 800 tons, came to grief in bad weather when only five days out from Glasgow, on a voyage to New York. She was in ballast at the time; but her ballast had shifted, pitching her on her beam ends, thus rendering her unmanageable. Master and crew eventually got ashore in their small boat at Village Bay. Although there was almost a famine on St. Kilda at the time, due chiefly to the factor's boat having failed to turn up with provisions owing to storms, the inhabitants rallied to the aid of the castaways who, for five weeks, were accommodated by the 16 families then comprising the commonwealth of St. Kilda. And now to the point of Finlay's story: while the Austrian sailors were on the island, every native was smitten with the *cnatan nan gall,* the strangers' cold, or cough.

There now intervened some days of mist and rain. It was fully expected that the morning of August, 27th, 1930, would have found the *Dunara Castle* at anchor in Village Bay. Banks of fog had detained her. Everyone on St. Kilda was getting restive. So low lay the mists that scarcely could we see the nearest cleits in front of the cottages. Dùn, which lies immediately opposite, was obscured completely. A hundred yards off, one heard the breathing of an invisible sea. The small window of my room was covered with big blobs of rain. Everything was damp and musty. The very sheets of paper upon which I took the notes that have been expanded to fill these pages seemed saturated, for so heavy is the atmosphere when mist hangs low over Hirta.

In the little room I occupied, a turf fire was kindled for me. It assisted considerably in dispersing the gloom; and it enabled me to jot down in comfort sundry observations that otherwise might have slipped my memory. At the other end of the house a spinning-wheel was droning in the preparation of a small piece of homespun for a mainland enquirer who, a few days earlier, had sent a modest postal-order. Less than a week previously, every house in "Main Street" had had its active *beart*, its weaving-loom.

About four in the afternoon, when the mists were at their densest, a small boy came running in to assure us that he had heard a steamer's whistle. More than an hour elapsed, however, ere any vessel came in sight. Her anchor was released approximately where the *Hebrides* had ridden so recently. Even from the quay, only half of her masts could be seen in the fog. A flutter now ran through the village: the transportation of the sheep became everyone's concern. In the interval imposed upon us by the state of the tide, the shepherds occupied themselves in arranging them in such a way as to facilitate their transference to the *Dunara Castle* when an opportunity occurred. All able-bodied men and women on the island now lent a hand with the launching of the island's boat. By making several trips, we brought ashore a great number of interested tourists, and the last mails. Though most of the tourists were already armed with handfuls and pocketfuls of postcards purchased aboard, they now besieged the tiny village post-office to procure more, together with postage stamps. As Neil Ferguson was too busy with the sheep to attend to such formalities as dispensing stamps and postcards, I assumed the responsibilities of postmaster. Within an hour, I had disposed of some hundreds of postcards—the entire stock of the village store, together with the requisite stamps. The little letter-box, consisting of a huge carton placed under a slit in the wall of the post-office shack, was filled to overflowing every few minutes. So many inquirers and souvenir-hunters crowded into the office that I had to request a number to queue outside until the rush was over, since the window was a small one, and their crowding in upon me threw the office into darkness. Before long, the penny stamps had run out; but by this time I had acquired such excellent salesmanship as to have been able to convince many that the occasion justified their placing three-halfpenny stamps on their postcards. Numbers of them demanded halfpenny stamps, and were disappointed that our supply did not allow of their adding to the postmaster's labours in this respect. Halfpenny stamps were in demand among those desiring that their communications should bear at least *two* St. Kilda stamp marks. With stamping this last mail to leave St. Kilda, my hands and arms were quite sore. It was unquestionably the biggest outgoing mail St. Kilda ever had known.

Among those who had come ashore this day was the examiner of

Registration Records—records of the island's births, deaths, and marriages. He arrived to check the entries, and to collect the books now to be transferred to the Register House at Edinburgh for preservation.

*　　*　　*

After 9 p.m. the evening sun, still hidden from view, illumined the mists with a warm pink. In the evening calm the jagged line of Dùn stood out against the afterglow. By this time we had begun to ship the sheep. Among the villagers' were a lamb or two belonging to MacLeod of MacLeod. These we segregated, confining them in a cleit with the intention of releasing them to the hills in the morning. Some of MacLeod's already were running wild on Hirta. He had in addition, of course, his immense flock on Soay, which in no way concerned us. The natives assured me that Soay's sheep were wilder even than Boreray's, since they had been left even more to their own devices.

About midnight I became lantern-man at the jetty, along which one scarcely could move because of sheep, kists, chattels, and bits of furniture. There I stood, at its very edge, using the lantern's light to guide the small boats plying unceasingly between the shore and the *Dunara Castle*. By this time the enclosure above the glebe was like a field on which a mighty soccer match had been played during heavy rain, for so harassed had been the wretched sheep by men and dogs. When, at 1 a.m., we drew up the island boats by lantern-light, it was dead calm. It required nine of us—all fairly strong fellows—to drag them sufficiently above high-water mark. This surely demonstrated how impracticable waning man-power had made life on St. Kilda for this shrinking community.

Home to the village we trekked about 2 a.m., under the stars. I now assisted Neil in finishing off odd postal duties. Dealing with the hundreds of letters and postcards and with innumerable parcels, as well as packing and sealing the mail-bags, constituted an arduous undertaking, having regard to the brevity of time now at our disposal, and to the absence of any competent help. Nearer 3 a.m. than 2, "The Books" were brought out for the last time. We droned a few verses of a Gaelic psalm to the tune, *Wiltshire;* but the household was so tired that we contented ourselves with a short reading and a shorter prayer. In the small hours we dragged ourselves to bed, knowing that at daybreak we had to resume the shipping of the sheep.

At break of day the *Dunara's* siren roused the already exhausted St. Kildans. They were not long in responding. Before the mists had rolled off the hills, the last of the sheep were aboard. The morning became wonderfully clear and calm. About 7 a.m. a speck was sighted on the horizon. Time proved this to be the Admiralty vessel, *Harebell*, under the direction of Commander Barrow, making for Village Bay to enact the final scene. As the last batch of sheep was being towed out, the *Harebell* dropped anchor. Then came the villagers through the grasslands above the shore, driving their cows and calves to the jetty, enticing them every now and then with handfuls of soda scone. This was the saddest spectacle of the whole evacuation. The four calves were ferried over to the *Dunara Castle* in one boat; whereas the ten cows were compelled to swim behind the small boats, each having a noose affixed in such a way as to keep her mouth sufficiently above water. The transference of these poor creatures was rendered all the more terrible by the scarcity of slings.

As a vegetarian I could endure no longer the sight of this shipping. So I went off by the Cambir toward Soay, where the prodigality of bird-life renders the beholder speechless, if not senseless. Up the flanks of the Mullach Sgar I climbed, passing over by the Mullach Geal into Hirta's Great Glen. Hills and valleys were now deserted. Not a bleat was there. Nothing could be heard but the faint breath of the North Wind soughing among the long, wet grasses round the shieling there. The whole island now diffused an air of oppression. As I wandered through this deserted wilderness, the loneliness became ominous. I found myself getting into such perilous country that I decided to proceed barefoot. On the Cambir the mists enshrouded me. Yet, on and on I pushed, determined to have a final view of Soay and the sound intervening.

About noon the *Dunara Castle* sailed for Oban with sheep, cattle, and shepherds. In approximately seventeen hours' time, she lay alongside the quay. A few hours later the inhabitants were taken off by the *Harebell*. I was present at the unloading of the St. Kildans' sheep at Oban in the darkness. Poor, wretched creatures! They were filthy and exhausted with the knocking about they had received. Almost every one of them was flung upon the steep gangway, to scramble up as best it could. The sight of the whole business was utterly revolting.

Then came the ten cows, followed by four timid calves. The bleating of St. Kilda's wild sheep could now be heard in the streets of

Oban as drovers and sundry others harassed them through the sleeping streets. Little wonder sheep and cows fetched such ridiculously low prices at the Oban marts. Little wonder so many of the sheep died afterwards, and I am still a vegetarian!

Here endeth my account of the removal of the remnant of a race that had struggled to maintain itself upon these barren rocks for a thousand years and more. Demographically, Hirta had now become as meaningless as remote Rockall. In this wise was the human history of nine centuries brought to a close. For wellnigh three-quarters of the year, an island no more than 110 miles from the Scottish mainland was as inaccessible as the White Sea in the dead of winter. In an era when man boasts of the way in which he has conquered distance and overcome the asperities of Nature, he finds himself obliged to retreat before its onslaught. In a long struggle for the supremacy of St. Kilda, Nature outwitted man; and man, in the manner described, retired from the contest.

The removal of this small community meant that Scotland contracted demographically by about 40 miles, while the Atlantic gained to that extent. In the summer people returning to Hirta on pleasure-cruises find the natives gone. The doors of their homesteads they no longer find locked: they now find them fallen. Peat-ash lies on dead hearthstones. The soot of centuries clings to buried swees. In a room or two, open to the sky, rots the islanders' humble furniture, just where it was left, as though some terrible calamity had wrenched them from their homes. Until a few years ago the more observant traveller landing on Hirta might have found on the schoolroom's shelves the saturated lesson-books of bygone days. In the pews of the building that served as the church lie the seared bibles and psalmodies left there by the islanders after their last service. It was not without a sense of deep emotion that the loneliest of Britain's island-dwellers resigned their heritage to the ghosts and the seabirds, ringing down the curtain on haunted homes and the sagas of the centuries.

*   *   *

As long ago as 1875 the matter of St. Kilda's evacuation, to the declared advantage of its inhabitants, was discussed, if somewhat tentatively, in relation to the suggestion that they might be re-settled in Canada. This suggestion was revived a decade later when Malcolm MacNeill, Inspecting Officer of the Board of Supervision, proceeded there to interview the natives and report on their condition and wishes. MacNeill spoke at length with the island's minister, school-master, and groundofficer, and also with the natives themselves. In the spring of the following year (1886) his findings were published. According to these, the islanders on the whole were well off, and quite able to meet the isolation and hardship inseparable from the approaching winter, since they already were "amply, indeed luxuriously, supplied". MacNeill did concede, however, that the pro-vision of a landing-place would have improved appreciably their lot, and that the possibility of assisting them to emigrate was worth con-sidering, particularly as most of them seemed to regard such a pros-pect as not altogether undesirable.

In this connection let us recall how Anthony Trollope, contem-poraneously, and also *prophetically,* expressed himself. "I think it may be taken as a rule that no region can be of real value, the products of which must be eked out by charity from other regions. Many a rich and useful country will not provide itself with all that it wants; but no country can be rich and useful unless it can provide itself by supplying its own wants, or can purchase what it requires by the sale of its own products. This certainly is not the case with St. Kilda."[1]

One should mention that the condition in which the crew of the *Henry Melling* reported the St. Kildans to be (already referred to at page 137) was nothing new. From time to time the skippers of Aberdeen trawlers, storm-stayed in Village Bay, brought to the main-land similar news of hunger and distress among them. Tom Steel, in his painstaking volume, *The Life and Death of St. Kilda,*[2] recalls a memorable occasion. On May, 18th, 1912, James Rennie, skipper of

[1] *How the 'Mastiff' went to Iceland,* London, Virtue & Co., Ltd., 1878. (Chapter II). In *Celtica,* the catalogue published by the National Library of Scotland in 1967 in connection with its splendid Exhibition of manu-scripts and printed books of Celtic interest acquired by the Library during its three centuries of existence, the note accompanying Item 96 runs as follows:

Anthony Trollope, the novelist, was one of a party who made a trip to Iceland in 1878 aboard the "Mastiff", a vessel built for the Scottish and Irish Royal Mail Service. The picture, drawn by Mrs Blackburn, a member of the party, shows the owner of the "Mastiff" delivering H.M. Mail bag (containing one letter) to St. Kilda. Readily recognisable are the minister and the sister of McLeod of McLeod, the proprietor of the island. It was Trollope's reluctant conclusion that the islanders should be re-settled elsewhere.

[2] A noteworthy publication of the National Trust for Scotland, 1965, typography and production by Tom Steel, its author's father.

Village Bay, St Kilda, showing the aerial masts of the wireless station erected there in 1913. In the background lies the island of Dùn
(*Page 171*)

Neil Ferguson (standing) watching Dudley Ward-Millar of British Telegraph Instruments, Ltd., operate the radio transmitter gifted in 1913 to the St Kildans by *The Daily Mirror*

Rockall on a wild day in May, 1942 with the ocean breaking beyond that part of Hazlewood Reef known as Leonidas Rock

Rockall from the northwest

the trawler, *Strathmore,* brought to Scotland the news of the St. Kildans' famishment owing primarily to months of Atlantic gales rendering impossible any contact with them, even by trawler. To this, the *Daily Mirror* responded by organising immediately a relief expedition, although, from the point of view of assembling provisions promptly, this news reached London rather inconveniently on a Saturday. Nevertheless, thanks to the prompt and substantial generosity of donors like Sir Thomas Lipton, Sir Joseph Lyons, and Gordon Selfridge, the situation was saved when, on May, 20th, the tug, *Victor,* reached Village Bay. "Dear Editor," wrote an appreciative St. Kildan to the *Daily Mirror,* "A thousand thanks for your great kindness to the lonely St. Kildans in their distress for the want of provisions. Your help reached us unexpectedly, and left us more than thankful for it."

In 1930, that which so many for so long had succeeded in staving off had to be faced in a realistic way. Conditions and circumstances, such as Trollope and others had found, no longer obtained. A viable economy, even with a measure of charitable assistance, had become impossible. In Tom Steel's concluding words, "the attempts of those to stave off evacuation were noble and well-intentioned, but bore the pathos and futility of working against that which must come about. St. Kilda was unique. It stood in the Atlantic, the changeless amid the changed, the changed amid the changeless. All that could be done was to wait and allow the men and women of Village Bay the courtesy and privilege of making for themselves the decision that would make Nature's defeat of man a reality."

So the solution lay in a single word—*evacuation.* In accepting this, one cannot but recall Trollope's ill-worded question of 1877: "Who shall say that these people ought to be deported from their homes and placed recklessly upon some point of the mainland?" he asked. "I have not the courage to say. They themselves, if they were consulted, would probably be averse to such deportation. Were they so deported, each individual would suffer, at any rate for a time, by the change."

There was nothing of deportation about the removal of the St. Kildans in 1930. Nor was there any reckless dumping of its last inhabitants on the mainland. On the contrary, a great deal of official sympathy and forethought went into their re-settlement. I feel that this ought to be stated here, and unequivocally, if only to forestall in some small degree those historians who, a century or two hence, and after the traditional manner of their predecessors, will mis-read, read into, and unconcernedly distort, even in face of available facts, not to mention such as are deliberately suppressed with monstrous terms of penal servitude awaiting those who divulge them. Napoleon defined history as agreed fiction—which, of course, it is! Anybody conscientiously engaged in historical research among such documentary evidence as has not been purposely destroyed is aware of this. So long as history is primarily the concealment of official roguery, and the expression of this or of that nationalism, the most unreasoning and distorting of mankind's emotions, it will continue to be so.

* * *

A true account of the St. Kildans' subsequent fate makes pathetic reading. Unable, largely because of old age, to fit themselves into an environment so strangely new and conventional, they spent the years following their removal in yearning to return to their life of isolation and simplicity. Indeed, some of the menfolk actually returned for spells during the months of ensuing summers. Tom Steel, in the volume already alluded to, quotes from a letter written to the Earl of Dumfries ten years after the evacuation by Alexander Ferguson, Neil Ferguson's brother: "Last Friday I hired a motor-boat to go to Shillay, and, standing on the top of that island, I saw St. Kilda under a white cap of summer haze. I felt like Moses when he viewed the Promised Land from Pisgah's heights." From seal-haunted Shillay, northernmost of the enchanted isles in the Sound of Harris, Alick Ferguson gazed westward to what for him, throughout his long and active life, was *Tir-nan-Og*.

* * *

Very soon after the evacuation, several of the natives were dead, some of old age, others of broken heart. During the Second World War four of the few eligible men served in the army, and three in the navy. For a time one of the former was a prisoner in Germany. None of the St. Kildans served in the First World War. Consequently, as I remarked in *A Last Voyage to St. Kilda*, Hirta must be one of the few islands of Britain then peopled to be without a war memorial in the conventional style.

In 1934, four years after the removal of Hirta's population to the Scottish mainland, Sir Reginald MacLeod, in whose family St. Kilda had been for so many centuries, sold it to the Earl of Dumfries, subsequently the 5th Marquis of Bute, upon whose demise in 1956 it passed by bequest to the National Trust for Scotland. At the present moment it is leased by the Trust to the Nature Conservancy, which meantime is conducting a precise ecological survey of it, while having leased to the Ministry of Defence part of Hirta for purposes connected with one of our more costly and less sane enterprises, namely, the tracking of those deadly missiles retained on the usual and highly plausible pretext of national defence.

Once the conserving hand of man has been withdrawn from scenes like St. Kilda, restoring unchallenged scope to those unrelenting conspirators, time and epigene weathering, even the boldest and most enduring evidence of human occupation soon gets buried, obliterated, and forgotten. Were it not for the voluntary working parties organised each summer by the National Trust for Scotland, little of what remained standing on St. Kilda at the time of the evacuation in 1930 would have survived, visibly or otherwise. But for such enthusiastic endeavours, the sites of the cottages comprising its village, as also those of its byres and cleits, would already be as difficult to locate and distinguish as will be the sites of North Rona's homesteads in half a century.

*   *   *

Just as my visits to the late Robert M. Adam, immediately after a spell in the Hebrides, seemed an extension of such, so likewise did visits to another friend in that same city of Edinburgh contribute, in a very real sense, to my preöccupation with St. Kilda. That friend was the late Dr. A. M. Cockburn—Alexander Murray Cockburn— hereinafter referred to as Alick. Our friendship began in the 1920s. It originated with our sharing an interest in a number of things, half a dozen of which I recall very clearly:

(1) Geology, especially in the field of Vulcanism.
(2) Kirk-Yetholm, in the Scottish Borderland, and its Gypsies.
(3) The Pentland Hills.
(4) Coleridge-Taylor's music.
(5) Agreeable gossip about Edinburgh University and such of its professoriate as we both had had dealings with.
(6) St. Kilda.

Geology we had studied under the same professor, and had received tutorial instruction from the same lecturers and demonstrators.

Both of us had associations with Kirk-Yetholm and with Town-Yetholm. Having holidayed there, we had made friends with the same natives, and from them had collected a good deal of Border lore and many amusing anecdotes concerning the last of the Gypsies, whose headquarters for centuries had been at Kirk-Yetholm. In addition to this, Alick and I had traversed the Cheviot hills and fells often enough to have shared an intimate topographical knowledge of them. Of our Pentland interests, I need only mention their literary associations and their hill-walks, and Alick's own authoritative investigations into their volcanic rocks.

Of our enjoyment of Coleridge-Taylor's music, I have a tangible reminder in the gramophone records he handed over to me one evening in his home, on the pretext that he wanted to devote the space they occupied to more recent recordings by other composers. On the other hand, he may well have had enough of the *Petite Suite de Concert* by the end of a memorable ten days' visit I once paid him, during which I put on this entire composition at least once a day! On our University gossip I need not dilate. Accept my assurance that it was more academic than unkind.

As for St. Kilda, I shall return to this topic in a moment when I have told you more about Alick in other contexts. Suffice it to say at this juncture that if, in going to St. Kilda, I was following in the Keartons' footsteps, I was following even more closely in *his*.

This worthy son of Edinburgh was born there in 1901. Except for a certain amount of foreign travel undertaken primarily for geological reasons, he lived and worked in and around his native city. There he died early in 1959, a few weeks after his having been incapacitated by the fatal illness that so unexpectedly and undeservedly terminated his distinguished career. Receiving his early education at Edinburgh's Royal High School, he entered Edinburgh University, graduating in 1924 with First Class Honours in Geology. Enlightened generosity thereafter on the part of his father, an architectural engineer, enabled him to set out the following year on a geological *wanderjahr* of his own choosing. The highlights of this, to quote from the Appreciation of him by the late Professor Arthur Holmes in the 1958–1959 Year Book of the Royal Edinburgh Society, were the volcanoes of Hawaii, and the Coast Ranges of British Columbia. From these distant places he returned to Edinburgh in 1926, in time to become the successful candidate for the Falconer Memorial Fellowship.

In accepting not long afterwards the invitation of my father's old

friend, John Mathieson, geographer and cartographer, he was to
travel in the Keartons' footsteps. Five months' intensive application
culminated in the joint completion of the first detailed topographic
map of the St. Kilda group of islands, published in 1928 by the
Ordnance Survey, its Gaelic toponomy carefully supervised by
Mathieson, a native Gaelic speaker.

St. Kilda henceforth was to be one of the greatest interests in
Alick's life. In order to extend his preliminary geological studies and
to make a geological map, he returned there alone in 1928. His
Geology of St. Kilda, published in 1935 in the *Transactions* of the
Royal Society of Edinburgh, lies before me as I write. He had done
for the geology of this remote group what the Keartons had done
for its biology, so many years previously. He had discovered these
islands to be the peripheral remnants of an igneous complex six or
seven miles across, the remaining visible fragments displaying so many
of the phenomena characteristically associated with the ring structures
of Mull and Ardnamurchan, lending weight to the theory that
St. Kilda also has been the great centre of Tertiary volcanic
activity.

But I must not weary you further with such matter, nor yet with a
catalogue of Alick's academic achievements and distinctions in this
and in allied fields. The latter you will find faithfully set forth in the
late Professor Holmes's estimate of him as a quiet, painstaking
scientist, and as the most lovable and unassuming of colleagues. For
myself, I cannot hear mention of St. Kilda without Alick's immediately coming to mind. Nobody at any time knew so much as he did
about it in so many ways, and about its inhabitants. His prolonged
sojourn there provided him with those unique opportunities of which
he fully availed himself. His only child he christened Ewen after his
athletic companion, Ewen MacDonald, the St. Kildan who, with
boat, rope, and geological hammer, accompanied him on all his
excursions.

In my mind's eye I see Alick Cockburn now, exercising on
Blackford Hill (at the base of which lay his home in Ladysmith
Road) the very lovable mongrel, Kilda, he had brought home with
him to Edinburgh as a puppy at the conclusion of his geological
work in that distant field.

Alick Cockburn was a worthy follower in the Keartons' footsteps;
and I myself, in turn, was fortunate in having been able to follow in
his. It was gratifying to have had the St. Kildans accept me as Alick's

friend, and to have given me so freely their amusing versions of incidents that had occurred during his memorable stay among them. Alick, to the end of his life, or of theirs, kept in touch with the St. Kildans settled on the Scottish mainland. Evenings with him at Ladysmith Road, frequently interspersed with tea and toast and a little Coleridge-Taylor, passed very agreeably. There were our mutual friends, the St. Kildans, to discuss. There were Alick's photographs of them and of their ancient heritage to finger our way through yet again.

In 1940, at the age of 85, Finlay Gillies, oldest of the surviving St. Kildans, died at Poyntzfield, in Easter Ross. Finlay was one of those who signed the petition to the Secretary of State for Scotland, praying that the islanders might be taken off before the onset of another winter.

In 1944, at the age of 68, Neil Ferguson died at Kincardine-on-Forth. When, at an odd time, I come upon that puffin-gin he gave me, I am instantly transported to those hectic days in the autumn of 1930, when we were all preparing feverishly for the arrival of the ship that was to bear us away. Indeed, that gin carries me back a good deal farther, at any rate in imagination—back to 1896, the year in which the Keartons landed there and collected the material for the book which, as it happened, was to foster in me a lasting interest in Britain's remotest isles, and bequeath many cherished associations, and memories amaranthine.

*   *   *

In 1934, four years after the evacuation of Hirta, Sir Reginald MacLeod sold the St. Kilda islands to the Earl of Dumfries who, on the death of his father in 1947, became the fifth Marquis of Bute, and who, at his own death nine years later, bequeathed them to the National Trust for Scotland, together with what is now known as the Bute Collection—that considerable corpus of documents, diaries, deeds, papers, and literary matter in manuscript form which he himself had collected or had been given during his twenty-two years' ownership of St. Kilda. In the last category come the manuscript writings of the naturalist, George Atkinson, who visited St. Kilda in 1831; of George Murray, a graduate of Aberdeen who was schoolmaster on the island from 1886 till 1887; of John Ross who succeeded him in that capacity the following year; and of Ann MacLachlan, wife of the missionary on St. Kilda between 1906 and 1909.

In January, 1957, after discussions between representatives of the Air Ministry, which had been negotiating with the late Marquis for a number of small sites on Hirta with a view to erecting radar installations as part of its South Uist Guided Missile Range, and of the Nature Conservancy in regard to the protection of these islands' unique wildlife and flora, the National Trust for Scotland announced its unconditional acceptance of the late Marquis's offer, and also its intention to create by public appeal—primarily for preserving objects of archaeological and antiquarian significance—an endowment to be known as the St. Kilda Fund. Following upon this acceptance, the three interested parties agreed to the Trust's leasing the entire St. Kilda's group to the Nature Conservancy, and to the latter's subleasing to the Air Ministry roughly a dozen acres on Hirta, placing the Ministry under obligation to reduce to a minimum, during its occupation, the disturbance to wild-life, and to clear the site at its departure—whenever that may be, having regard to mankind's present mental condition! The Ministry claimed that such installations as it had in view were a critical feature of its rocket-range scheme in so far as St. Kilda lay on the flank of an area of fifty square-miles of clear ocean into which rockets from South Uist would be launched, their flights measured, tracked, and plotted by radar on St. Kilda.

Recognising that road-making and the works of construction then envisaged for this R.A.F. radar station would mean the employment on Hirta of as many as 300 persons, the Nature Conservancy, on the plausible pretext that they might disturb, inter alia, its fulmar colonies, and perhaps exterminate the St. Kilda field-mouse, stated that none of them would be permitted to keep on the island either dog or cat. Furthermore, every precaution had to be taken against the entry of rats, an even greater danger from the ornithologist's viewpoint. In the interim, Kenneth Williamson, formerly director of the Fair Isle Bird Observatory, agreed to carry out the duties of warden on St. Kilda until a permanent warden was appointed.

In the field of natural history the Conservancy's preöccupation has been with these islands' immense seabird colonies—with the world's largest gannet colony, as we have seen, with the oldest and largest of Britain's fulmar colonies (having a total population far exceeding that of the gannets), and with puffins numbering some hundreds of thousands. Two other species of bird have received from the Conservancy special attention, namely, the St. Kilda wren and Leach's rare petrel, colonies of the latter having been discovered there about 1956.

The three unique mammals granted comparable treatment are the St. Kilda field-mouse, the St. Kilda house-mouse already alluded to, and Soay's wild sheep. A fourth now falls to be mentioned. When we left St. Kilda in 1930, the great Atlantic seal was scarcely ever seen there or thereabouts. Today this mighty mammal breeds between August and November on part of the shoreland of Village Bay and elsewhere on Hirta. Observant R.A.F. men estimate that at least a hundred pups are born there annually. Here we have another example of this seal's moving to new breeding-grounds among remote islands as human beings move out. Commercial exploitation had so depleted the population of this species that it had to be given statutory protection. Half a century ago its numbers throughout the world were thought to have been reduced to less than 1,000: today they are put at 60,000. This is still the world's rarest seal, however.

How many St. Kilda wrens are there? Kenneth Williamson asked this question a few years ago, at the commencement of the Nature Conservancy's tenancy of St. Kilda. How many of that unique species to which, in 1884, the Quaker ornithologist, Henry Seebohm, appropriately gave the scientific name of *Troglodytes hirtensis*? On the basis of the 115 males on Hirta during the dawn-song survey of 1957, Kenneth put the number then at 230 pairs for all the St. Kilda islands.

The R.A.F.'s. activities on Hirta have rendered it more favourably situated for scientific investigation in several fields than at any time in its existence. The extent to which this is the case is seen in *St. Kilda Summer*,[1] that exhaustive volume in which Kenneth Williamson and J. Morton Boyd collaborated so acceptably. In the meantime the National Trust, anxious to locate and preserve Hirta's largely buried and almost forgotten antiquities, was able to do so with the assistance of the servicemen stationed there, and through the coöperation of Edinburgh University's School of Scottish Studies, handsomely encouraged by a grant from the Russell Trust. "The place was a paradox," wrote the thoroughly competent professional naturalists I have named, "so tiny on the map, yet of overpowering immensity when you walked there in the village, shut in by the soaring sky-line behind: so minute a speck in the geography of Britain, yet replete with superlatives—the highest sheer cliff, the tallest sea stacks, the

[1] Published by Hutchinson & Co. in 1960.

world's biggest gannetry, Britain's biggest fulmar colony, the haunt of unique forms of wren and mouse and sheep."

*   *   *

When we left St. Kilda in 1930, we were unable for one reason or another to take off with us either the flock of several hundred blackface sheep pastured in summer on Boreray and still flourishing there, or the wild, long-legged, and quite primitive sheep on Soay which for centuries have bred there, virtually unattended by man, and which therefore may be regarded as a relic of aboriginal domestic sheep.They are light in weight, have a short, brown, woolly coat, and a short tail. The rams carry rather heavy, dark horns. These curve outwards and downwards in a single plane, seldom showing any spiral. The ewes, according to Dr. Peter Jewell of the Zoological Society of London, who in recent years has made these Soay sheep his special study, may be horned or not.[1] How they originally got to Soay, an island upon which it is just possible for the most agile human being to land on the calmest of summer days, is not known. It has been suggested that their progenitors were placed there in pre-Roman times by early, prehistoric settlers on Hirta, the only island of the St. Kilda group upon which man, isolated, could subsist for any length of time.

Sheep were first domesticated in the Near East in Neolithic times, the Asiatic moufflon having been their wild ancestors. Neolithic herdsmen are believed to have brought the first domesticated animals to Britain about 3000 B.C. In 1931, the year following the evacuation of St. Kilda, 107 of Soay's wild sheep were caught and transported to Hirta, where they were let loose. A casual count in 1948 showed this wild flock to have increased there to a little over 1,000. In 1951 its number had fallen to 710. By 1959 it had risen again to 1,300 or thereabouts. A census taken in May, 1960, recorded only 610. Tom Weir put the number in 1964 at over 1,600.

To this cycle of increase and heavy mortality among the Soay sheep on Hirta, Dr. Jewell and the Nature Conservancy are now giving particular attention. Jewell attributes the cause of death to an enterotoxaemia common among sheep, especially in the late spring, when they are usually in poor condition. Sudden changes of weather or a flush of new grass, he states, can provoke the pathogenic flare-up of gut organisms. The exact pre-disposing factors in this cyclical

[1] See his contribution on St. Kilda's Wild Sheep to *The New Scientist*, vol. 2, 1964.

F

mortality among this, the most important herd of primitive sheep left in the world, would still have to be determined, however. What we see, then, is a steady increase in numbers, over a period of five or six years, of a mammal roaming wild on a strictly limited area, reaching a maximum density of population at the end of that period, and then falling by disease to about half that density before beginning to increase again.

The study of the Soay sheep population is made particularly attractive because the ecology of the island presents a fairly simplified system. The sheep is the only herbivore grazing its pastures and swards. Although there are no trees, there is plenty of well distributed shelter. As there are no predators, the population's limit is set by what food is available. This means that the system is somewhat unstable. Big fluctuations in the numbers of sheep occur, rising periodically to over 1,500, and crashing as periodically to as low as 600. The determining factor is the availability, or otherwise, of food in late winter. At this time, when the population is high, a great many sheep die of starvation. This situation provides the opportunity for making an intensive study of the manner in which a natural food supply can regulate numbers. It may be contrasted with the more natural one found on the mainland of Britain in early times, when elk, deer, wild cattle, and wild boar would have formed a community of herbivores using forest and grassland, and wolf and fox would have been important predators. Because of the great complexity of such a system, peaks and crashes in the numbers of animals would be less likely to occur. One sees the finest development of these complex systems in Africa. There, today, as many as twenty species of large herbivores graze and browse in a single environment, using *all* the vegetation, from the roots and tubers to the tree-tops. Preying upon them are lion, leopard, cheetah, hunting dog, and hyaena. This means that there are many regulating factors at work in such a complex system. Their buffering ensures that populations can be maintained at fairly stable numbers.

*   *   *

How unpredictable are the ways—nay, the waywardnesses—of man! Little could I have imagined as I sailed away from Village Bay that autumn evening in 1930, so fully occupied with transmitting by ship's wireless two telegrams, each roughly 1,600 words in length, to *The Times* as its Special Correspondent, that so few years afterwards the scene I had left to loneliness and desolation was to become one of reöccupation on a grand scale—that the day wasn't so very far off when the derelict meadowlands between village and bay were to be crowded with huts, marquees, tents, caravans, bulldozers, cater-pillar tractors, lorries, generating plant, mechanical shovels, and mighty stone-crushing and earth-moving devices—that beach-landing craft would lie on the sands of Village Bay when the tide receded; that in the storm-beach I so often had trodden high explosive would blow a gap designed to expand a beach-head little altered during hundreds of centuries; that a road would traverse the steep mountain-side of Ruaival, up which I had clambered so laboriously with my camera on a number of occasions; that Ordnance Survey engineers would display powerful beacon-lights from the summit of Conachair when fixing the triangulation point which was to raise St. Kilda to national-grid status in recognition of its rocket-tracking importance; that each summer, on a patch of comparatively level ground by the fringe of Village Bay, there should be held the Hirta Highland Games where tug-o'-war and tossing-the-caber are conducted along tradi-tional lines, and with a zest excelled not even at Aboyne or Braemar; that the thirsty contestants would retire to the NAAFI to drink beer and watch "the telly"; and that the humble manse and factor's house of former years, now replete with baths, showers, washhand-basins, water-closets, and a few hundred gallons of thermostatically heated water constantly on tap, would be the last word in mod. cons.

All this missile-tracking and the like, at a time when thousands of millions of pounds are being devoted competitively to lunar aero-nautics, and mankind's mass miseries here on earth are simultaneously increasing beyond all hope of alleviation, I would wish to leave to those less critical than myself. In existing circumstances, I am unable to work up for them much enthusiasm. For me, they foretoken man's merited extinction.

Notwithstanding, a visit to St. Kilda can still be one of life's most enriching experiences. Each summer the National Trust for Scotland organises from Greenock an Adventure Cruise of roughly 1,300 miles, and at a cost of about £30. *The itinerary always includes St. Kilda.*

CHAPTER EIGHT

St. Kilda's Mail-boats

EXCEPT FOR an occasional trawler driven in storm-time to anchorage in Village Bay, not for nine months of the year did the St. Kildans have anything in the nature of regular communication with the rest of mankind. When they desired to transmit to the outer world any particular piece of news, they gouged out of a piece of driftwood, which they fashioned like a toy boat, the cavity in which they placed a sealed bottle or small tin containing a letter, together with the request that the finder should take it to the nearest post-office. A penny was enclosed to cover postage. If the sealed receptacle held more than one letter, a corresponding number of pennies accompanied them. Over the cavity was nailed a wooden lid upon which were carved the words PLEASE OPEN. To this toy boat, launched in a westerly wind, was attached an inflated sheep's bladder. In this way the St. Kildans kept the rest of mankind informed of how they were faring throughout the months that no vessel other than an occasional trawler reached them. Two-thirds of these St. Kilda Mail-boats, as they were called, were picked up eventually on the shores of the Orkneys and Shetlands, of the Long Island, or of Scandinavia, whence their contents were forwarded to the persons to whom they were addressed.

There are one or two historic occasions when the St. Kilda mail was delivered in this manner. On September, 28th, 1885, a crofter on Taransay, a fairly large island lying roughly a mile west of the Harris mainland, in the Outer Hebrides, found on its shores a plank about three feet in length, fitted with a small sail and a metal keel. Crudely carved on the lid covering the cavity chiselled out of this plank were the words, "St. Kilda—Please Open". Inside the cavity lay two small, sealed bottles. These the finder took to Alexander Sutherland, Taransay's schoolmaster at that time. Each bottle contained a letter. One of these, written by the Rev. John MacKay, St.

Kilda's Free Church minister, was addressed to Dr. Robert Rainy, then Principal of New College, Edinburgh, and convener of that denomination's Highland Committee. This letter evoked much interest throughout Scotland because of *The Scotsman's* having reported a few days previously the arrival at Uig, in western Lewis, of a letter from St. Kilda similarly delivered, written by Alexander Ferguson, one of that island's crofters, to a friend who once had been schoolmaster there:

> "My Dear Sir—I am now going to write you a letter, and sending her in one of the little ships in which we were sailing on the shore, as you know, to let you know all the knews [sic]. The men were building a house, just a little house for the cows; a great storm came on and all the corn and barley were swept away by the storm, and one of the boats was swept away by the sea; the men of St. Kilda is nearly dead with the hunger. They send two boats from St. Kilda to go to Haries [sic], not the fishing boats, but little piece[s] of wood like the little one which I send. I sent [sic] my best loves unto you."

The view widely current that Ferguson's letter was a practical joke had to be re-considered in the light of that reaching Dr. Rainy so soon afterwards. Regarding his at the outset as a fake, Dr. Rainy sent it to the Home Secretary, who was inclined to agree with him. However, a more careful perusal of what the reverend gentleman had written raised doubts. He had said that on Saturday and Sunday, September, 12th and 13th, a storm of exceptional violence had struck St. Kilda, had destroyed its crops, and had damaged seriously all of its sixteen cottages. "And I can honestly say that I never saw anything that could come near it." True though it was that MacLeod of MacLeod, the proprietor, had sent the St. Kildans a supply of oatmeal only a couple of weeks previously, both Rainy and the Home Office believed that they were in some need. While the latter was considering what should be done, a number of magnanimous men in Glasgow, coöperating with the Highland & Agricultural Society, sent food and seed from that city aboard the *Hebridean* to the island's 77 inhabitants, 20 of whom where children under fourteen years of age. A fortnight after the receipt in London of Dr. Rainy's letter, Malcolm MacNeill, an official of the Board of Supervision, under the Poor Law in Scotland, landed at St. Kilda from the gunboat,

Jackal. The report he made on what he found there hardly confirmed what MacKay had stated. Whilst conceding that the island had experienced a severe storm, MacNeill found no loss of life, injury neither to man nor to beast, no really serious damage to cottages, no agricultural destruction, and no shortage of food. On the contrary, each household still had an appreciable quantity of the meal landed there early in September. In view of this and of what the islanders in their traditional way had salted down of bird and beast for consumption during the ensuing winter, MacNeill, having seen neither evidence nor likelihood of starvation, stated in conclusion that "I have thus no doubt that the inhabitants of St. Kilda are amply—indeed luxuriously—supplied".

To describe such a community as luxuriously provided for at any time was, of course, quite ridiculous. On the other hand, having regard to such matters as its excessive rate of infant mortality and its proportion of rheumaticky and infirm, its general condition hardly could have been deemed satisfactory. What, then, lay behind such a statement? The belief, perhaps, that only such a message was likely to receive prompt attention? What readers may be unaware of is MacNeill's mentioning that in his view nothing short of evacuation could solve the inhabitants' problems arising primarily from their isolation, problems in the nature of things liable to recur periodically. "Within the past 18 months," he wrote, "a strong desire to emigrate has sprung up and, with the exception of one or two old men, I found none who was not anxious to be transferred either to the mainland or to Australia." Yet, a dwindling population was to hang on here for another forty-five years. The elderly taken off St. Kilda in 1930 were among the young who, according to MacNeill's report, had been willing to quit in 1885.

*　　*　　*

Among the first recovered mail-boats of this kind was that for the launching of which, on February, 5th, 1876, the radical journalist, John Sands of Ormiston, author of *Out of the World* (1878), was responsible. It came ashore twenty-two days later on a sandbank at Poolewe, in Wester Ross. From then onwards, either to announce an emergency or as an idle ploy, they were committed to the sea at irregular intervals right up until the eve of St. Kilda's evacuation in 1930. The mail-boat despatched my myself from Village Bay that autumn, duly delivered at Dunvegan Castle and now on show there, was the last. In the accompanying photograph of it you may just discern a fragment of my handwriting. It faces page 136.

A state of emergency actually arose on St. Kilda while Sands was marooned there. In January, 1877, the Austrian vessel, *Peti Dubrovacki*, went on the rocks there and became a total wreck. For more than five weeks her crew of nine lived on the islanders, eating food the latter could ill afford to spare. Three of the shipwrecked resided with the minister: the remaining half-dozen were distributed in turn among the villagers. A servere strain already had been placed on the St. Kildans' supplies when it was decided to launch, in a watertight bottle by the St. Kilda Post, a message seeking aid. When the wind veered to the westward, it was sent a-sailing, attached to a lifebuoy belonging to the foundered vessel. Picked up at Birsay, in Orkney, nine days later, it was forwarded to Lloyd's agent at Stromness. As the result of this, H.M.S. *Jackal* some days afterwards reached St. Kilda with directions from the Admiralty to provision the natives with food and coal, and to take off the shipwrecked Austrians.

*   *   *

To naturalists, the best known of St. Kilda's wind- and wave-borne letters is that which Neil Ferguson wrote to Richard Kearton in the spring of 1897. When Richard and his brother, Cherry, were leaving St. Kilda after their adventurous study of its natural history, particularly of its fantastic, oceanic bird-life, they requested that during the ensuing winter or spring, by which time they would be back in London, somebody on the island might communicate with them by means of 'The St. Kilda Mail'. And so, at 11 a.m. on March, 24th, 1897, with a nor'westerly blowing, Finlay MacQueen launched the tiny mail-boat picked up exactly a week later by a shepherd in a cove at Vallay, in North Uist. At this moment, while I type these pages, that very mail-boat lies eloquently by my elbow. One of the four letters it carried in a small, sealed tin was that addressed to Richard by Neil Ferguson. Now preserved in the records department of Post-Office headquarters in St. Martin's-le-Grand is the clearly expressed letter dated April, 1st, 1897 (the day after the shepherd's discovery at Vallay), which A. Stuart, then postmaster at Lochmaddy, wrote to Mr. Deane, at that time Secretary of the Scottish Region of the Post-Office in Edinburgh:

A small boat, less than 2 ft long, with buoy attached, was found at the island of Vallay, North Uist, yesterday—

On the 'deck' being removed a tin canister was found (in the 'hold') which contained 4 letters from St. Kilda. They were damaged by wet and the manager at Vallay re-covered, stamped, and posted them. The addresses reside in Ullapool, Glasgow, & London.

The distance from St. Kilda to Vallay is about 45 miles.

Perhaps this primitive yet ingenious method of 'mail service' may be of interest to you——

I am to claim the 'boat' but am doubtful about getting it.

A Stuart
Lochmaddy 1 Apl97

So far as I can make out, the extremely faint writing below Stuart's signature and the date reads "Submitted for the Secretary Information J. Macdonald". One assumes that J. Macdonald was the clerk who actually opened the letter and marked it for Mr. Dean's attention. I would imagine that the system prevailing then, as now, was that letters addressed to the Secretary, even when addressed to him by name, would be opened by a junior official in the first instance.

This letter forms part of about a dozen files which the Post-Office Scottish Region compiled on the subject of St. Kilda from the 1880s until 1930, when St. Kilda ceased to be of interest to it. These files in due course gravitated to the Central Registry in London, where a certain amount of material would have been weeded out, and the rest laid aside for preservation under terms of the Public Record Act of 1965. The Post-Office is one of the few Government Departments permitted by the Public Record Office to retain its own archives.

The superscription at the top of Stuart's letter, now seen to have been deleted, is the standard registration mark applied in Edinburgh Central Registry to all correspondence when it is received. This supplies the name of the region, the date of the receipt of the letter, and its serial number, the last mentioned being that used in all subsequent correspondence dealing with the matter. I imagine that, when this letter was laid aside for preservation in the Central Registry in London in comparatively recent times, this reference ceased to have any significance, and was therefore crossed out.

The letter this historic mail-boat carried for Richard Kearton found him in London by ordinary post a week after it reached Vallay. A reproduction of it appears among the several illustrations adorning Richard's minor classic, *With Nature & a Camera,* which Messrs. Cassell had the discernment to publish for him in 1899. Neil mentions in the course of his letter how, during a fowling expedition to the cliffs of Conachair earlier that day, he had killed fifteen fulmars, "but four of them was lost. I was thinking of the day I was with you and Cherry photographing when a big stone fall [*sic*] from your feet and nearly killed Cherry. I hope to see you yet; this is to be sent in a toy boat by the first north-west wind of which Finly McQueen is Captain. With best wishes. Remember me to your brother.—I remain, yours faithfully, Neil Ferguson."

We cannot compute what the naturalist's world would have lost had that descending stone deprived it so prematurely of Cherry Kearton. For our enrichment, he was to live another 43 years. Having survived Richard by twelve years, he died in 1940 while returning home from a Children's Hour broadcast during an air-raid on London.

Neil Ferguson, Finlay MacQueen, and Finlay Gillies were among the St. Kildans who, accompanying the Keartons on their hazardous exploits in these arduous islands, astounded them by the confidence and surefootedness with which they scaled the cliffs in pursuit of seafowl and their eggs. Each in his own day was a renowned cragsman, adept at snaring puffins and fulmars with their homemade snares and fowling-rods. Finlay MacQueen, the most intrepid of them, so despised the method of being let down the rocks by means of a rope held above by a fellow-cragsman that he often set out alone with fowling-rod and stave. The former he fixed for himself. To it he attached the rope wherewith he lowered himself to parts of the cliffs otherwise inaccessible. In his heyday he was one of the most famous rockers in all the world. The agility with which, when in his prime, he could leap on to almost perpendicular cliffs from a boat in a stormy sea is described in the writings of many who visited St. Kilda in his time. I well recall the day this fearless cliffsman proudly showed me the great dent in his head, received when, half a century earlier, a tumbling boulder struck him while he was fowling.

Not until 1877, when the sister-ships, the *Hebrides* and the *Dunara Castle,* owned by Messrs. MacCallum, Orme, & Company, that small but splendid concern, began to include, in its scheduled sailings from Glasgow's historic Broomielaw, its popular fortnightly calls at St. Kilda during the months of June, July, and August, was any

official postal service to and from St. Kilda established. That year the
G.P.O. gave to this noteworthy shipping company the contract for
the carrying of postal communications between the St. Kildans and
the world beyond them. Hitherto they had depended upon MacLeod's
factor when, as weather permitted, he arrived to collect their rents
and dues. In 1897 it was suggested that the factor, John MacKenzie,
whom I knew in my early life, should be paid a subsidy to convey
mails when, quite independently and spasmodically, he sailed there.
This never came to anything, however. By 1895 the G.P.O. was able
to guarantee six deliveries throughout the summer months. Mails
reaching or leaving the island during the rest of the year were taken
at erratic intervals by Aberdeen trawlers operating in these northern
waters and sometimes anchoring in Village Bay during storms or when
mending damaged trawls. In fact, in 1898 the G.P.O. actually
authorised the sending to Aberdeen of all mails destined for St.
Kilda.

In September, 1890, in response to an application made to the
G.P.O. by the factor the previous year, a sub-postoffice was established
in the factor's house on the island. The following year its Free Church
incumbent, the Rev. Angus Fiddes, was appointed sub-postmaster
at a salary of £5, with one or two bonuses. In this capacity he acted
until 1905, when he was succeeded by Neil Ferguson, who was to
remain St. Kilda's postmaster until we all left the island at the end
of August, 1930, and for whom I deputised during our final days
there. Throughout most of Neil's tenure, the postoffice was the
shack adjoining the east gable of his home at 5, Main Street, the
island's village. It had been moved from the factor's house in order
to provide room there for the installation by the Marconi Wireless
Telegraph Company, in the summer of 1913, of a radio transmitter
gifted to the inhabitants by the *Daily Mirror*, following upon that
newspaper's campaign for the amelioration of the islanders' hard-
ships. As early as 1906 the idea of furnishing St. Kilda with a telephonic or a wireless telegraphic means of communication had been
raised by my father's old friend, (James) Galloway Weir (1839–1911),
Liberal member for Ross & Cromarty. The Postmaster-General replied that the laying of a cable for the former and for the installation
of the latter would cost, respectively, £10,000 and £1,400. Moreover,
it was pointed out that the revenue-earning potentiality of either of
them would be too negligible to warrant such public expenditure. The
same objection, of course, might have been put forward when, not

long before, the Northern Lighthouse Commissioners installed the wireless equipment enabling the Flannan lightkeepers to communicate with those at the Butt of Lewis, roughly 40 miles to the north-east of them. Weir got no farther with his proposal.

Among the principal objectors to such a scheme for St. Kilda were these Commissioners. As James Alexander MacKay, the noted philatelist and postal historian, put it, "for years they had resolutely refused to allow their lighthouse steamers, *Pharos* and *Hesperus*, to call at St. Kilda in winter time, although they were accustomed to visit the Monach Isles and the Flannans, both less than four hours' steaming from St. Kilda. Now they flatly refused to allow wireless communication with St. Kilda to add to the preöccupations of the, no doubt, harassed keepers of the Flannan Light."[1]

Despite quantities of official red tape, the licence was granted in January, 1913, when St. Kilda lay beyond reach, in the grip of the North Atlantic winter, and its inhabitants were about to succumb to one of the worst influenza epidemics in their experience. A prolonged spell of unusually severe weather delayed matters for several months. Not until July, therefore, was the *Daily Mirror's* wireless equipment shipped to the island. This consisted of 1½ kilowatts petrol motor generator and a standard 10-inch coil transmitter with a range of 75 miles. Furnished by the Marconi organisation already mentioned, and installed by the London building contractors, Messrs. Kilby & Gayford, it reached St. Kilda on July, 10th. Less than a fortnight later, Dudley Ward-Millar of British Telegraph Instruments, Ltd., tested the transmitter, and instructed the island's missionary how to operate it. Early in the morning of July, 29th, 1913, its first messages were sent to King George V, to the *Daily Mirror,* and to James Hogge, then Liberal member of Edinburgh, East. Hogge, an earnest social worker, had long shown an interest in the St. Kildans' welfare.

Now that wireless communication had been established, Hogge asked the Secretary for Scotland to see that from time to time reports on the islanders' condition were made. At the beginning of October the wireless station broke down, due to a lack of technical skill on the part of the missionary and of Neil Ferguson. The *Mirror* carried out some improvements on the installation when a professional

[1] *St. Kilda: Its Posts & Communications,* published in Edinburgh by the Scottish Postmark Group in 1963, and *The Scots Magazine,* October, 1964.

wireless engineer—a German named Gustaf Flick—went out to St. Kilda to repair it and to operate it. For several months during the winter of 1913–1914 the station, on a frequency of 600 metres, remained in contact with Malin Head radio, when telegrams were sent and received at ordinary inland rates. In April, 1914, the *Mirror* invited the G.P.O. to take over the plant. This it declined to do unless a guarantor could be found to meet for twenty-one years the difference between the annual cost of working and maintaining it and the revenue from telegrams transmitted by it. The cost of the former, according to the G.P.O., amounted to £400 a year, whereas receipts from the latter came to no more than a few pounds. As no such guarantor could be found, the station, early in 1914, was closed down and to some extent dismantled, placing the St. Kildans as formerly. However, the outbreak of war that autumn meant the re-establishing of wireless communication when the Admiralty invited the Marconi Company to re-open the station. This was done; and in January, 1915, the Admiralty sent aboard the armed trawler, *Amsterdam,* a naval detachment to man it. This consisted of Captain Frank Athow (on the retired list since the Boer War), 2 petty officers, 12 ratings, and a batman. This original detachment remained on the island for eight months without any compensation in the way of leave. Thereafter its members were changed round every six months. They settled in with the St. Kildans very agreeably. "As often happens where servicemen are stationed," wrote James Alexander MacKay, "romance blossomed. Mary MacDonald, one of the island's belles, fell in love with Malcolm MacLean, a sailor from Port Glasgow; and their marriage in 1918 was one of the great events on St. Kilda that year." After the war Malcolm remained behind to run a croft there, although scarcely under conditions as felicitous as the islanders had enjoyed throughout the immediately preceding years, when a naval establishment in their midst meant good food freely given them, and most of their male members received monetary payment for coast-watching, trench-digging, cable-laying, and the like. Never had money been as plentiful on St. Kilda. With the cessation of hostilities and the consequent withdrawal of the naval detachment, the natives reverted to that comparative want which so often had been relieved by public charity.

*   *   *

The nearest the St. Kildans got to the First World War was when

it came to *them*. Until the spring of 1918, those manning their
island's wireless station worked unceasingly, observing and reporting
the movements of German ships and submarines. The Germans, not
unjustifiably, took the view that it had better be put out of action.
About 10 o'clock on the misty morning of May, 18th, there appeared
off Village Bay a U-boat. From its conning-tower a figure urged
the inhabitants by loud-hailer to quit their village because the shelling
of the factor's house—the wireless station—was about to begin. Instantly obeying, men, women, and children sought shelter in a deep
gully behind the village. Davis, the signaller on duty in the attic,
where the transmitter was, barely had had time to flash the news that
a German submarine was in the bay when at 10.40 the shelling
commenced. Just as he was escaping by the back door, one of a total
of seventy-two shells fired from the submarine hit the factor's house,
demolishing the porch at the front of it. The shelling continued for
about fifty minutes. Thereafter the U-boat retired into the mists.
Although there were no casualties among the islanders, the shells
damaged slightly the church-cum-schoolhouse, a couple of cottages, a
few cleits, and the storehouse down by the pier, ripping off its roof.
Despite the factor's house having been rendered untenable and the
Mirror's radio equipment put out of commission, wireless contact by
means of the Admiralty set was re-established by 5 p.m., when a
number of patrol vessels was directed to the scene. The Admiralty
now proceeded to erect a gun to command the entrance to Village
Bay. This gun, its emplacement, and its magazine, when I examined
them in 1930, were much as they had been at the cessation of
hostilities a dozen years earlier, except for the gun's rust. Among
the most cherished of Neil Ferguson's possessions was the nosecap
of a German shell found on a hillside sometime after the
shelling. The resumption in 1919 of the summertime calls of the
two Glasgow vessels mentioned encouraged the more active St.
Kildans to search for fragments of those shells that had burst
on their island. These they profitably disposed of to that summer's
tourists.

In August, 1918, three months after the U-boat's visit, the wireless
was repaired as part of the necessary defence of St. Kilda. In
February of the following year, three months after the plausible
cessation of hostilities, the Admiralty dismantled and removed most
of it. The gun, mounted on a concrete platform and commanding
the entrance to Village Bay, was left behind, however; but not before

G

a naval detachment had rendered it useless by dumping in the sea its breech-block.

Thus ended St. Kilda's wireless link with the outer world, albeit a declining native population was to remain there for a further eleven years. In 1957, twenty-seven years after its departure, as we have seen, St. Kilda was re-occupied, to be extensively and expensively developed as a missile-tracking station in connection with the rocket-range simultaneously established on South Uist. This, of course, necessitated the re-introduction of wireless on a large and highly efficient scale. When the Marconi experts were installing the radar stations there that year, they discovered near the factor's ruinous house the remnant of a weather-board shack in which lay bits of an old rotary converter, fragments of the original wireless equipment of half a century earlier. The souvenir significance of these they were swift to appreciate.

Epilogue: Among so much about St. Kilda still pressing in upon me for inclusion in these pages, one comparatively recent incident, I feel, ought to be mentioned. If ever you should find yourself at the Lochmaddy hotel, in North Uist, you may see in its Visitors' Book three significant entries:

14. 7. 53.   Neil Ferguson.   3, West Street, Glasgow, C. 5.
17. 7. 53.   D. G. Ferguson.   Free Church, Easdale, Argyll.
17. 7. 53.   A. G. Ferguson.   St. Kilda, Old Kilpatrick.

These three Fergusons (Neil, Donald, and Alick) are the kindred of Neil Ferguson so often referred to in these pages. In July, 1953, nine years after Neil's death, they arranged to meet at Lochmaddy in order to sail from there to St. Kilda aboard a motor-boat owned locally. They took with them a stone to mark the grave of my old friend, their kinsman. Immediately after erecting it, they set off on their long return voyage. A violent gale sprang up, however; and engine trouble added to their peril. They hoisted as much sail as appeared safe in the circumstances; but the gale ripped it and bore it away. By some miracle they reached Lochmaddy, long overdue and worn out.

CHAPTER NINE

Rockall

++

SITUATED IN the North Atlantic, precisely in latitude 57° 36′ 41″ North, and in longtitude 13° 41′ 25″ West, according to fairly recent Royal Navy and Royal Air Force reckonings, is a lone, barren, conical rock 70 feet in height, its summit conspicuously snow-white with guano. Calculations based on R.A.F. photographs taken between 1941 and 1945 give a maximum breadth of 83 feet, and a circumference at its base of 250. For centuries, this fragment of the ancient world, lying 224 miles west of the Outer Hebrides, and therefore 293 from the Scottish mainland, has been known to mariners as Roc(h)ol, or Rockall, or Rokabarra, or variants of these names. It is the highest point of what deep-sea fishermen, operating regularly in its vicinity for cod, haddock, hake, and halibut, have long referred to as the Rockall Banks, the name now applied universally to the submarine plateau from which it emerges, and which runs in a north-south direction for 150 miles.

Although Rockall lies so much closer to Britain than to any other land, it belongs physiographically, just as does Iceland, to the American continent rather than to the European. The ocean depths between Rockall and Iceland are comparatively shallow: none exceeds 600 fathom. Soundings between Britain and Rockall, on the other hand, give oceanic depths up to 1600 fathom. One appreciates the significance of this when recalling that, with the sole exception of the Faeroes, not one of the islands or groups of islands surrounding Britain—not even St. Kilda, the nearest land to Rockall—lies where the intervening ocean reaches a depth of 100 fathom. It was the knowledge of this that, as long ago as 1898, led Miller Christy to his conclusion that Rockall forms the easternmost outlier of North America, rather than the westernmost outlier of Europe, despite a location so very much closer to the latter.[1]

In 1945 this great depth between Britain and Rockall was given

[1] *The Scottish Geographical Magazine*, August, 1898.

official recognition when a hundred U-boats were towed out to it by naval tugs from 'the trots' at Loch Ryan and at Lissahally, near Londonderry, to be sent to the bottom, in a thousand fathom of ocean. The first batch was sunk off Rockall during weather so stormy that they could not be disposed of by explosive charges placed in the hull of each, as had been planned. They therefore had to be blown up by gun-fire from the destroyers accompanying them. All these submarines were of a brand-new type. According to our newspapers (never slow in 'featuring' such incidents, so long as their true implications haven't to be stated), German crews assisted in sending these submarines to the bottom. What a colossal waste of metal, if nothing else! Why collect for salvage hereafter the trifling metal caps from one's milk-bottles in face of the tens of thousands of tons of valuable metal deliberately placed thus beyond reach?

Although this solitary speck of the world is outwith the limits of most charts and sailing directions, its existence cannot be overlooked because of its lying directly in the track of so many ships traversing regularly the seas between North America and the north of Scotland and Northern Europe. During the Second World War its position was of considerable significance in so far as it lay close to the path of our Northern Naval Convoys and of the patrolling aircraft of Coastal Command. Its location was fixed as long ago as 1831 by Rear-Admiral T. E. Vidal, then captain of a naval vessel employed in charting in our northern latitudes oceanic fragments such as Rockall. When, a century and a quarter later, naval surveyors and oceanographers, with aviation and all manner of modern scientific equipment at their disposal, again announced its geographical position, one recalled with profound admiration the precision with which Vidal and his companions already had done so *without* those astonishing scientific aids employed nowadays as a matter of course.

The submarine plateau, of the existence of which Rockall is by far the most conspicuous piece of evidence above sea-level, is composed chiefly of a coarse, dark-coloured granite. That Rockall itself is almost entirely aegirine-granite has been confirmed by an examination of the rock specimens weighing in all about 20 lbs., chipped mostly off its top ledge by those members of the annexation expedition who were landed on it by helicopter on September, 18th, 1955. Only one very small piece appears to be of that dark variety to which the appropriate name of rockallite has been given. These specimens (to be mentioned later) may be seen at the Geological Museum, South Kensington, along with a number of earlier specimens such as those small chips collected by Moussard and Le François in 1921, and described so authoritatively by A. Lacroix.[1]

Despite Rockall's remoteness and the fact that a landing, other than by helicopter, is feasible only on two or three days in a year, references to its geology, particularly to its rockallite, are surprisingly numerous. At least four of Rockall's aegirine-granite specimens at South Kensington were collected by the party landed there by helicopter from H.M.S. *Vidal* in September, 1955, when this merest fragment of *terra firma* was officially annexed in the manner related toward the end of this chapter.

* * *

No less surprisingly numerous are the literary references to Rockall. They are to be found, often quite unexpectedly, in all sorts of publications—in books of travel, in seafaring narratives, in nautical journals, in the publications of learnèd societies, in geographical and geological proceedings, and in magazine and newspaper articles.

Probably the first knowledge we have of this oceanic speck is that contained in Martin Martin's *A Late Voyage to St. Kilda* (1698), wherein we read of "Rokol, a small rock, sixty leagues to the westward of St. Kilda," which the inhabitants of that island referred to as Rokabarra. This name the St. Kildans acquired from a company of French and Spanish survivors of a vessel wrecked on Rockall in 1686. Eventually reaching St. Kilda, they showed its inhabitants on a map which they had with them the position of Rokol. By pointing downwards with the forefinger, they indicated exactly where their ship had foundered.

The next reference to Rockall in point of time, so far as I have been in a position to ascertain, is that made by Captain Coates in *The Geography of Hudson Bay*. Coates made several voyages between this country and Hudson Bay between 1727 and 1751. "Rokele is a pyramid not unlike the stack," he writes, "but higher and bigger, and white from the same cause; and I had no ground at eighty fathom on the N.W. side, at the distance of a mile and a half, and I made E. 10° N. erly from this rock to Hoy heade."[2]

One of the earliest, and certainly one of the most important, visits to Rockall was that made in 1810 by Captain Basil Hall, R.N., F.R.S.

---

[1] *Comptes Rendus de l'Academie des Sciences*, 1921, vol. clxxiii.
[2] *Hakluyt Society, Vol. MDCCLII*, Edited by John Barrow.

The circumstances of this visit are set down fully in Captain Hall's own account, published originally between 1831 and 1834 in three series, each in three small volumes.[1] On the title-page of volume iii of the second edition, published in Edinburgh by Robert Cadell in 1831, there appears a vignette representing a dark, steep-sided mass of rock with a white, conical apex. This vignette was one of the very earliest attempts to portray Rockall. Probably the first view ever published, however, was that which appeared in Purdy's *Memoir of a Chart of the Atlantic* (1812).

Basil Hall's account, discursive and entertaining, explains the circumstance of his first acquaintance with the rock—with this "mere speck on the surface of the waters," as he describes it. Hall was lieutenant in H.M.S. *Endymion* between 1809 and 1812. This frigate at the time was under the command of the Hon. Thomas Bladen Capel. One day, while cruising in the North Atlantic, the *Endymion* chased what was thought to have been an enemy brig with very white sails aloft, and dark lower sails. On running close, however, the brig turned out to be Rockall, a lone block of granite which sailors at sea had ofttimes mistaken for a ship under sail. Officers and men of the *Endymion* already had been deceived by Rockall several times during that same cruise, even after they believed themselves thoroughly familiar with its aspect and location. Captain Hall informs us that he actually boarded three vessels in one day, each of which had included Rockall when reckoning the number of vessels it had sighted. Not until he directed their glasses to the spot did they realise their mistake.

The projecting rock itself, according to Captain Hall, is only seventy feet high, and not more than a hundred yards in circumference. He found it to consist of granite, topped by a snow-white coating and frequented by a myriad seabirds. Its distance he estimated at 184 miles very nearly due west of St. Kilda, the remotest of the Hebrides, at 290 miles from the nearest point of the Scottish mainland, and at 260 from the north of Ireland. Furthermore, he calculated it to be at a distance from the mainland greater than that of any other island, islet, or rock of the same diminutive size, to be found anywhere in the world.

Not until the *Endymion's* visit in 1810 was the position of Rockall accurately determined; and no doubt this visit was the occasion upon which Captain Hall came into possession of that piece of the rock

[1] *Fragments of Voyage & Travels, Vol. iii*, by Captain Basil Hall, R.N.

ever since labelled "Rockall, Capt. Basil Hall". The rock itself was visited from the *Endymion* by a party in two boats, while the frigate stood down to leeward. The party carried geological hammers, chronometers, sketch-books, and the like. Some members of it chipped off specimens of the rock: some circumnavigated the rock in one or other of the boats, in order to sound where the bottom could be found: some sought, by means of a cord, to measure the rock's circumference. The party worked assiduously, realising both the peril and the importance of its undertaking.

After it had been on the rock for some time, and had made several useful observations, a haze, and then a dense fog, descended. An increase in the swell, moreover, showed that the problem of re-embarking was likely to be as hazardous as the problem of landing had seemed simple earlier that day. With some difficulty the entire party succeeded in getting off; but, to its dire vexation, no one could locate the *Endymion*! Confusion now ensued as to where the frigate lay. No two members were in agreement as to the last direction in which she had been sighted. She evidently had drifted away to a considerable extent. The thickening of the fog now rendered her absolutely invisible. Eventually, it was decided to put ashore on Rockall again the nimblest of the party in the hope that, from the rock's highest point, he might have been able to locate the ship. But this outlook man could see nothing except the approach of a thicker bank of fog. The obvious thing to do in the circumstances was to cruise in the vicinity of the rock, and not allow the boats to drift away from the only point that remained fixed in this welter of sea, since it was reasonable to suppose that, sooner or later, the *Endymion* would find the rock again. Indeed, Rockall was the only landmark she had any chance of picking up!

"I see the ship!" shrieked the outlook man some hours later, as he sat perched on the peak of Rockall. A temporary lane in the fog had revealed her afar off, crowding all sail and beating to windward. Without delay the outlook man, numb with cold and exhausted by his long and trying vigil, was brought off the rock. The occupants of both boats now rowed vigorously in the direction in which the ship lay. Barely a quarter of a mile had they proceeded when the fog, closing in behind them, obscured Rockall. To begin with, this seemed to matter little, since the *Endymion* still was in view; but, when she tacked a little later and was again lost in fog, it was patent that those aboard her had sighted neither the rock nor the boats, and were still searching the seas. Neither Rockall nor ship was now to be seen. In this predicament it was decided to turn round, and attempt to locate Rockall once more. By a stroke of good fortune, the boats ultimately succeeded in finding it. The sun had gone down by this time. Visions of having to remain all night, either on the rock or in the open boats, were looming ominously when, as if by a miracle, the fog lifted and the vessel came in view once more. Almost simultaneously, those aboard her sighted the rock; and the vessel immediately came about. It was almost dark by the time she had picked up her boats and rescued their benumbed occupants.

"Why did you fire no guns to give us notice of your position?" was the first question put to the men on the *Endymion* by their overjoyed companions.

"Fire guns?" they answered. "We have done nothing but blaze away every ten minutes for these last five or six hours!"

Not a single discharge was heard by the occupants of the boats—so readily does dense fog absorb sound.

*   *   *

In 1819, Dr. John MacCulloch, the tiresome 'Stone Doctor', made a passing reference to Rockall. "St. Kilda," he wrote, "solitary in structure (trappean) as it is in position, since the nearest rocks on the east side consist of gneiss, and the first we meet with on the west, Rockall, is formed of granite."[1]

Rockall's appearance of a ship under sail was also noted by Surgeon Alexander Fisher, R.N., in May, 1819. Fisher believed the rock to be the summit of a very extensive submarine mountain.[2] At a range of four or five leagues, he was deceived into thinking it was a sailing-ship. When in this locality, Fisher and his companions spent some time in searching unsuccessfully for the Sunken Land of Busse. They attempted to sound at one particular spot under which they imagined this Lost Land lay; but, even with 1220 fathom of line out, they could find no bottom. They concluded, therefore, that they had mistaken the longitude of the place at which an earlier oceanographer had sounded at a fourth of that depth what was thought to have been this Sunken Land.

A later reference to the Sunken Land of Busse is made by the

---

[1] *A Description of the Western Isles of Scotland, 3 vols., 1819.*
[2] *Journal of the Voyage of Discovery to the Arctic Regions in His Majesty's Ships 'Hecla' & 'Griper', 1819–1820.*

marine biologist, Dr. G. C. Wallich (1815–1899), who mapped out Rockall as rising from the Rockall Shoal 315 miles west of the Hebrides, and who elaborates on the relation of this Shoal to the sunken area shown with great precision in many old charts, and including the Sunken Land of Busse. Wallich, too, mentions that, in similarity with another North Atlantic rock, Rockall, when viewed from certain points of the compass, resembles a ship under sail.[1]

* * *

In 1831 the vicinity of Rockall was visited by Captain Vidal, R.N., in H.M.S. *Pike*. On Vidal's Chart the rock is shown to consist of coarse granite. Compass variations noted very near to it during this visit induced the supposition that it was highly magnetic. If this were true, it must have arisen from the subterranean mass, and not from Rockall itself, since magnetic basalt, the chief cause of local attraction, does not exist on Rockall, so far as is known at present.

Rockall was visited again in 1862. In the summer and autumn of that year, H.M.S. *Porcupine,* with R. Hoskyns as master and surveyor, carried out a series of deep-sea soundings and pertinent scientific investigations in its neighbourhood. The rock itself was first observed at noon on August, 14th. Several fishing-smacks were operating off it at the time; but, as heavy seas were breaking, rendering it perilous to approach within measurable distance of the rock, the *Porcupine* was obliged to heave-to for the night. Observation was considerably better the following day; and, as the swell was less dangerous, an attempt was made to land a party. The only member of the party to obtain a footing was Mr. Johns, the boatswain. But he succeeded at a point from which the summit was inaccessible. With the sounding-lead thrown to him, Johns broke off four or five geological specimens. These he wrapped in his neckerchief, and threw into the boat.

By the middle of the nineteenth century the position of Rockall was familiar to many mariners. Gradually it found a place in European cartography and oceanography, although a number of early 17th-century charts of the North Atlantic already had denoted it. On Gulielmus Jansonius's map of 1606, for example, it appears as Rocol. On a chart of the Atlantic drawn up on parchment in 1618 by Domingo Sanches, and now preserved in the *Bibliothèque Nationale*

[1] *The North Atlantic Sea-bed, comprising a Diary of the Voyage on board H.M.S. Bulldog in 1860.*

in Paris, it appears as Rochol. On Janson's *Atlas* (Amsterdam, 1650) it is entered as Rocol.

For all that, shipwrecks still occurred upon this lone outpost, or upon those off-lying perils, Hazelwood Rock and Helen's Reef. How many vessels may have gone to their doom between the time of that mentioned by Martin as having been wrecked there in 1686 and the early years of the nineteenth century, we have no means of ascertaining. We do know, however, that on April, 19th, 1824, the Dundee brigantine, *Helen*, bound for Quebec and Montreal with a general cargo, was lost by striking a sunken reef about six miles east-north-east of Rockall, showing that this area of the ocean is far from being free of danger to navigation. The vessel sprang a serious leak in consequence. After thirteen hours' incessant pumping, she sank in deep water.

Then, about Christmas-time, 1839, a Hull vessel, *Charlotte*, captained by one, John Bremman, was wrecked on Rockall. Here was another occasion on which the St. Kildans received a contingent of shipwrecked mariners. Eighteen survivors of the crew took to a boat and found their way to a cave in the west bay of St. Kilda. There they remained for two days and two nights at the base of cliffs they could not scale. Their plight was discovered by a herd laddie who, from the edge of the cliffs above the cave, chanced to observe the boat in which they had arrived. With the aid of the St. Kildans' fowling ropes, the survivors, one by one, were rescued. They were conducted to the village, where they received hospitable treatment. For eleven days the inhabitants housed, clothed, and fed them. Thereafter one of the St. Kildans accompanied them in their boat to Pabbay, in the Sound of Harris, and thence to Portree, in Skye. At Portree they bequeathed their boat to the St. Kildan, who immediately sold it locally for nine pounds, and returned home to St. Kilda in another. Though the captain of the *Charlotte* had promised to see that the St. Kildans were suitably rewarded for their prolonged hospitality to him and his crew, it is said that they never received a farthing. Perhaps the owners of the vessel considered that the boat given to the St. Kildan was sufficient recompense.

Less fortunate than the *Charlotte's* survivors were the passengers aboard the S.S. *Norge*, of Copenhagen, when she ran into Rockall on June, 28th, 1904, and perished with six hundred lives. In the old burying-place down by the sea at Sandwick, near Stornoway, and within a few yards of my own Hebridean kinsfolks' burial-ground, may be seen a granite stone erected to the memory of ten survivors from the *Norge*. Most of these were children. They were landed at Stornoway on July, 4th. But, owing to the exposure they had endured, they succumbed later in the Lewis Hospital.

Several other references to Rockall are to be found in 19th-century annals; but these are mostly from hearsay and guesswork. In any case, they are of minor importance in comparison with that which resulted from a scientific expedition's attempts to land on the rock in 1896. However, it should be mentioned that, in or before 1888, the skipper of a Grimsby smack succeeded in landing on Rockall, and, having climbed its steep face with a line, estimated its height at 78 feet. The top, he noted, forms a ridge running from east to west. The west side is almost perpendicular, whereas the east side slopes less abruptly to the sea. Fleetwood and Grimsby trawlermen frequently visit the Rockall Bank; and in the Natural History section of the British Museum may be seen a collection of marine organisms attached to the loose stones and pebbles obtained near Rockall by these Grimsby fishermen.

* * *

In the course of the winter of 1895, some correspondence passed between the ornithologists, Richard M. Barrington and J. A. Harvie-Brown, with reference to the importance of planning an expedition to Rockall. Suggestions were made regarding Rockall's being a possible site for a meteorological station: its situation seemed admirably suited to such a purpose. It was agreed, therefore, that some actual knowledge of the structure and configuration of this rock was primarily necessary. The bird-life also attracted those contemplating an expedition; and it was thought that a visit to Rockall might solve the mystery then surrounding the life of the great shearwater, whose nesting-place had never been discovered. Ornithological, geological, meteorological, and other considerations prompted those interested to approach the Royal Irish Academy, an institution that warmly supported the idea, and made a generous grant in aid of it. This grant covered roughly half the expenses of the expedition. The deficiency was met by J. A. Harvie-Brown and Richard Barrington.

Plans for reaching Rockall developed apace. Due account was taken of the fact that the objective lay some 240 miles away from the Irish coast, in the bosom of the North Atlantic, and that the undertaking therefore involved some hazard, and would be anything but a pleasure cruise. The Congested Districts Board's S.S. *Granuaile*, gross tonnage 380, and in charge of a certain Captain Quirke, was chartered to the Royal Irish Academy with the consent of the owners, and on terms as generous as were consistent with the financial responsibilities placed upon the Board in the administration of its duties. This vessel had been designed mainly for carrying cargo in connection with the Board's activities on the west of Ireland. She had some limited passenger accommodation. Since the members interested in ornithology had thought June a better month for their purpose than May, on June, 3rd, 1896, the party assembled aboard the *Granuaile* in the tiny harbour of Killybegs. The anchor was hove-to about midnight; and the vessel duly put out to sea with a favourable wind from the eastward.

The ornithological aspect of the expedition was entrusted to J. A. Harvie-Brown and Richard Barrington, already mentioned. The latter also rendered a conspicuous service during the voyage by taking samples of sea water, with temperatures. Messrs. Robert Lloyd Praeger, Vismes Kane, and Jamieson attended to the examination of matters biological and geological, and bore away many specimens.[1] A certain Charles Green acted as official photographer. He photographed Rockall from several angles and under several aspects. Captain, mate, and crew also threw themselves with zest into the work, and did much to ensure the success it achieved. The expedition's equipment consisted in the main of two beam trawls, several dredges, one Agassiz deep-sea trawl, several hundred fathom of wire rope, a steel wire sound machine, a rope ladder, boxes and jars for specimens, photographic paraphernalia, sufficient coal in the bunkers to enable the vessel to return to Killybegs, and a harpoon gun with a special projectile resembling a small grapnel, and with 40 fathom of 1½-inch rope for the purposes of establishing contact with the rock, and of assisting in scaling it, once a landing had been accomplished.

At 6.30 a.m. on Friday, June, 5th, the expedition sounded and, finding bottom at 130 fathom, realised that, wherever the vessel was, she had certainly reached the Rockall Bank, and had crossed the tremendous abyss of ocean dividing Rockall from the European plateau. The sea at the time was running high. Driving rain from a north-easterly airt spoilt any chances of distant visibility. An hour later the crew sounded in 80 fathom. This raised hopes of Rockall's

[1] In *The Way that I Went*, published by Methuen in 1937, Praeger gives his own account of this splendid endeavour.

proximity, though it still remained invisible. A further sounding of 100 fathom at 8 a.m. justified the conclusion that the vessel had passed her objective. As the day remained overcast, the sextants were of no avail. The hope that a glimpse of sun might have enabled the expedition to fix its position accurately faded with the passing of noon. After consultation, it was agreed that there was no alternative but to lie-to until conditions improved. The vessel's head, therefore, was brought round to the north; and she now moved ahead slowly, pitching and rolling heavily, and meeting wild seas on her starboard bow.

To locate the loneliest speck of rock in the world under such circumstances seemed impossible. Spasmodic soundings during the early afternoon revealed depths ranging from 120 to 140 fathom. On finding a bottom of fine sand about 3 p.m., it was decided to try a scrape of the trawl. But, unfortunately, as the trawl was being shot, the sea's wash brought it into contact with the propeller, which tore it so badly as to render it useless. Three hours later, members of the party sighted a ketch-rigged fishing-smack, head-reaching under close-reefed canvas. The *Granuaile,* steaming up as close to the smack as was consistent with safety, discovered that it hailed from the Shetlands. To the question as to the direction in which Rockall lay came the answer, "Sou'west". Noisy seas prevented those aboard the *Granuaile* from hearing the distance which the expedition had to proceed to reach its objective. However, the ship's head was put about to run before wind and tide in a south-westerly direction for roughly twelve miles, during which distance the appearance of several great shearwaters whetted the expectations of the ornithologists aboard. Toward close of day they sounded in fifteen fathom; and, since impending dark made it perilous to approach any closer, either to Rockall itself, or to off-lying Helen's Reef, the anchor was dropped with fifteen fathom of chain, so as to serve as a drag. The vessel drifted to leeward during the night; and at dawn on the following day the captain sighted Rockall in a direction south-by-east. At first sight, any hope of being able to effect a landing seemed utterly impossible. To the observers at 3.30 a.m. on this June morning, the rock of their quest resembled a haycock, infinitesimally small in a welter of turbulent sea.

Some idea of the impression this discovery made upon the expedition may be had from the narrative of the cruise supplied by the Rev. W. Spotswood Green, F.R.G.S. "Girt in seething foam," he wrote, "the great swells, as they struck it, sent up single jets of spray, sometimes higher than its summit, and, as they met around its lee and dashed together, completely enclosed it in their embrace. I quickly summoned all the party on deck, and having made a preliminary survey of the main rock and the Hazelwood rock close by, over which the seas broke heavily, we looked out for Helen's Reef. The waves everywhere were crested with foam, which rendered our search somewhat difficult, but, when we saw a huge roller break, we were satisfied that we had at last located it definitely. The engines were once more stopped, it being desirable to save coal as much as possible, and we drifted to leeward in the trough of the sea, hoping that, sooner or later, the storm would abate. After breakfast the sun came out, giving us a good chance for photography, so we steamed up again, and took a series of photographs and sketches from various points of view. Some of us closely examined the structure of the rock, while others observed the various species of birds perched on it, or swimming on the water close by. The tangle, possibly a Laminarian, which hung like drapery in the foam, with a fringe of green alga above, were objects of interest, but it seemed certain that no land-plant could exist on Rockall."[1]

The *Granuaile* was allowed to drift away for about a mile, and a sounding was taken in 60 fathom. Although high seas were still running, it was decided to attempt to scrape the bottom with a large dredge, to which tangles were attached. Unfortunately, the dredge was lost; but some fragments of coral and the like were brought up by the tangles. On the chance of being favoured with better weather, the remainder of that day was occupied in steaming slowly to windward, and drifting back to leeward, never losing sight of the rock. Lying-to in a westerly direction were four ketch-rigged fishing-smacks.

At sunrise on June, 7th, the seas were still breaking heavily around the rock. A conference was summoned, at which it was agreed to abandon any idea of effecting a landing. Determined not to allow the expedition to return to Ireland without something to show for its exertions, the chart was now consulted with a view to locating a possible dredging-ground. When seventeen miles had been covered in a direction east-by-south, they sounded in 130 fathom, and shot the Agassiz trawl. But the nature of the ground gave some cause for alarm. The trawl, therefore, was promptly hauled aboard

[1] *Transactions of the Royal Irish Academy, Vol. XXXI.*

again. It was found that coral, fragments of which were still clinging to the meshes, had torn the net badly. Apart from these pieces of coral, this brief attempt brought up nothing but a few star-fish.

* * *

It was the intention of the expedition to have paid a visit to St. Kilda on the homeward voyage. But, when the engineer intimated that the bunkers now contained just enough fuel to enable the *Granuaile* to reach Killybegs, every effort was made to save distance. Therefore, at 10 a.m. a course was set for the coast of Donegal; and on the evening of the succeeding day—June, 8th—the vessel arrived at Killybegs. There the members of the expedition broke up; and most of them returned to Dublin—but with the understanding that, if weather conditions improved, they should embark on another attempt on Saturday, June, 13th. Arrangements were made in the meantime for the further services of the *Granuaile*. Moreover, communications were established by wire both with Tory Island, and, through the Meteorological Office, with the station on Sumburgh Head, in the Shetlands, so that regular weather forecasts might be obtained. On Friday, 12th, weather reports from distant stations seemed propitious; and on the Saturday evening the same enthusiasts found themselves at Killybegs aboard the *Granuaile*. The anchor was weighed at 11.30 p.m., and the vessel again steamed out toward Rockall. Most of the following day, which opened with promise of auspicious conditions, was devoted to the arranging of gear. Toward the late afternoon an ominous swell from the west began to make itself felt.

It was not until 4.30 a.m. on the following day (June, 15th) that Rockall was once more sighted. A strong wind was blowing at the time from a south-westerly direction; and the atmosphere was dark with mist and rain. A couple of hours later, though the seas were breaking furiously against the rock, it was possible to select the spot at which a landing might have been made from a small boat, had the seas been less boisterous. But even this remote possibility had to be abandoned when, a little later, the wind, in shifting to the westward, strengthened considerably. To attempt a landing now was out of the question; and once more the expedition was forced to content itself with circumnavigating the rock at a distance from it ensuring the vessel's safety in such conditions. From all points of the compass the rock was photographed and sketched. Another endeavour was made to dredge some biological and geological specimens from the bottom. This resulted in the loss of another dredge. The vessel then steamed some fifteen miles due south; and a sounding was taken in a hundred fathom. As the bottom here proved to be of fine sand, the Agassiz trawl was shot. Only a brief scrape was made, however, because of the danger of again losing or damaging the nets. When the trawl was brought up, it was found that the bag contained a great assortment of shallow-water shells which gave the appearance of having been dead for a very long time. Their discovery lent strong justification for the theory that, at a time not very distant, geologically speaking, the portion of the ocean now dominated by Rockall must have exhibited more land than to-day is represented merely by the rock and one or two outlying reefs, that this land must have been fringed by a coast-line less deep and less precipitous than it now is, and that, in all probability, Rockall itself is a speck in the centre of extensive sand-banks—"the only speck acting as a memorial stone to what tradition has called the Sunken Land of Busse."[1]

However, the argument was advanced that the molluscs, the shells of which were dredged from the bottom, might have been carried to this area as bait by line-fishermen operating at the Rockall Bank, a fishing-ground so wellknown to the fishermen of many nations. But the mixed character of the shells did much to discredit that argument. Some consideration was also given to the theory that possibly these shells had been carried thither by icebergs that had grounded in bays in the Arctic regions. But it seemed improbable that the area of Rockall had been visited by bergs at a period sufficiently recent to have explained the presence on the ocean's floor of these shells.

Another short scrape with the trawl was made in 110 fathom. This time several species of sponges, corals, echinoderms, and shells were retrieved from the bottom of the ocean. Among the shells were found some living specimens of *scaphander lignarius*.

As the *Granuaile* again steamed round Rockall, Harvie-Brown shot a couple of shearwaters and a tern, and Barrington a kittiwake of immature plumage. With some difficulty, and in considerable peril, the dinghy was lowered in order that these birds might be retrieved. Only one shearwater and the kittiwake were recovered. So high was the swell at the time that those in the dinghy were unable to see even the tops of the *Granuaile's* masts.

Night was now falling; and it was hoped that before morning the

[1] *Transactions of the Royal Irish Academy, Vol. XXXI.*

wind would have abated somewhat. But dawn on the 16th revealed
a sea more turbulent than ever. Once more the dinghy was lowered
in an endeavour to obtain a specimen of the tangle off the rock; but
the sea was so disturbed, and the danger of being sucked in toward
the corners of the rock so great, that it was found impossible to
approach within twenty yards.

No sooner had the dinghy been hoisted aboard than again it was
decided to bid farewell to Rockall. By breakfast-time the *Granuaile's*
head was turned to S.E. by E.; and she steered for St. Kilda. In the
small hours of June, 17th, approximately twenty hours later, the
anchor was dropped in Village Bay. Members of the expedition went
ashore for an hour or two; but, as it rained heavily, and the wind
took a turn for the worse, it was decided to return to Ireland with as
little delay as possible. At sundown the wind became so trying that
the vessel was forced to shelter for the night under Berneray (Barra
Head), the most southerly of the Outer Hebrides. At daybreak on the
morrow she steamed southward. That evening she berthed safely at
the quay in Londonderry.

*   *   *

So far as I have been able to ascertain, no qualified British geologist
has landed on Rockall, although the first three specimens obtained at
various times from this weird and fascinating mass of rock have been
subjected to a good deal of study and scientific speculation. All appear
to have been broken off by sailors, and brought home by the officers
of surveying ships. The first specimen, known as the "Basil Hall
Specimen," and already alluded to, is but a fragment, and appears
to be a portion of that collected by Captain Basil Hall in 1810. The
second specimen is labelled the "Hoskyns Specimen". It received its
name from Commander R. Hoskyns, R.N., of H.M.S. *Porcupine*,
who visited Rockall in 1862. So high were the seas at this time that,
as already related, only Johns, the boatswain, was able to land. This
specimen is one of the few fragments that the boatswain knocked
off the rock during the brief and perilous time he spent on it. It is
now among the geological exhibits at Queen's College, Galway. The
"Inskip Specimen" is the name given to the third. Captain Inskip
was a lieutenant on the *Porcupine* when she visited Rockall. For
many years this fragment of the ancient world was mislaid. In any
case, it could not be located toward the close of the nineteenth century.
For all I know, it may have been traced by this time.

Notes of a highly scientific character regarding these rock specimens, as also regarding the geological and biological specimens
dredged from the bottom of the ocean around Rockall, may be referred to in the *Transactions of the Royal Irish Academy* by those
interested in scientific detail. Information regarding the specimens
collected during the first cruise of the *Porcupine* in 1862 is also
available.[1]

In June, 1896, Harvie-Brown and Richard Barrington estimated
the bird population of Rockall itself at roughly 250 guillemots, 50
kittiwakes, 30 puffins, 10 gannets, eight of which were immature,
and one or two razor-bills. Of the nineteen specimens observed, all
were marine with the exception of a solitary dunlin, which was
sighted about a quarter of a mile from the rock, and was believed to
have been a stray bird from the Long Island, where its tribe is found
in considerable numbers. At this time it was thought that the
guillemot was the only bird to nest on Rockall. But for ornithological
details, as well as for particulars obtained by the expedition of 1896
concerning *mollusca, crustacea, chaetopoda, echinodermata, polyzoa,
hydrozoa, actinozoa, spongida,* and the rest, I again refer you to the
Transactions.

*   *   *

In the small hours of a summer's night in 1921, while holidaying
with kinsfolk on the fringe of Stornoway Bay, I awoke, without any
apparent reason, to observe in the wardrobe mirror, near the foot of
my bed, the reflected navigation lights of a vessel creeping stealthily
into our harbour. It was a night of stars and of great stillness. I
watched these lights as they moved across the mirror to come to rest
in a corner of it, as it were. Soon I heard the plop of anchor and
the rattle of anchor-chain. Morning revealed the presence of a three-
masted schooner at anchor in our spacious bay, a mile or so offshore.
In no time I was afloat in my own lugsail, resolved to examine this
strange visitor at close quarters. I found her to be Dr. Jean Charcot's
expeditionary ship, *Pourquoi-Pas?.* Charcot and some of his crew
were leaning lazily over the ship's side as I hove-to and, in such
French as I could muster, sought to engage them in conversation.
Charcot was not long in inviting me aboard his famous ship, and in
telling me that some ten days earlier, and on two different occasions,
he had succeeded in landing a member of his crew on Rockall, and

[1] *Proceedings of the Royal Society of London, Vol. XVIII.*

had obtained thereon several geological and ornithological specimens.
For a number of years *Pourquoi-Pas?*, on her voyage between St.
Malo (where she was built) and the Arctic, used to anchor for several
days each summer in Stornoway harbour. Charcot was a familiar
figure in Stornoway, where he had many friends. Though his vessel
had a powerful auxiliary motor, she always carried her yards. Astern
and at the yardarm she flew the Tricolor. The inhabitants of St.
Malo held her in special esteem; and great numbers of them always
assembled on the quay to witness her departure each summer on her
three months' exploration in distant and perilous waters. She was to
St. Malo what the *Victory* is to Portsmouth.

Although every schoolboy, in scanning the map of north-western
Europe in his atlas, must have noticed that tiny speck in the North
Atlantic, against which the name, Rockall, occurs in quite small
print, my real interest in this, the most isolated, fragment of Britain
dates from this visit of mine to Charcot and his *Pourquoi-Pas?* I
was reminded of it in the autumn of 1936, when this noted French
explorer and all his companions, save one, were lost with their vessel
off the west coast of Iceland.

"*Men Caor!*" (Rock of the Devil) Charcot's Breton seamen
muttered when, on the horizon, they first observed Rockall, for all
the world like a derelict ship at the mercy of the swell. "This double-
pointed helmet," wrote Charcot, "65 feet high, was probably the
summit of a mountain several thousand feet high. Its dazzling crown
of eternal snow has been replaced by a covering of guano."[1] By means
of a tow-net of the Bale & Forbes type, Charcot's men raised from
the ocean's floor large fragments of rock, some of them hundreds of
pounds in weight—a feat that, in the estimation of M. Lemoine of the
Académie des Sciences, opened up a new field for that great science,
submarine geology.

On June, 29th, 1921, the adventurous ex-circus clown, Moussard,
remained alone on Rockall for half an hour. The landing on
July, 1st, was made by Pierre Le Conte and by a member of the
crew named Bonnichon. Acting under the direction of M. Hamel,
the expedition's naturalist, they made a series of detailed observations
as to the portions of the rock occupied by the different species of
bird.

[1] An excellent account of Dr. Charcot's life, written by Marthe Oulié,
and entitled *Charcot of the Antarctic,* was published by John Murray in
1938.

In answer to a letter from the late Sir Hugh Gladstone, the ornithologist, who enquired whether he had made any notes on the birds seen on Rockall, Charcot replied from Neuilly-sur-Seine in December of the same year that his landing was specially for geological purposes and for oceanographical observations in the neighbourhood. "Nevertheless," he added, "we took interest in all the details concerning this curious rock. My love for animals is such that I never let one be killed or even bothered, when it is not absolutely necessary either for science or for living. We have in our collections samples of all the birds that we saw on Rockall, so we let them to their business, and very thankful they became very friendly."[1]

From a communication on the birds of Rockall made by James Fisher in 1941, at the 404th meeting of the British Ornithologists' Club, we learn that Le Conte, responding to "indications" given him by M. Hamel, set down a series of details and observations on the "emplacements" occupied by the different species of bird, which lived by "milliers" on the Rock, and belonged to the following five species:–

(1) *la mouette tridactyle* (kittiwake)
(2) *le puffin majeur ou à face blanche* (great shearwater)
(3) *le macareux moine* (puffin)
(4) *le fou de Bassan* (gannet)
(5) *le guillemot à capuchin* (guillemot)

Charcot wrote Gladstone that there were *"quelques sula bassana sur le sommet"*, and that kittiwakes, guillemots, and puffins were also present. He does not mention the great shearwater as having been on the Rock, though it occurs in Le Conte's list. "Of course, the Great Shearwater," says Fisher, "did not occupy any *emplacement* on Rockall, and never has done so, to the best of any reliable person's knowledge."[2]

* * *

While travelling between King's Cross and Edinburgh a few years ago, I happened to fall into conversation with a passenger who mentioned that in 1917, during the First World War, the men of the British destroyer, *Nepean,* mistook Rockall for an enemy vessel, just as the men of the *Endymion* had done more than a hundred years

---

[1] *British Birds,* January, 1937 (Messrs. Witherby).
[2] A summary of Dr. James Fisher's paper will be found in the *Bulletin* of the British Ornithologists' Club, No. CCCCXXXIX, 1941. (Vol. LXII).

earlier. For particulars of this incident I immediately wrote to Commander Malcolm Farquhar of H.M.S. *Courageous,* who replied that he "had little enough to communicate about Rockall, because I've never seen it by daylight".

In the autumn of that year the *Nepean,* of which Commander Farquhar was then sub-lieutenant, was on her way back to Scapa, having escorted a convoy of oilers to longtitude 12° West. During the middle watch, while he lay in his bunk, the alarm buzzers rang for action stations. In his capacity as torpedo control officer, he rushed to the bridge. A dark shape resembling a ship without lights had been sighted; and all was made ready to open fire instantly, should she fail to answer the *Nepean's* challenge. However, as the destroyer approached, it was discovered that she had her guns trained on Rockall! "And it wasn't long," concludes Commander Farquhar's letter, "before I was back in my warm bunk again! That was my first—and last—sight of Rockall!"

* * *

Now we revert to more recent times.

In April, 1941, James Fisher, acting on behalf of the British Trust for Ornithology, asked the Commander-in-Chief of Coastal Command whether any of his aircraft, when flying near Rockall, might make some observations regarding its bird-life. The result was that, during a series of flights in this neighbourhood the following summer, some excellent photographs of the rock itself were taken from different angles and altitudes, and helpful observations made. An analysis of the photographs, Fisher tells us, "shows the gannets were present in small numbers (up to about 6), occasionally settling, but not breeding; kittiwakes were certainly not breeding, but sometimes used the Rock in numbers (up to about 140) as a resting-place; up to 50 guillemots could be found on the broad south-west ledge—though eggs could not be seen, they were possibly breeding."

A further series of photographs taken from Coastal Command aircraft in 1945 shows clearly that on May, 27th, there were 24 or 25 guillemots on the broad ledge. Some eight weeks later, Flight-Lieutenant R. A. Hinde flew over Rockall, spotting 8 guillemots on the ledge, 6 of which flew off. Though he made a dozen runs over the Rock, the remaining two stayed where they were. Fisher thinks it just possible that they were incubating eggs. On this occasion ten kittiwakes and two immature gulls were also seen on the Rock.

As part of a scheme inaugurated by the British Trust for Ornithology, which has collated all the data obtained, aerial photography of other isolated bird colonies was also carried out by Coastal Command during the Second World War. St. Kilda, Sùla Sgeir, Ailsa Craig, and the Flannan Isles were among the remote outposts photographed in this way. Thus at last it was proved that the fulmar breeds on Eilean Tighe, one of the Flannans, and that gannets frequent the Scar Rocks, in Wigtownshire.

In the summer of 1946, under ideal conditions, Seton Gordon was flown out to Rockall. From the air, he said, it resembled a tilted haystack, the top of which seemed tightly tied round with a wisp of white grass. Although several runs were made over it, some of them quite low, neither solans nor puffins were seen upon it. Kittiwakes were using it as a resting-place; while half a dozen guillemots showed so little inclination to quit their particular ledge, even when the plane roared repeatedly over them, that he concluded they were sitting on eggs.

Seton thinks that the strange bird which fishermen say they see on the rock from time to time—they call him Rockall Jack—may be the great shearwater, which frequents Rockall in summer and, so far as is known, nests only on one of the Tristan da Cunha group of islands.

*   *   *

On September, 21st, 1955, the Admiralty announced the formal annexation of Rockall, said to have been rendered necessary, according to *The Times,* on the ground that it was likely to enter the orbit of the guided missiles range then projected on South Uist and now a senseless *fait accompli.* Though Rockall hitherto had been claimed by no nation, it was now annexed by Britain to eliminate embarrassing counter-claims that might have arisen when the rocket-station on South Uist was completed. The annexation was carried out on the authority of the Queen by a landing-party from H.M.S. *Vidal,* the 2,000-ton survey ship commanded by Commander (now Captain) Richard Connell, R.N., and equipped with the helicopter which simplified the landing.

"When our ship, *Vidal,* is in all respects ready for sea, and all necessary personnel has embarked," the royal orders directed, "you are to leave Londonderry on September, 14, 1955, or the earliest date thereafter. Thence you will proceed to the island of Rockall. On

arrival at Rockall you will effect a landing and hoist the Union flag
on whatever spot appears most suitable or practicable; and you will
then take possession of the island on our behalf. You will keep a
record of your proceedings. When the landing has been effected and
the flag hoisted, you will cement a commemorative plaque to the
rock."

The annexation was given the name of Operation Rockall.

The first man to be lowered on to the rock from the ship's helicopter was Sergeant Brian Peel, a Royal Marine commando, and an
expert cliff-climber. He was set down on a ledge 20 feet long by 6
feet wide, which cuts into the rock a dozen feet below its summit.
Peel was followed by Corporal Alexander Fraser, another commando,
a Scot from Granton. Then came the ornithologist, James Fisher,
and, lastly, Lieutenant-Commander Desmond Scott, of Whitstable,
First Lieutenant of the *Vidal*. Scott was in charge of the landing-
party.

After three arduous hours spent on Rockall, a pre-fabricated flag-
mast eight feet in height was erected. On this, Scott hoisted the
Union flag, taking formal possession of Rockall with the words:
"In the name of Her Majesty, Queen Elizabeth II, I hereby take
possession of the island of Rockall." While the annexation ceremony
was being conducted, the *Vidal* steamed slowly past the rock, firing
a salute of 21 guns. A brass plaque cemented to the rock duly recorded the annexation in the following terms:

By authority of Her Majesty Queen Elizabeth the Second, by the
Grace of God, of the United Kingdom of Great Britain and Northern
Ireland, and of her other realms and territories, Queen, Head of the
Commonwealth, Defender of the Faith . . . and in accordance with
Her Majesty's instructions dated the fourteenth day of September,
One Thousand, Nine Hundred and Fifty Five, a landing was effected
this day upon this Island of Rockall from H.M.S. *Vidal*. The Union
Flag was hoisted and possession of the Island was taken in the name
of Her Majesty.

(Signed) R. H. Connell,
Captain, H.M.S. *Vidal*,
18th, September, 1955.

As was only to have been expected, Fisher, with the aid of Peel
and Fraser, improved his shining hour by collecting periwinkles,
algae, lichens, and other matter of interest to the marine biologist. A
good chunk of rockallite was also obtained. Unofficially, but none-

theless appropriately, the ledge on which the helicopter dropped the party was named Hall's Ledge, in memory of Captain Basil Hall of the *Endymion,* from which, as we have seen, the first recorded landing on Rockall was made in 1810, nearly a century and a half earlier. Hall's Ledge, running flat along Rockall's south side and curving a little way along its west, roughly a dozen feet below its splintering apex, is now accorded an oceanographical status well merited.

When, early in August, 1959, officers and ratings from the destroyer, *Cavendish* (Captain P. U. Bayly, R.N.), landed on Rockall, they were unable to find the metal plaque erected there four years previously, although they remained on the rock for at least an hour. The *Cavendish* at the time was on passage to the west of Ireland from the Iceland area, where she had been on fishery protection duties. The suggestion that the plaque lay invisible under a covering of bird-lime could not be accepted as a possibility, since the spot to which it had been cemented was known precisely to members of the party ashore, led by Lieutenant-Commander C. P. R. Collis, of Cheam. The Admiralty, having eliminated the idea that some souvenir-hunter had carried it off, proffered no theories as to what had happened to it. Only one leg of the tripod flagstaff erected by the *Vidal's* party still stood where it had been placed in 1955. Near it were found a second leg and the flagstaff's base. According to an Admiralty statement, the *Cavendish's* party fixed on Rockall its own tablet. The vessel approached within two cables of the rock; and the party went ashore in a whaler towing a rubber dinghy. "Four of us got into the dinghy, and scrambled ashore on the south-east corner of the rock over the seaweed," Lieutenant Peter Cheshire, of Harrow, informed *The Times.* "We had a line on the dinghy, and pulled four more from the whaler on to the rock. With Electrical Mechanic S. T. Nisbet, of Narberth, Pembrokeshire, Able Seaman W. M. Symons, of Weymouth, and Radio Electrical Mechanic D. J. Sale, of Birmingham, I got to the top, and we threw down a line and hauled up some quick-drying cement. We set it in a gully and wrote 'H.M.S. *Cavendish.* 1959'."

Thereafter the Union flag was lashed to the remaining leg of the *Vidal's* tripod. "There was no trace of *Vidal's* plaque, although we searched for it." The base of the flagstaff, discovered loose on the rock's summit, was shipped, to be sent by the *Cavendish* to the *Vidal.* Symons, while climbing the rock, fell about 10 feet into the sea; but he regained a footing, and was the first of the party to reach the summit. Sale was washed off the rock as he landed, but managed to swim back to it.

So far as I am aware as we go to press, no official explanation as yet has been given for the disappearance of the *Vidal's* plaque. Only those of us who have made a close study of the power which the surging ocean can exert have any conception of the colossal weight and magnitude of what crashing waves are capable of dislodging and carrying away.

Rockall nowadays is audibly familiar to millions of us through the B.B.C. In 1949 the Admiralty and the Ministry of Agriculture & Fisheries agreed with the Air Ministry that the boundaries of some of the sea areas used in the weather forecasts for shipping should be altered. Smaller areas enable closer consideration to be given to local variations. Consequently, the forecast for a restricted area can be more detailed and precise. This sub-division entailed the introduction of a few additional names, some of them geographical, some self-explanatory. Among the former is Rockall, now denoting that sea area lying to the west of the southern half of Scotland and of the northern half of Ireland, between the areas designated Bailey and Shannon.

And here we must leave Rockall, that merest dot occupying less of the world's surface than does my concluding dot in relation to the area of this final page.

Index